AF784826

Arbitration Awards: Generic Features and Textual Realisations

Arbitration Awards:
Generic Features and Textual Realisations

Edited by

Vijay K. Bhatia, Giuliana Garzone
and Chiara Degano

CAMBRIDGE
SCHOLARS
PUBLISHING

Arbitration Awards:
Generic Features and Textual Realisations,
Edited by Vijay K. Bhatia, Giuliana Garzone and Chiara Degano

This book first published 2012

Cambridge Scholars Publishing

12 Back Chapman Street, Newcastle upon Tyne, NE6 2XX, UK

British Library Cataloguing in Publication Data
A catalogue record for this book is available from the British Library

Copyright © 2012 by Vijay K. Bhatia, Giuliana Garzone and Chiara Degano and contributors

All rights for this book reserved. No part of this book may be reproduced, stored in a retrieval system, or transmitted, in any form or by any means, electronic, mechanical, photocopying, recording or otherwise, without the prior permission of the copyright owner.

ISBN (10): 1-4438-4091-2, ISBN (13): 978-1-4438-4091-0

TABLE OF CONTENTS

Part Two. Exploring the Hypothesis of the Colonization of Arbitration Discourse by Litigation

CHAPTER ONE

ARBITRATION AWARDS: GENERIC FEATURES AND TEXTUAL REALISATIONS. AN INTRODUCTION

VIJAY K. BHATIA, GIULIANA GARZONE
AND CHIARA DEGANO

1. Introduction

This volume is one of the end products of an international research project on international commercial arbitration, and focuses on the arbitration award as a genre that embodies the final outcome of a complex sequence of discursive and professional inquiry and negotiation practices, i.e. arbitration proceedings, in the same way as the judgment represents the end product of the lawsuit or the court trial. Similarly to the judgment, the arbitration award – today an increasingly conventionalised and codified genre – is a complex discursive artefact, which has the main purpose of announcing the arbitrator's or the arbitral tribunal's decision. In order to do so, it not only states their final decision, but also narrates the circumstances that have led to the arbitration itself, and above all provides justifications for such a decision, relying on hard facts and on reasoning. Thus, the arbitration award is a very interesting object of investigation for the discourse analyst as well as for the jurist and the rhetorician, being a still relatively unexplored genre. With the growing popularity of arbitration as a form of dispute resolution, research on the award can also contribute to shedding light on its evolution in recent times.

All the studies collected in this volume share the methodological assumption that texts and genres can be investigated only within the context of the institutional and professional practices in which they originate. Therefore, before going on to discuss the contents of the book more in detail, a few contextual considerations regarding international commercial arbitration are in order.

1.1. International commercial arbitration and relevant practices

International commercial arbitration was established by the United Nations General Assembly in 1966 to favour the harmonization and unification of international trade practices, and was intended as 'alternative to litigation' to resolve cross-border commercial disputes. Some years later, the United Nations General Assembly introduced the UNCITRAL (United Nations Commission on International Trade Law) Model Law on International Commercial Arbitration (1985), which has greatly contributed to harmonization, being adopted integrally by a number of countries and incorporated, with more or less substantial modifications, into the legislation of many others.

Today, international arbitration is the most popular form of alternative dispute resolution (ADR) for the settlement of commercial disputes the world over (cf. among others Hunter, Marriot, and Veder 1995; Mattli 2001). As envisaged in the UNCITRAL Model Law, international commercial arbitration crucially depends on the parties' decision – usually expressed in an arbitration clause included in their agreement – to resolve disputes through private adjudication by a single arbitrator, or a tribunal of more than one. The practice of international arbitration has developed in a manner to allow parties from different legal and cultural backgrounds to resolve their disputes without any judicial interference. More importantly, arbitration is supposed to provide a mechanism for commercial dispute resolution that is not only economical, speedy and confidential, but also universally enforceable, just like any court decision.

In arbitration, parties often appoint legal counsels to present their arguments to an impartial arbitration tribunal to resolve the dispute. Unlike other forms of alternative dispute resolution, such as conciliation and mediation, which do not suggest or impose any specific decision to resolve the dispute, arbitration is meant to issue a decision, known as 'award', which is binding on the disputing parties, i.e. it is generally non-appealable in a court of law, except on procedural grounds under a very restricted set of conditions. In arbitration, the parties to the dispute have considerable input in the selection of arbitration tribunal, and also in the choice of processes and procedures they would like the tribunal to follow, including the choice of language, the seat of arbitration, as well as the arbitration rules within which the resolution is negotiated, while in litigation they would have absolutely no control over the decision-making process.

Although the outcome of arbitration is final and enforceable, the parties to a dispute often look for opportunities to go to court when the outcome is not to their liking. They often choose arbitrators on the basis of their legal, rather than technical, expertise, as lawyers are likely to be more accomplished in exploiting opportunities to challenge a particular award (Miles 2003). As Bhatia *et al.* (2012: 303) point out, this brings in the crucial involvement and role of legal experts in what was supposed to be a non-judicial practice. Nariman rightly emphasizes that "there is just too much legal baggage [in International Commercial Arbitration]… it moves slowly and ponderously… [it] has become almost indistinguishable from litigation, which it was at one time intended to supplant" (Nariman 2000: 262). Similarly, Kerr (1997) points out that international arbitration seems to have acquired the pejorative sobriquet, *arbitigation,* which signals large scale 'judicialization' of arbitration. In practice, this overwhelming influence of litigation results in an increasing mixture of discourses as arbitration becomes, as it were, 'colonized' by litigation practices, and threatens to undermine the integrity of arbitration itself, thus compromising its spirit as a non-legal practice. However, there is relatively little research evidence for such impressions and observations, except the opinions and statements from experts in the field, like those quoted above.

1.2. The research project

In the light of these developments, the idea emerged that it would be desirable to conduct an evidence-based investigation of the extent to which arbitration practices are influenced by litigation procedures and practices. This was the main focus of the international project funded by the Research Grants Council HKSAR under their Competitive Earmarked Research Grant, entitled *International Commercial Arbitration Practice: A Discourse Analytical Study*,[1] in collaboration with more than twenty international teams of researchers, drawn both from the legal and arbitration practice, and from discourse analysis. One of the key objectives of this project has been to investigate the 'integrity' of current international arbitration practices by analysing various sets of complementary textual, and discourse data, to asses the extent to which arbitration practices have

---

[1] For a more extensive description of the project and a discussion of the relevant issues, cf. *Bhatia et al.* 2012. Cf. also the project's website at <http://enweb.cityu.edu.hk/arbitrationpractice/.

been interdiscursively influenced by litigation, especially in terms of intention and purpose, processes and procedures adopted, and also in terms of the shared expertise expected on the part of the participants in specific cases. In order to achieve these objectives, the project used a multi-perspective and multidimensional genre analytical framework (Bhatia 2004) to integrate analyses of data. Three main perspectives were adopted:

1) Intertextual and interdiscursive relationships among discursive practices in arbitration.
2) Narratives of experience of key practitioners tested against other stakeholders.
3) Comparative analyses of arbitration and litigation documents, focusing on critical moments in the discourses of arbitration practice.

The studies collected in this book, mostly authored by members of the project, draw mainly on the third perspective, being text-based, but also occasionally consider aspects included in 1) and 2). They focus on different aspects of arbitration awards, which have been traditionally kept confidential, hence made not easily available in the public domain. In more recent years, however, some of the established international institutions, like the International Chamber of Commerce and the International Court of Arbitration, have taken the initiative to publish some of these awards, in sanitised or abridged form to preserve confidential information about the parties. This has made it possible to collect corpora of arbitration awards for research purposes.

Corpora of this kind, in various languages (English, French, Italian, Chinese), collected from some of the most important arbitration institutions in various countries, are the point of departure of most chapters of this book. Many of them focus on international arbitration awards, but in some cases (e.g Antelmi and Santulli, and Tessuto), the analysis is based on awards resulting from national arbitration in order to outline a more comprehensive picture of the award as a genre.

In some cases, corpora of court judgments have also been relied on for comparison in order to identify various textual and discursive indicators – from syntactic traits to argumentative patterns – and describe contrastively the discursive mechanisms at work as well as the move structure and the rhetorical strategies enacted in each of these two genres. At the same time, the comparison of awards with court judgments has made it possible to assess the degree of interdiscursivity and hybridization between them, as an indicator of colonization.

The exploration of these themes has theoretical relevance too, as it provides interesting insights into the mechanisms that preside over the contamination and hybridization among genres in professional practice.

2. Contents of the volume

The volume is divided into two Parts. The studies presented in Part I introduce the distinctive features of the arbitration award as a discourse genre, examining its move structure, the recurrent rhetorical patterns and the use of linguistic resources, in some cases comparing it with judgments as a germane genre, thus also providing a fundamental background for the subsequent chapters. Part II takes up the issue of the possible contamination of arbitration discourse by discursive patterns typical of litigation, already marginally touched upon in Part I, and tackles it squarely in the various chapters, each of which examines one or more features of awards in different languages and contexts, looking for evidence that may confirm or disprove the main hypothesis of a blurring of boundaries between the discourse of arbitration and the discourse of litigation.

Part I opens with a chapter that deals with the general issue of the language of arbitration. Authored by MANLIO FRIGO, a practicing lawyer and arbitrator, it discusses the general problem of language use in arbitration proceedings and in the drafting of final awards, a problem that is crucial for the sake of the recognition, enforcement and free circulation of these pronouncements. Special attention is given to the possible interference, interaction or conflict between the language used and the applicable law chosen. Among the issues examined, prominent is that of the approach to be adopted in legal translation, given that in many cases in international arbitration the problem of the language is solved through certified translation. In light of his own experience as a practitioner, and examining the relevant provisions set forth in international conventions, Frigo recommends trans-conceptual translation, which focuses on the contents of the award, rather than on its linguistic formulation. He also recommends that, in order to avoid problems of non correspondence across legal systems, parties' and arbitrators' choice of the language of the arbitration be consistent with the applicable law chosen.

In the second chapter, which starts the discussion of the structure and discursive organization of the arbitration award, VIJAY BHATIA and JANE LUNG focus on the rhetorical and cognitive move-structure of this genre, which they explore in a corpus of arbitration awards collected from different countries, namely Iran, Russia, Austria, China, France, America and Sweden, all drafted in English. On this basis they identify a discursive hierarchical pattern, in which moves are embedded in four main discursive patterns: background information, details of the dispute, review of contentions and claims, and closure, containing the decision. The chapter also makes an attempt to set these findings in relation with the nature and communicative functions of the arbitration award, and especially with its being a consensual private dispute resolution process. The authors conclude that, although arbitration does not take place in a court, it is still a legal process, so international commercial arbitration awards can be considered a distinctive genre in legal discourse in their own right.

Narrowing the focus on some distinctive pragmatic features of legal discourse, the expression of performativity and deontic modality is the main object of investigation in the following chapter, authored by CHIARA PREITE. Through the analysis of a corpus of awards in French issued by the International Chamber of Commerce (ICC) of Paris, it is shown that normativity is conveyed by means of thetic and athetic performativity, highly relevant in decisions, and by deontic modals, which can be found all across the texts examined in the form of Obligation, Permission, Prohibition and, to a lesser extent, Facultivity. For this purpose a wide range of more or less explicit markers are utilized – modal verbs, para-synonymical forms, periphrastic expressions, simple present and future tense. This variety of realizations is not peculiar to French arbitration awards only, but characterizes other forms of deliberative texts, e.g. judgments passed by the Court of Justice of the European Union.

In her chapter GIULIANA GARZONE, working on a corpus of ICC awards in English, and occasionally on a corpus of Lords' Judgments for reference, draws on the notion of polyphony to examine arbitration awards as argumentative texts in which arbitrators construct their arguments giving account of the parties' views and making reference to relevant texts. In so doing, they also respond to all possible objections and anticipate counterarguments by incorporating them in their decisions. In particular, Garzone looks at concessive constructions, including modals and disjuncts with a concessive/dialogic value, as a form of dialogism which enables the arbitrator to meet his/her interlocutors on their own ground, acknowledging their possible objections, and discusses the pragmatic inferences, or implicatures, that such constructions license. Garzone concludes that recourse to this type of discursive resources is all the more crucial in arbitration awards as arbitrators do not have the same absolute authoritativeness and authority as judges; rather, they are delegated their authority by the parties themselves, so they have to justify their decisions extensively, demonstrating that all the arguments put forth by both parties – also those put forth by the party to which the award is unfavourable – have been taken into due account.

The discussion of dialogism in arbitration awards is developed further in the next chapter, authored by DONELLA ANTELMI and FRANCESCA SANTULLI, who examine a corpus of arbitration awards issued in Italy, in order to single out some of the distinctive features of the realization of this text genre in an Italian context, thus identifying the aspects in which they differ from court judgments. After showing that various forms of dialogism are deployed in these texts in order to introduce different 'voices' – mainly the parties' and legislation – whose claims are then examined, on the basis of their analysis the authors conclude that the arbitration award as a text genre is similar to the judgment, but displays a larger number of elements and structures that express the different enunciative stance of arbitrators. Their linguistic texture, with its more or less explicit argumentative structures, is a clear consequence of the juridical debate on the nature and validity of arbitration, which has been a constant in the Italian academic and forensic tradition. The writer of an award must reduce the risk of challenge, but at the same time he/she must discursively create his/her own credibility, objectivity and impartiality.

The theme of the strategies used by arbitrators in order to discursively construct their own credibility and authoritativeness continues in GIROLAMO TESSUTO's chapter, which is based on a small-size corpus of Canadian awards. Drawing on (meta)discourse and genre analytical literature, this study examines the generic-move structure and the linguistic resources used by arbitrators to encode their identity and authoritativeness in the organization and rhetorical patterns of the genre, shedding light on the intergeneric relationship between arbitration awards and legal judgments. Although the analysis of the move-structure points to similarity between awards and court judgments in a certain limited number of rhetorical and discursive devices, essential distinctions between the two genres remain. These concern in particular the construction of the sender's and receiver's identities, with the judges' voices fitting with their status and hierarchy in the court procedure, while the arbitrators' voices are the result of their being appointed by the parties. As for the receivers, arbitrators seem to interact more effectively with the intended readers by adapting and anticipating their values, interests and expectations, thus involving them in the institutional, professional and organizational practices of discourse.

The elements that have emerged in Part I, outlining the distinctive generic features of arbitration awards, and the occasional observations concerning the similarity or difference between arbitration awards and court judgments and associated practices, represent a point of departure for the more systematic and focalized discussion of the hypothesis of a gradual colonisation of arbitration practices by litigation put forth in the chapters collected in Part II of the book. Here evidence for or against the colonization of arbitration awards by litigation is looked for by focusing on different aspects of award drafting, which broadly speaking cluster around two main lines of research: the logical structure of awards, on the one hand, with a focus either on cognitive structure or on argumentative features, and, on the other hand, discursive strategies related to the (Hallidayan) interpersonal function, with special regard for the construction of authorial stance in relation to other voices.

Along the first line of research, VIJAY BHATIA and HAN ZHENGRUI's chapter compares arbitration awards and litigation judgments issued in the People's Republic of China, revealing that the two genres tend to display the same moves, arranged in the same sequential order, with both arbitrators and judges committed to reporting conclusions rather than negotiating their decisions. The sole difference, according to the authors, lies in the degree of standardization, as judgments are more structured and standardized than arbitration awards. On this ground, the authors conclude that, although in arbitration practices considerable freedom is left for the parties to negotiate while in judgments the State's power exerts greater influence, not much material difference exists between arbitration awards and legal judgments. And such similarity is interpreted as an effect of interdiscursivity, which in turn is dependant on the context of production, given that arbitrators listed by various Chinese arbitration commissions are mostly law professors and lawyers.

In the next chapter, CHIARA DEGANO relies on a corpus-based analysis of the arguments used in arbitration awards to seek evidence of a colonization of international commercial arbitration – in theory independent of any specific legal system – by the common law litigation tradition. Resting on the assumption that the widespread use of English in international arbitration ends up bringing with it an influence of the Anglo-Saxon legal culture as well, and considering that arguments based on analogy are the foundation of precedent-bound case law, Degano asks whether recourse to case-based logic in international arbitration awards has increased over time, as a possible effect of the influence of common law. The results of the computer-assisted analysis, carried out using linguistic indicators to retrieve occurrences of arguments by analogy, suggest an increase in the recourse to such forms of reasoning parallel to a reduction in the frequency of references to statutory sources of law, two data which taken together can be seen as a step towards confirming the initial hypothesis.

Tackling both reasoning structure and rhetorical strategies, MICHELE SALA focuses on the use of argumentation in arbitration awards, taken as a yardstick to assess to what extent and through which discursive resources experts of the legal profession interpret and transform the conciliatory nature of arbitration. Based on a corpus of Italian commercial arbitration awards, the analysis examines the argumentative strategies which are used by arbitrators to support their claims, substantiate their final decision, and confer authority and definitiveness on their judgment, focusing primarily on the use of standardized and formulaic language, the frequency and distribution of syntactic indicators of argumentation such as consequential or contrastive markers and, finally, the rhetorical strategies used by the drafters to express evidentiality, epistemic and interactive meanings. The findings confirm the hypothesis of an influence of litigation, which according to the author might be due to the presence of lawyers on the Board of Arbitrators, but may also be purposefully intended to attach a specific deontic connotation to the award, so as to make it recognizable and acceptable as a normative text.

Along the second line of research, focusing on discursive strategies related to the interpersonal function, IGNACIO VÁSQUEZ and DIANA GINER explore intertextuality in arbitration awards and court judgments, considering it both in the prototypical form of quotations embedded in a text, and in the more indirect form of hedges and boosters as markers of interactional metadiscourse whereby the authors modulate their distance from, or commitment to, the words of the parties to the dispute that they decide to report in their final pronouncements. Results show that hedges and boosters are commonly used both in awards and judgments, with a twofold move-specific function: when appearing within the reasoning sections, they seem to be strongly related to the justifying function of the language, while in the conclusions and finding sections, there is a tendency to use boosters to make the tone more authoritative, with a clear declarative function. On this basis, the authors conclude that the two functions that Maley (1985) identified in the language of judgments are also present in the language of arbitral awards, thus reducing the gap that one might expect to exist between awards and judgments, as a consequence of their profoundly different rationales and procedures.

The last two chapters of the book deal with the same issues, but the object of investigation is a special form of international arbitration, i.e. sports arbitration.

PAOLA EVANGELISTI ALLORI's chapter looks in particular at the construction of the parties' identity in the text. She compares the authorial stance of arbitrators and judges in sport arbitration awards and judgments respectively, looking in particular at the reporting verbs these professionals use to represent actions undertaken by the parties to the procedure, and in so doing they implicitly convey their own view of the parties themselves and of their position within the case. The analysis, carried out on two specialised corpora of legal discourse, i.e. final pronouncements given by court judges and by sport arbitrators in international appeal cases, highlights remarkable differences in the use of reporting verbs, which is interpreted by the author as a clue to the existence of different drafting conventions for the practices of court litigation and (sport) arbitration. The findings reveal that in both genres reporting verbs play a significant role in the section dedicated to the exposition of the facts and the subsequent pronouncement of the judging body. However, a difference emerges in narrative styles, with a reverberation, in particular, on the image of the party who sets the legal appeal procedure in motion. While arbitrators tend to project an image of the Appellant as a dynamic and alert participant in the procedure who strives eagerly to have his/her point of view accepted by the judging body, the court judges project an image of the Applicant as a more static, almost detached participant in the background.

The issues involved in sports arbitration are explored also by MICHELA MENGHINI in the final chapter of the book. She focuses on the use of intertextual devices and their functions in awards issued by the Court of Arbitration for Sport between 1991 and 2010, with the purpose of establishing whether significant differences can be found between older and more recent awards, and whether such differences can be ascribed to the influence of litigation, as recently hypothesized for commercial arbitration. The analysis suggests that colonization by litigation practices has not (yet) conspicuously affected sport arbitration. However, few but interesting differences in terms of intertextual features might indicate that a recent trend in this sense is under way. Particularly noteworthy is the use of integral citations, which in recent awards are almost invariably present and distributed through the various sections, unlike in older awards. Since integral citations as markers of intertextuality in awards perform the function of signaling textual authority, their increase might indicate an incipient concern for sport arbitrators to assert authority and make their decisions as explicit and conclusive as possible, and this could be seen as an effect of the influence of litigation.

3. Concluding remarks

The picture of the award that emerges from this volume is one of a cohesive genre which, with the due differences across cultures and traditions, is quite codified in terms of macro-textual organization and cognitive structure.

At the level of micro-discursive features, too, the analyses presented in the various chapters consistently reveal a cluster of distinctive traits, which seem to be the result of two main extra-linguistic factors: the necessity for arbitrators to be accountable to the parties who appointed them, and the layering of procedural steps through which the arbitration process unfolds with the relevant discursive formations.

The first factor, i.e. arbitrators' accountability to the parties, determines their recourse to a complex nexus of rhetorical strategies, aimed at the discursive construction of the participants' identities. From the viewpoint of the writer/sender, arbitrators tend to emphasize their authoritativeness and credibility, while at the same time endowing their decisions with an aura of reasonableness and conclusiveness. At the other end of the continuum, the drafting takes into account the positions of the parties, anticipating their expectations and trying to accommodate their points of view, even when the final decision runs counter them.

As for the second factor, i.e. the discursive complexity of arbitration and its impact on the final pronouncement, the fact that the award is issued at the end of a composite process determines a stratification of discourses produced at various stages of the arbitration itself, which are represented in different degrees in the final document.

This, also partly associated to the concern for the parties' points of view, gives rise to a polyphony of voices skillfully orchestrated by the arbitrators, playing the double role of deliberators and of narrators (but also selectors) with regard to previous facts and discourses.

With regard to the initial hypothesis of the impingement of litigation on arbitration, the results of the researches presented in the volume suggest that even if the two genres retain some distinguishing features in their own respect, differences are a matter of gradualness, with court judgments displaying a higher degree of standardization, possibly as a consequence of their being more deeply institutionalized than arbitration. However, also arbitration, with its transformation from the original "town elder model" (Rivkin 2008) to its contemporary legalized form, has become increasingly institutionalized —hence a consolidation of the award as a genre—, drawing on the conventions of the court judgment. While in commercial arbitration such a process is well into its consolidation stage, in sports arbitration the signs of an influence of litigation are at a more seminal phase, but are nonetheless present, suggesting that even this type of arbitration is not immune from litigation contagion.

References

Bhatia, Vijay K. 2004. *Worlds of Written Discourse: A Genre-Based View*. London: Continuum International.

Bhatia, Vijay K., Christopher N. Candlin, and Maurizio Gotti 2012. "Contested Identities in International Arbitration Practice." In *Discourse and Practice in International Commercial Arbitration: Issues, Challenges and Prospects*, edited by Vijay K. Bhatia, Christopher N. Candlin, and Maurizio Gotti, 301-318. London: Ashgate.

Hunter, Martin, Arthur L. Marriot, and V.V. Veder. 1995. *The Internationalisation of Arbitration*. London: Graham and Trotman.

Kerr, Michael. 1997. "Concord and Conflict in International Arbitration". *Arbitration International* 13, no. 2: 121-143.

Maley, Yon. 1985. "Judicial Discourse: The Case of Legal Judgment". In *The Cultivated Australian,* edited by John E. Clark, 159-175. Hamburg: Buske.

Mattli, Walter. 2001. "Private Justice in a Global Economy: From Litigation to Arbitration". *International Organization* 55, no. 4: 919-947.

Miles, Wendy. 2003. "Practical Issues for Appointment of Arbitrators: Lawyer vs. Non-Lawyer and Sole Arbitrator vs. Panel of Three or More". *Journal of International Arbitration* 20, no. 3: 219-232.

Nariman, Fali S. 2000. "The Spirit of Arbitration: The Tenth Annual Goff Lecture". *Arbitration International* 16, no. 3: 261-278.

Rivkin, David W. 2008. "Towards a New Paradigm in International Arbitration: The Town Elder Model Revisited". *Arbitration International* 24, no. 3: 375-386.

PART ONE.

ARBITRATION AWARDS: GENERIC STRUCTURE AND DISCURSIVE FEATURES

CHAPTER TWO

FREE CIRCULATION OF ARBITRAL AWARDS AND INTERACTION BETWEEN STRUCTURE OF THE LAW AND STRUCTURE OF THE LANGUAGE

MANLIO FRIGO

1. Introduction: language related problems in international arbitration

When we try to outline the advantages of arbitration we usually take into consideration some factors, typically:

- binding nature of the arbitral awards: they are not subject to appeal and the grounds of challenge available against arbitral awards are very limited;
- better enforcement: arbitral awards have easier and greater international recognition than judgments of national courts, thanks to the 1958 New York Convention on the Recognition and Enforcement of Foreign Arbitral Awards (130 States) and several bilateral agreements;
- expertise: the parties can appoint their arbitrators;
- rapidity;
- confidentiality: arbitration hearings are not public, awards are not published;
- equal footing: parties are on an equal footing with reference to the place of the arbitration, the procedures, the nationality of the arbitrators, the language of the arbitration.

However, with respect to international commercial arbitration the 'equal footing guarantee' might conceal some traps. This is particularly the case with problems pertaining to language and translation. Some scholars have stressed the fact that international commercial arbitration is a "*trans-cultural venture*" and that the need to bridge language differences is part of the process, and this is also true when considering that post-award court proceedings must also meet language-related challenges (Varady 2006).

1.1. Impact of the linguistic factor

The linguistic factor is of great importance in fostering the spread of arbitration mainly in what concerns:

a. the possibility of appointing arbitrators of different nationalities (and in particular coming from States different from the State where the proceedings will take place);
b. the choice of a language different from the language of either party as the language of the arbitration and, accordingly, of the arbitral award.

Does the structure of the language used in arbitral proceedings affect the structure of the applicable law? Does the applicable law have any impact on the language used in the proceedings and *vice-versa*?

1.2. Language-related issues and award recognition

It is a common feature of both international and domestic law rules that they face "language-related problems" by means of specific provisions concerning the recognition of arbitral awards. Just to quote an example, the *Arrangement Concerning Mutual Enforcement of Arbitral Awards between the Mainland and the Hong Kong Special Administrative Region* provides that, in order to obtain the enforcement by the relevant court, the applicant shall submit i) an application for enforcement, ii) the arbitral award, iii) the arbitration agreement. Furthermore it provides that "Application for enforcement made in the Mainland shall be in the Chinese language. If the arbitral award or arbitration agreement is not in the Chinese language, the applicant shall submit a duly certified Chinese translation of it".[1]

---

[1] Article 3.4. of the *Arrangement Concerning Mutual Enforcement of arbitral Awards between the Mainland and the Hong Kong Special Administrative Region* of July 14, 2006.

The main multilateral agreements on the subject matter provide for similar solutions, namely article 4 of the 1927 Geneva Convention on the Execution of Foreign Arbitral Awards, and Article IV of the 1958 New York Convention on the Recognition and Enforcement of Foreign Arbitral Awards contain the same rule and require a translation certified by an official or sworn translator or by a diplomatic or consular agent.[2] Incidentally, also the Italian civil procedure code, consistently with the above international agreements, provides for the same requirements.[3] From this point of view, the solution of any linguistic problems relies therefore upon the "certified translation" of the original document.

2. Translation in international arbitration

The translation and its certification do not ensure a proper solution when a "non-merely-linguistic problem" is at stake. In other words, what happens when differences between legal systems or even specific legal institutions occur? According to a famous definition, legal translation is not merely a conversion from a juridical system to another, but rather "translation consists in superimposing, through the intermediation of two concordant terms which refer to two different juridical concepts, two correspondent or equivalent notions, linked to two different orders".[4]

As has been observed by some legal scholars, the translator can make a choice between two or three alternatives: translating the text, reconstructing the thought of the author, or rendering what – in his view – is the "objectively" correct sense of a legal text written by somebody else in the original language.

The situation may even be more complicated, for instance because the text has more different juridical meanings and therefore a strictly juridical interpretation appears to be necessary. Furthermore, any language aims at describing the legal institutions or the legal phenomena of the country where that language is spoken. If we take the example of English expressions such as *equitable interests* or *consideration*, it is quite clear that other languages lack equivalent expressions as they are spoken in

---

[2] See article IV of the New York convention. With a slightly different wording article 4 of the Geneva Convention requires a translation "… certified correct by a diplomatic or consular agent of the country to which the party who seeks to rely upon the awards belongs or by a sworn translator of the country where the award is sought to be relied upon".

[3] See article 839 of the Italian *Codice di procedura civile*.

[4] See Ricoeur 2006: 1ff.

countries where *equitable interest* and *consideration* simply do not exist (cf. Sacco 1999: 129ff.).

2.1. Issues involved in legal translation

Legal translation has to face some difficulties barely known to other kinds of translation. Broadly speaking, the translation of a notion into another notion is possible and legitimate when the two notions express the same concept, but this is not always the case in the juridical world. The concepts elaborated in the law making process or in any case defined by the jurists in a given legal system do not necessarily correspond to those elaborated or defined in another legal system. If this is the case, one should envisage the need for what may be defined as a *trans-conceptual translation*.

This problem may arise in cases where the same language is used in different legal systems: the *Besitz* of the Germans and the Swiss does not coincide with the *Besitz* of the Austrians, as the latter not only implies the control of the person on the object, but also his intention of being the owner of the object.

In other cases, there are notions that are at first sight identical in two different languages *and* in two different legal systems, but in actual fact they are different in certain respects. For instance, the *contract* of the British common law does not have a precise equivalent in the *contrat* of the French, where basically there is no trace of the notion of "consideration".

Should then one conclude that the translation of legal texts is impossible or illegitimate, or simply unreliable? Of course not, as there are various solutions available. According to some proposals aimed at overcoming these difficulties, in order to translate a term involving problematic juridical notions it could be advisable to dismantle them by means of componential analysis, highlight the elements that have no reciprocal correspondence in the relevant legal systems, elaborate a language in diagrams in which the semantic unit contains all the characteristics to be considered in order to distinguish one notion from the other (cf. Vanderlinden 1995; Sacco 1996: 659).

Even without going so far, when problematic cases arise are there any legal criteria or principles applied in the international practice?

2.2. Rules for the interpretation of juridical norms

International law has its own rules concerning the interpretation of juridical norms, including at least partially the translation issue. As far as international treaties are concerned, Article 31 of the Vienna Convention of 1969 sets out a general rule of interpretation which provides that

> A treaty shall be interpreted *in good faith* in accordance with the ordinary meaning to be given to the terms of the treaty in their context and in the light of its object and purpose.

This statement, far from being conclusive, raises a few issues:

a) First: what is the 'ordinary meaning' of a word used in a treaty, considering that the expressions used in a treaty are technical?
b) Second: what is the exact meaning of 'good faith'? Is there a universally accepted notion of good faith, or is it, again, a technical notion the meaning of which may be slightly different according to the legal system it is referred to? The paradox, here, is that the good faith criterion is aimed at preventing that one of the parties to a treaty may take advantage from an ambiguous term, but the use of this term can turn out to be ambiguous in itself (Bariatti 1986: 175).

The issue of interpretation is expressly connected to the linguistic topic in another provision of the Vienna convention. Pursuant to its article 33, the interpretation of treaties authenticated in two or more languages is subject to two main rules:

1. "the terms of the treaty are presumed to have the same meaning in each authentic texts" (article 33.3), and
2. "Except when a particular text prevails in accordance with paragraph 1, when a comparison of the authentic texts discloses a difference of meaning which the application of articles 31 and 32 does not remove, the meaning which best reconciles the texts, having regard to the object and purpose of the treaty, shall be adopted" (article 33.4).

The first rule provided for under article 33.3 can be of some help in this discussion, as the principle set forth in it should be followed by the interpreter when the difference between the original text of the award and its translation may affect the post-award proceedings.

2.2.1. An example

Very recently, in the *Continental Casualty Co. v. Argentina*[5] ICSID case concerning the 1991 Argentina-US BIT (Bilateral Investment Treaty), the arbitral tribunal had to face a problem of interpretation of an escape clause. Pursuant to article XI of the BIT the obligations that either party had undertaken under the treaty as to the treatment of investments and investors of the other party "*shall not preclude*" the application of "*measures necessary*" for the pursuit of three types of national interests listed therein, among which namely: "a. the maintenance of public order", and "c. the protection of its own essential security interests".[6]

In its award of September 5, 2008, the Tribunal was confronted by a narrow interpretation by the claimant and a broader definition by the defendant of the terms '*public policy*' and '*essential interests*'. It is noteworthy that, with reference to the former expression, the tribunal held that "the expression 'maintenance of public order' indicates...rather clearly that public order is intended as a broad synonym for public peace, which can be threatened by actual or potential insurrections, riots and violent disturbances of the peace". Moreover, "this is the ordinary and principal meaning of "*orden publico*" in the Spanish text of the BIT corresponding to the same meaning in the French legal concept of '*ordre public*' in public and criminal law".[7] In this case, in rendering its decision the Tribunal brilliantly tried to provide an interpretation of the "ordinary meaning" of the wording by making recourse to a broad notion of public order, possibly slightly beyond its strictly legal meaning, but in all likelihood more in keeping with the spirit of the interpretation criteria set out in the Vienna Convention.

This example shows quite clearly how the above criteria can be properly applied in interpreting a normative text.

---

[5] See *Continental Casualty Company v. Argentine Republic*, ICSID Award of September 5, 2008, at <www.worldbank.org/icsid>.

[6] The other principle, not relevant to this discussion, is "the fulfilment of its obligations with respect to the maintenance or restoration of international peace or security".

[7] As a consequence: "Thus in the Tribunal's view, actions properly necessary by the central government to preserve and repress illegal actions and disturbances that may infringe such civil peace and potentially threaten the legal order, even when due to significant economic and social difficulties, and therefore to cope with and aim at removing these difficulties, do fall within the application under Art. XI". (see, § 174)

2.3. Trans-conceptual translation

Going back to the recognition and enforcement of arbitral awards, it is quite unlikely that errors in translation may be relied on as a ground for challenging the validity of the award. If we look at the 1958 New York convention's provisions, it is clear that the refusal of recognition and enforcement can only be justified for reasons concerning either the contents of the award (see article V.1.c,[8] and article V.2.b[9] with respect to the public policy of the country where recognition and enforcement are requested), or the subject matter of the arbitration in case it is not capable of settlement by arbitration under the law of that country (see Article V.2.a).

It is to be added that the seriousness of this problem can be particularly appreciated in case the law applied by the arbitrators is not the law of the country where the recognition is requested. In this respect an error in translation might only lead the interpreter to a refusal based on a *prima facie* consideration of the conditions, as the norm clearly requires that the consideration be effected on the documents (award and/or "agreement in writing") and not on their translation. Should this be the case, the refusal could be easily overcome by making recourse to the ordinary legal tools provided for by the law of the country concerned.[10]

On the other hand things would be different in case of trans-conceptual translation. Should the award (and not its translation) refer to legal institutions and/or juridical notions having a different meaning or being

[8] Pursuant to article V.1.c. of the 1958 New York convention recognition and enforcement of the award may be refused at the request of the party against whom it is invoked, only if that party furnishes to the competent authority where the recognition and enforcement is sought, proof that "... the award deals with a difference not contemplated by or not falling within the terms of the submission to arbitration, or it contains decisions on matters beyond the scope of the submission to arbitration, provided that, if the decisions on matters submitted to arbitration can be separated from those not so submitted, that part of the award which contains decisions on matters submitted to arbitration may be recognized and enforced".

[9] Pursuant to article V.2.b of the 1958 New York convention recognition and enforcement of the award may be also refused if the competent authority in the country where recognition and enforcement is sought finds that "The recognition or enforcement of the award would be contrary to the public policy of that country".

[10] In the Italian legal system, article 287 of the Civil Procedure Code admits the possibility of the correction of an error (*errore materiale*, 'material mistake') by the same judge who had rendered the decision.

absolutely unknown in the country where the award is supposed to be recognized or enforced, two different outcomes could be foreseeable:

a) the interpreter recognizes the award, translating the problematic notion into a notion expressing more or less the same concept (i.e. a similar legal *régime*);
b) the interpreter considers that the award cannot be recognized due to the impossibility of "translation". This is an extreme and certainly not desirable solution, but in this respect it is to be pointed out that this option was recently confirmed by the Italian Supreme Court when stating that a foreign award of punitive damages – which are not contemplated under Italian positive law – cannot be recognized in Italy, being contrary to the country's public policy. In such a case a *trans-conceptual translation* was considered simply impossible, not because of the absence of a theoretical equivalent, but rather due to inconsistency with the public policy – that incidentally only broadly speaking is an equivalent of the Italian *ordine pubblico* – meant as a general limit to the recognition of foreign legal and juridical values not consistent with the Italian legal system.[11]

3. Conclusion

In conclusion, it is the main task and responsibility of the arbitrators to ensure that their award can circulate as provided for under the applicable norms. The relevant international law rules are, in this respect, sufficiently clear in highlighting the exclusive importance of the *contents of the award* (and not of its translation) as a ground for challenging the award and refusing its recognition.

In this regard one should read the relevant provisions contained in the most significant legal texts concerning the language of the arbitration as a call for responsibility of both the parties and the arbitrators in taking into consideration the effects of their choice. According to an ordinary rule in international commercial arbitration, arbitrators are empowered to determine the language (or languages) of the arbitration in the absence of an agreement by the parties.[12]

---

[11] See Cass. n° 1182 of January 19, 2007; the Supreme Court had confirmed the decision of the Venice Court of Appeal that had dismissed the claim for recognition of a judgment of the District Court of Jefferson, Alabama.

[12] See article 5 of the Arbitration Rules of the Chamber of National and International Arbitration of Milan, Article 22 of the 1985 UNCITRAL Model Law on International Commercial Arbitration (as amended in 2006), article 16 of the

Moreover, it is also commonly admitted that arbitrators can supplement the parties' agreement as to the choice of the law applicable to the merits, particularly when their choice is open, as in cases where the arbitral clause provides for a multiple choice, e.g. the choice of more than one national applicable law as well as international law.[13]

As the two things frequently go together in international practice, for the sake of the free circulation of arbitral awards – and to some extent this is a truly common target – it would be of some importance that the parties and the arbitrators make a choice of the language of the arbitration which proves to be consistent with the (choice of the language of) the applicable law.

References

Bariatti, Stefania. 1986. *L'interpretazione delle convenzioni internazionali di diritto uniforme*. Padua: CEDAM.

Ricoeur, Paul. 2006. *On Translation*, translated by Eileen Brennan, London, Routledge (*Sur la traduction.* Montrouge: Bayard 2002).

Sacco, Rodolfo. 1996. "Comparer les droits. A propos de l'ouvrage de J. Vanderlinden". *Revue internationale de droit comparé* 3: 659-668.

—. 1999. "Langue et droit". In *Les multiples langues du droit européen uniforme,* edited by Rodolfo Sacco and Luca Castellani, 163-185. Paris-Torino: L'Harmattan.

Vanderlinden, Jacques. 1995. *Comparer les droits*. Bruxelles: Kluwer-Belgique/ Story Scientia.

Várady, Tibor. 2006. *Language and Translation in Commercial Arbitration: From the Constitution of the Arbitral Tribunal through Recognition and Enforcement Proceedings*. The Hague: TMC Asser Press.

Rules of Arbitration of the International Chamber of Commerce of Paris (ICC), which also provide that the choice of the language or languages of the arbitration is to be made "… due regard being given to all relevant circumstances, including the language of the contract".

[13] See as an example the decision of the Stockholm Court of Appeal 15 May, 2003, in case n° T 8735-01 *The Czech Republic v. CME Czech Republic B.V.*, in *Rivista dell'Arbitrato*, 2003, 815; cf. article 17 of ICC Arbitration Rules, and article 3 of Rules of the Milan Chamber of National and International Arbitration.

CHAPTER THREE

ANALYSING INTERNATIONAL COMMERCIAL ARBITRATION AWARDS AS GENRE

VIJAY K BHATIA AND JANE LUNG

1. Introduction

Although legal genres have been extensively researched both in their spoken and written forms with a focus on rhetorical and cognitive move structures (Bhatia 1982, 1993, 2004; Lung 2008), there has been relatively little research in the analysis of arbitration discourse. This chapter aims to fill this gap by analyzing the genre of arbitration awards. The term arbitration refers to a non-litigative method of resolving disputes between two parties. This is essentially carried out by an impartial tribunal consisting of one or more arbitrators, not necessarily legal experts, but often knowledgeable in the areas of dispute. At the end of what is generally known as arbitration trial, the tribunal delivers an award, somewhat similar to a court judgment. This chapter will examine a corpus of awards in order to discover the nature of its organisation in terms of rhetorical moves and the manner in which these moves are embedded in a discursive pattern and how typical such patterns are. The chapter will also make an attempt to show how this discursive hierarchical pattern can be explained by taking into consideration the nature and communicative functions of arbitration awards.

As to the nature of arbitration, it is interesting to note that arbitration falls into the category of a consensual private dispute resolution process. It is consensual in that parties agree to submit their disputes to be resolved by an arbitral tribunal, and the resulting award is viewed as final and binding. Turner defines the arbitration award as

> the decision of the arbitrator based upon the submissions made to him in an arbitration. It can be made orally, but an oral award is not covered by the provisions of the Arbitration Act 1996 ("the 1996 Act") and oral awards

are rare, or an exceptional ad hoc measure in conditions of urgency – followed by the same in writing. An award must be the consequence of an arbitrator deciding as between opposing contentions, having weighed the evidence and submissions. (Turner 2005: 9)

2. Data and methodology

This study employs a genre analytical framework to examine the cognitive and rhetorical features of arbitration awards. The data used for this study draw on arbitration awards collected from different countries, namely Iran, Russia, Austria, China, France, America and Sweden. Although the arbitration trials were conducted in various countries, the awards were reported in English. Genre and discourse analyses take a number of factors into consideration in order to explain both institutional and social community goals. This study considers genre as a typical "staged, goal-oriented" (Martin 1985) "social action" (Miller 1984) serving a specific communicative purpose (Swales 1990; Bhatia 1993).

3. Discursive hierarchical patterning in arbitration awards

This section examines some of the typical rhetorical and cognitive patterns one may find in arbitration awards, illustrating how such patterns are presented, and discussing what kind of information is textualised through what can be viewed as a discursive hierarchical pattern (DHP). A discursive hierarchical pattern can be defined as individual discursive patterns organized hierarchically in terms of three aspects: textual, generic and social. The textual aspects include the use of linguistic resources such as lexico-grammar and discourse markers, whereas the generic aspects relate to the generic moves which realize communicative purposes. Social aspects, on the other hand, have a direct bearing on how language is used and interpreted socio-critically.

The analysis reveals that arbitration awards tend to favour the following typical discursive hierarchical pattern (see Figure 1 below), consisting of four individual patterns (DHP 1-4).

Figure 1 shows that Arbitration Awards tend to display a typical Discursive Hierarchical Move Pattern, which begins with the opening Move "Heading" (ArbDHP-Pre-1) meant to be a brief guide to the award. "Heading" is followed by the first Move "Recitals" (ArbDHP-1) offering the essential background information about the award. ArbDHP-1 includes four steps, "Introducing the parties" (ArbDHP-1-S1), "Competence of the tribunal" (ArbDHP-1-S2), "Pre-hearing proceedings and applicable law"

(ArbDHP-1-S3) and "General statements of a dispute" (ArbDHP-1-S4). This is generally followed by Move 2 entitled "Details of the dispute" (ArbDHP-2), consisting of three steps, "Summary of agreed facts" (ArbDHP-2-S1), "Submissions and claims and/or counterclaims by the parties" (ArbDPH-2-S2), and "Relief sought by the parties" (ArbDHP-2-

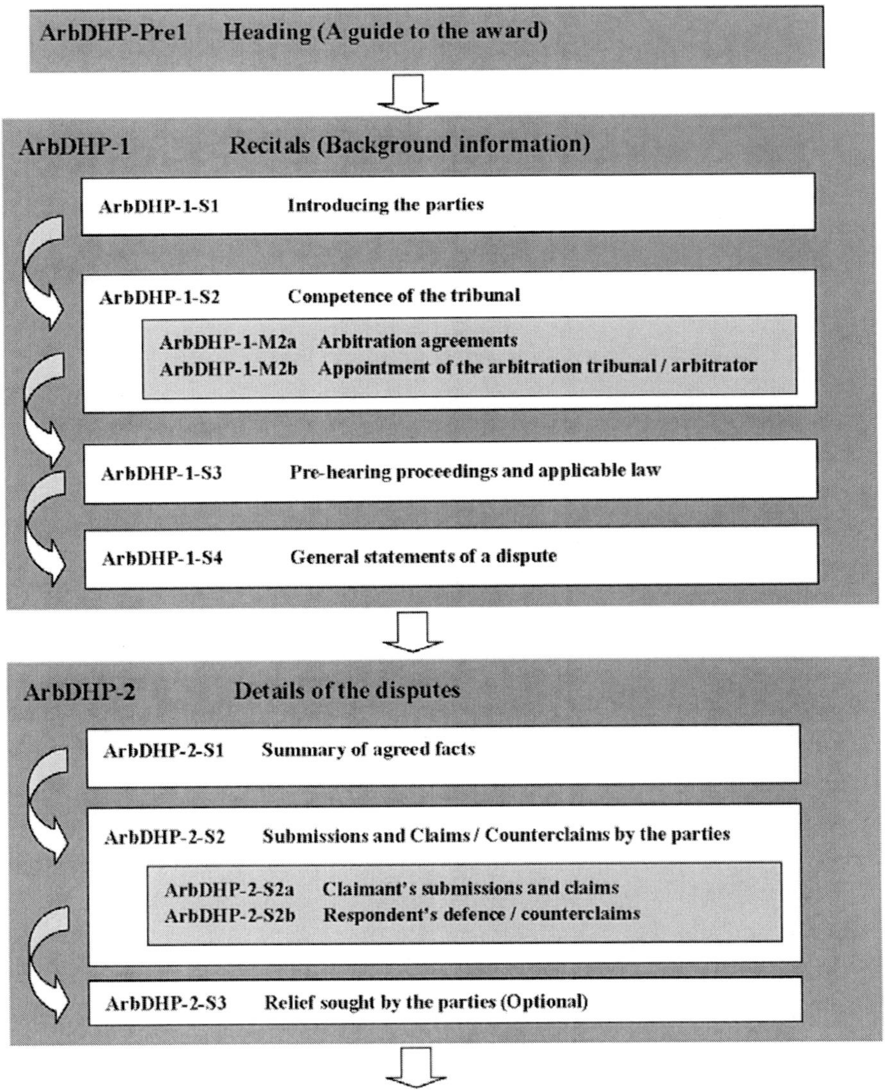

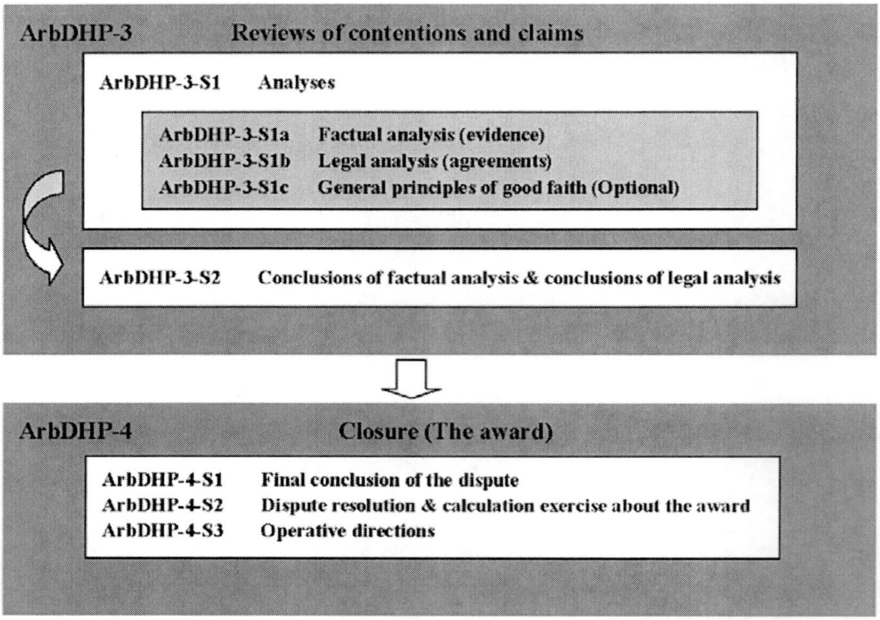

Figure 1. Discursive hierarchical patterning in arbitration awards.

S3). Having given the details of the disputes and the awards, then Move 3 "Review of contentions and claims" (ArbDHP-3) follows, which, once again consists of several steps, especially "Analyses" (ArbDHP-3-S1), such as "Factual analysis" (ArbDHP-3S1a), "Legal analysis" (ArbDHP-3S1b), and "General principles of good faith" (ArbDHP-3S1c). The second step of Move 3 consists of "Conclusions of factual analysis and conclusions of legal analysis" (ArbDHP-3-S2). The final Move 4 "Closure (The award)" (ArbDHP-4) incorporates three steps: "Final conclusion of the dispute" (ArbDHP-4-S1), "Dispute resolution and calculation exercise about the award" (ArbDHP-4-S2), and "Operative directions" (ArbDHP-4-S3). The following sections will illustrate the discursive hierarchical patterns in arbitration awards in greater detail.

3.1. Heading (ArbDHP-Pre-1)

All arbitration awards carry a heading (ArbDHP-Pre-1), which includes standardized information identifying it as an arbitration award, at the same time providing other helpful information such as the identification of the tribunal, e.g. *Iran-United States Claims Tribunal*, the legislation under which the arbitration is conducted, the date *28.07.1989*, and the name of the parties to the dispute, as in *Watkins-Johnson Co. & Watkins-Johnson Ltd. v. The Islamic Republic of Iran & Bank Saderat Iran,* indicating also their status (i.e. *claimant* and *respondent*). In addition, it often contains some reference to the seat of arbitration. Here are some typical examples:

(1) Date: 28.07.1989
Country: Arbitral Award
Number: 370 (429-370-1)
Court: Iran-United States Claims Tribunal
Parties: Watkins-Johnson Co. & Watkins-Johnson Ltd. v. The Islamic Republic of Iran & Bank Saderat Iran
(nf_1989.07_Iran_measures)

Or

(2) Date: 12.12.2007
Country: Arbitral Award
Number: 50181T 0036406
Court: American Arbitration Association
Parties: Macromex Srl. v. Globex International Inc.
(American arbitration association)

3.2. Move 1 - Recitals (Background information) (ArbDHP-1)

After the heading – corresponding to ArbDHP-Pre-1–, arbitration awards proceed to the first Move called "Recitals" (ArbDHP-1) which provides the context for the dispute and sets the scene for the award by giving background information. The main purpose of this Move is to account for the initial phase of the arbitration process indicating the appointment of the arbitrator, with reference to the arbitration agreement, often setting out the sequence of events leading to the appointment. This typically incorporates three main steps, which introduce the disputing parties, establishing the competence of the tribunal, many of the preliminary considerations as well as the applicable law, finally concluding with an overall summation of the dispute being negotiated. The following are the typical steps in Move 1.

ArbDHP-1-S1: Introducing the parties
ArbDHP-1-S2: Competence of the Tribunal
ArbDHP-1-S2a: Arbitration agreements

ArbDHP-1-S2b: Appointment of the Tribunal / arbitrator
ArbDHP-1-S3: Pre-hearing proceedings and applicable law
ArbDHP-1-S4: General statements of a dispute

We will now consider some typical illustrations of each step.

3.2.1. Introducing the parties (ArbDHP-1-S1)

At this stage the parties are identified through almost formulaic statements, as in the following case:

(3) A. The parties
1. The claimant … is a limited liability company incorporated and existing under the laws of The People's Republic of China [hereinafter Buyer].
2 The Respondent [and Counterclaimant … is a company incorporated and existing under the laws of the Republic of Brazil (hereinafter Buyer]
3 [Buyer] and [Seller] are together referred to as the "Parties" in this Award. (*Sweden*)

The communicative purpose here is first to assign functional roles to the parties. The narrative often moves forward to the historical account of the dispute, giving details as to how and when the parties entered into an agreement/contract. In terms of lexico-grammatical resources, this step typically makes use of nominals or nouns, such as *seller, buyer, company(ies), arbitration, contract(s)/agreement(s)* etc.

3.2.2. Competence of the Tribunal (ArbDHP-1-S2)

After introducing the parties, the award proceeds to step 2, which establishes the competence or jurisdiction of the tribunal to arbitrate the dispute, almost always based on the interpretation of the arbitration clause in the agreement or contract agreed to by the parties. This move may involve discussion of two issues, the agreement (ArbDHP-1-S2a: Arbitration agreements) and the appointment of the tribunal (ArbDHP-1-S2b: Appointment of the Tribunal/arbitrator), which will now be illustrated separately.

Arbitration agreements (ArbDHP-1-S2a) - At this stage of the award reference is made to the arbitration agreement, without which there can be no basis for arbitration at all, as arbitration is a creature of the agreement between the two parties to a dispute. It is for this reason that arbitration is often seen as a consensual process mutually agreed upon by the parties so that if a dispute should arise, it would be resolved by arbitration. The arbitration agreement provides the basis for an arbitrator's jurisdiction (e.g. *the Rules of the Arbitration Institution of the Stockholm Chamber of Commerce ("SCC Rules")*). It also states the place (or the "seat") of arbitration (e.g. *Stockholm, Sweden*), the applicable arbitration rules, the language in which the dispute is going to be negotiated during the proceedings (e.g. *English*), the number of arbitrators (e.g. *one arbitrator*) and how they are to be appointed (e.g. *appointed by the Arbitration Institution of the Stockholm Chamber of Commerce ("SCC")*). Typical lexico-grammatical devices include *arbitration* (e.g. *arbitration clause, arbitration agreement, arbitration commission* and *arbitration tribunal*), *arbitrator* (e.g. *...which invites the arbitrator to determine the law applicable to the merits of the dispute, the sole arbitrator believes that..., the arbitrator must, in order to resolve the dispute, determine an applicable law.* A typical example is the following:

(4) "Pressure Sensor Agreement ('Agreement') which was concluded by the Parties in Houston, USA on 25 April 2002.
Article 17 (a) of the Agreement reads as follows:
"Any disputes arising out of ... this Agreement shall be settled ... by one arbitrator, the award being final and binding. The arbitration shall be held in Sweden. The language ... shall be English."

Appointment of the arbitral tribunal / arbitrator (*ArbDHP-1-S2b*) - Having discussed the arbitration agreement, the award then moves on to discuss the "Appointment of the tribunal" (ArbDHP-1-S2b), which gives a brief account of the sequence of events leading to the appointment of the tribunal, and sometimes the appointing authority is also mentioned. The main communicative purpose is to show that the arbitrator's appointment was in accordance with the arbitration agreement, as made explicit by the formulaic expression *In accordance with the arbitration clauses in their contracts*. The arbitral tribunals can be either appointed by the parties, or by an appointing authority chosen by the parties (e.g. *the Arbitration Commission*). The composition of the arbitral tribunal may vary, consisting of a sole arbitrator, or two or more arbitrators, and with or without a chairman. The number of arbitrators is usually stated in the arbitration clause or agreed to by the parties after a dispute has arisen. A single arbitrator is usually appointed by the agreement, but, in the case of three arbitrators, each party appoints one arbitrator, and the two arbitrators thus appointed then select a neutral third arbitrator, who presides over the trial. Here is a typical example from the corpus.

(5) In accordance with the arbitration clauses in their contracts ...The [Seller] authorized the Chairman of the Arbitration Commission to appoint Mr Liu Wenjie the Arbitrator for the [Seller]. … the Chairman appointed Ms Zhou Xiaoyan the Arbitrator for the [Buyer] … the Chairman appointed Mr Wang Shengchang to act as the Presiding Arbitrator …. The three arbitrators formed the Arbitration Tribunal (*China*)

3.2.3 Pre-hearing proceedings and applicable law (ArbDHP-1-S3)

After establishing the arbitration tribunal, the award moves on to the next important step which indicates "*Pre-arbitration hearing proceedings*" often discussing the "*applicable law*". The main function of the pre-hearings is to identify the issue(s) to be resolved at the arbitration hearing, to decide the procedures to be followed, to make directions and to prepare a timetable (e.g. *set out a first timetable to be followed by the Parties in this arbitration*) for the conduct of the arbitration trial, as well as to consider any other preliminary matters such as fees, costs and deposits, including a copy of exhibits and documentary evidence that each party plans to introduce at the hearing. Thus, by referring to the pre-arbitration hearings, ArbDHP-1-S3 achieves its communicative purpose, that is, testifying firstly that a number of matters have been agreed on and settled in the pre-hearings; secondly, that the parties are ready to proceed with the hearing; thirdly, to explicitly re-state the parties' agreement on the applicable law in the arbitration concerned (e.g. *the UN Convention on Contracts for the International Sale of Goods ("CISG")*). Since ArbDHP-1-S3 specifies that certain rules are to be applied and why they are to be applied, certain words and expressions are then foregrounded, such as *The arbitral tribunal first determined the applicable law, the applicable law in this arbitration shall be, the Convention applies when..., according to Article...the Convention would also be applicable if..., suffice to exclude the application of the Convention*, as indicated in the following extract:

(6) Procedural Order No. I … sets out a first timetable … confirms the Parties' agreement that the applicable law… shall be the UN Convention on the International Sale of Goods ("CISG") (*Sweden*).

And,

(7) The proceedings were bifurcated and it was agreed that the arbitral tribunal would in the first stage determine the matters of applicable law and limitation periods.

> The arbitral tribunal first determined the applicable law. Because the 1980 Convention on the International Sale Goods (CISG) … the Convention applies when both contracting parties have their place of business in Contracting States. … according to Art. 1(1)(b) the Convention would also be applicable if the rules of private international law led to the application of the law of a Contracting State. … Nor did the fact that the parties had agreed on a limitation period different from that in the CISG suffice to exclude the application of the Con. (*ICC-Paris*)

3.2.4. General statements of a dispute (ArbDHP-1-S4)

After discussing the applicable law, the next step (ArbDHP-1-S4) follows with some general statements of dispute(s) involved. It briefly defines the main issues, thus outlining the dispute and providing the prelude for Move 2 (ArbDHP-2) which gives the *Details of the disputes*. The general statements of the dispute (ArbDHP-1-S4) also identifies precisely what the dispute is about (e.g. *failure to take delivery*) and who initiated (e.g. *brought by Seller*) the action against whom (e.g. *against Buyer*). Typical lexico-grammatical features of the narratives used in this part of the award are, *[Buyer] brought a claim against [Seller], this action was brought by [Seller]…against [Buyer], the insurer subsequently instituted arbitration against the [Seller], such requests were refused by [Seller], respondent rejected this request, respondent had not fulfilled its obligations on the basis of (two) contracts, a dispute arose as to the price of…, respondent terminated the Agreement* as indicated in the following examples.

(8) This action was brought by [Seller], a Pakistani company, against [Buyer], a Russian company, in connection with failure to take delivery of the second lot of goods prepared for shipment …. (f_2000_02_russian_reduce damage).

And,

(9) … the insurer indemnified the buyer for the damage. The insurer subsequently instituted arbitration against the [Seller]. *(ICC-Paris)*

3.3. Move 2 - Details of the disputes (ArbDHP-2)

After giving the background about the tribunal appointment in Move 1 *Recitals* (ArbDHP-1), Move 2 (ArbDHP-2) gives the *Details of the disputes*. This Move is generally realized in terms of three steps, as indicated below:

ARbDHP-2-S1: Summary of agreed facts
ARbDHP-2-S2: Submissions and Claims / Counterclaims by the parties
ArbDHP-2-S2a: Claimant's submission and claims
ArbDHP-2-S2b: Respondent's submission and defence / counterclaims
ArbDHP-2-S3Relief sought by the parties

3.3.1. Summary of agreed facts (ArbDHP-2-S1)

The first step in Move 2 summarizes agreed facts (ArbDHP-2-S1) not necessarily in full detail; the focus, as in legal judgments, is often on "material facts", not on all facts. It must be pointed out here that this stage identifies facts that are not disputed and simply offers a kind of recap of the documentary evidence supplied by the parties. The recap may include all relevant dates and contract/agreement numbers in a clear, concise and chronological manner, such as in *On 19 February 2001, the [Seller] and the [Buyer] reached another agreement, Contract No. 21041*; *On 17 April 2001, the [Seller] entered into a new Contract No. 21041A)*. These facts may also include the payment (e.g. *the [Buyer] paid only US $9,900.00 as a token payment*) and the quantity of the consignment (e.g. *a total quantity of 650,090 tons form part of two consignments of cold-rolled sheet, a partial consignment of 350,090 tons*). Other facts may also include the shipment dates (e.g. *The shipment dates were expressly established in each order as follows: No. 38268-38297: 4/24/06 +1-2 weeks; No. 38298-30297: 5/1/06 +1-2 weeks…As such, all products were to be shipped no later than May 29, 2006.*)

All these facts then lead on to a brief initial account of the dispute, its nature and issues at stake, i.e., *The [Seller] withheld the amount of US $ 29,700.00 on its account to date; The fact that the respondent did not settle the invoices [...] in question should be regarded as an infringement of its obligation under Art. 53 of the CISG to pay the price for the goods.* Some of the preferred lexico-grammatical expressions include *it may be disputed between the parties; an infringement of its obligation under Art. XX of the GISG; the [Seller] believed the [Buyer] would not be able to fulfill its payment under Contract No. xxx; [Buyer] is liable for failure to perform contractual obligations; under the CISI [Seller] should have taken such measures; the [Seller] failed to ship to it in a timely manner; according to this Agreement; in accordance with the Agreement; pursuant to the Agreement.* Here is a good example:

(10) On 19 February 2001, the [Seller] and the [Buyer] reached another agreement, Contract No. 21041. … the [Buyer] paid only US $9,900.00 as a token payment. The [Seller] believed that the [Buyer] would not be able to fulfill its payment obligation under Contract No. 21041, … and agreed to cancel Contract No. 21041. On 17 April 2001, the [Seller] entered into a new Contract No. 21041A directly with the ultimate customer, the American Company D, who agreed to pay the [Seller] US $100,080.00 including US $29,700.00 which should be paid to the [Buyer]... The [Seller] withheld the amount of US $ 29,700.00 on its account to date. (China)

3.3.2. Submissions and Claims / Counterclaims by the parties (ArbDHP-2-S2)

Step 2 of Move 2 "Submissions and Claims / Counterclaims by the parties" (ArbDHP-2-S2) as the name suggests accounts for the relevant information about the parties' submissions and claims or counterclaims. In view of the fact that arbitrators are impartial and knowledgeable persons in the areas of controversy, it is essential for them to allow each of the parties to have sufficient opportunity to make submissions on the evidence and to present their cases. When it comes to defining an arbitration claim, it could be summed up as a statement of injury along with a request for compensation. This compensation might be in the form of an estimated or exact amount of money. A claim is presented by the party demanding arbitration, and the respondent files a Response to the Demand which may or may not include a claim for compensable injuries. Step 2, thus, is composed of two sub-moves: Claimant's submission and claims (ArbDHP-2-S2a) and Respondent's submission and defence / counterclaims (ArbDHP-2-S2b).

Claimant's submission and claims (*ArbDHP-2-S2a*) ArbDHP-2-S2a sets out a brief but precise summary of the parties' contentions in a statement of claim (e.g. *set forth in the Statement of Claim)* by describing what happened (e.g. *failing to provide Sensors that can meet warranted technical specifications*), why liability does or does not exist (e.g. *warranted technical specifications set out in the Agreement*), what the issues to be resolved are (e.g. *[Seller] has fundamentally breached the Agreement*). When describing the details of the disputes, relevant laws or rules are referred to (e.g. *Article 11(d)*). The conclusion is then drawn (e.g. *by failing to perform its contractual obligations and breaching the warranties given under Article 11(d), [Seller] has fundamentally breached the Agreement*).

Words and phrases which are commonly used in ArbDHP-2-S2a include *set forth in the Statement of Claim, set out in the Agreement, Claimant has taken the view, Claimant contends that, Claimant also contends that, Claimant further submits/stated that.* Other expressions include *should be assessed according to (Italian) law, fails to perform (Article 1218) in respect of individual performances, regarding the Agreement signed between claimant and respondent, respondent had no right to terminate the Agreement,* as illustrated below:

(11) [Buyer]'s Case and Claims

> 75. [Buyer]'s fundamental case, as set forth in the Statement of Claim, is that by failing to provide [Seller] Sensors that can meet warranted technical specifications set out in the Agreement and failing to cure the material defects found in [Seller] Sensors within a reasonable period of time, [Seller] has fundamentally breached the Agreement.

The Claimant's claims follow, accompanied by the reasons that support and justify them. These claims could include lost profits (e.g. *it is therefore entitled to be compensated for the profits it lost due to [Seller]'s breach of the Agreement)*, and/or the actual cost and expenses incurred for the transaction (e.g. *it is entitled to be compensated for the costs and expenses wasted due to [Seller]'s breach*). Sometimes the Claimant may also demand the recovery of the arbitration fees paid and the legal expenses. Words and expressions which are commonly used include *breach of contract, the breaching party, the non-breaching party, its breaching behavior*, and *it is entitled to be compensated,* as seen in the following example:

(12) 82. [Buyer] contends that a party who suffers damages as a result of another's breach of contract is entitled to be compensated for the profits which would otherwise have been gained from such contract if it is duly performed. [Buyer] submits that it is therefore entitled to be compensated for the profits it lost due to [Seller]'s breach of the Agreement. ... Therefore, [Buyer] claims that it is entitled to be compensated for the costs and expenses wasted due to [Seller]' s breach. (*Sweden*)

Respondent's defence/counterclaims (*ArbDHP-2-S2b*) - After Claimant's submission and claims in ArbDHP-2-S2a, ArbDHP-2-S2b provides the opportunity for the Respondent to make defence/counterclaim submissions and present his/her case. A transition phrase or sentence usually links the submissions of the Claimant and the Respondent. These transition devices include *The [Seller] objected to the [Buyer]'s claims*, or *The [Buyer] objected to the claims upon which of the [Seller] based his / her assertions, inter alia, on [Buyer]'s breach of the contract conditions*, or *In its Statement of Defence, Set-off claims and Counterclaims, [Seller] put forward a quite different story.* The Respondent then starts explaining and putting forward his/her defence or counterclaims. Let us look at a typical example of Respondent's defence:

(13) 84. In its Statement of Defence, Set-off Claims and Counterclaims, [Seller] put forward a quite different story. Based on its own version of the facts, [Seller] asserts that it has not breached the Agreement and denies its liability with respect to the performance of the Agreement in its entirety. [Seller] also sets out two set-off claims and further brings its counterclaims against [Buyer] for infringement of [Seller]'s proprietary and confidential technology. (*Sweden*)

3.3.3 Relief sought by the parties (Optional) (ArbDHP-2-S3)

Steps ArbDHP-2-S2a and ArbDHP-2-S2b are sometimes followed by ArbDHP-2-S3, in which Arbitrators may state the relief sought by both parties, by citing the Statement of Claim.

The relief sought by Claimant could include the kind of award that Claimant would like to seek from arbitrators (e.g. *a declaratory award*), what he/she would like arbitrators to declare (e.g. *by failure to provide goods as warranted in the Agreement, [Seller] has fundamentally breached its obligations to [Buyer] under the* Agreement), the amount that Claimant wants Respondent to pay (e.g. *US $300,000 for those defective pressure sensors*).

The relief sought by Respondent could include dismissing Claimant's claims (e.g. *dismiss [Buyer]'s claims, with prejudice, in their entirety*), enjoining the Claimant from doing something (e.g. e*njoin [Buyer] ... from unauthorized use and disclosure of [Seller]'s confidential information*), and awarding Respondent his / her incurred cost and expenses (e.g. *award [Seller] his / her costs and expenses, including reasonable attorneys' fees, incurred in defending against [Buyer]'s claims and in pursuing [Seller]'s counterclaims*).

The excerpts below provide an example of relief sought by the claimant and the respondent respectively:

(14) Relief sought by [Buyer]

113. In its Statement of Claim, [Buyer] seeks from me ... a declaratory award ... an award that [Seller] be ordered to take back the defective pressure sensors already delivered ... and repay to [Buyer] US $300,000 for those defective pressure sensors ...(*Sweden*)

(15) Relief Sought by [Seller]

115. In its Statement of Defence, Set-off Claims and Counterclaims, [Seller] requests that I:

a. dismiss [Buyer]'s claims, with prejudice, in their entirety;

b. set off an award, if any, in favour of [Buyer] and against [Seller] in the amount of

i) approximately US $40,000, due to [Buyer]'s retention of a number of [Seller] Sensors; and

ii) US $25,000, representing the amount remitted by [Seller] as an introduction fee;

c. enjoin [Buyer], its officers, agents, servants, employees, attorneys, successors …

i) unauthorized use and disclosure of [Seller]'s confidential information; and

ii) development, manufacture and sale of sensors that are based upon [Seller]'s proprietary technology;

d. direct [Buyer] to account to [Seller] for its profits arising from the conduct complained of herein;

e. award damages to [Seller] in an amount to be determined at the conclusion of this arbitration proceeding;

f. award [Seller] its costs and expenses, including reasonable attorneys' fees, incurred in defending against [Buyer]'s claims and in pursuing [Seller]'s counterclaims …(*Sweden*)

3.4. Move 3 - Reviews of contentions and claims (The tribunal's reasoning) (ArbDHP-3)

Move 3 *Reviews of contentions and claims* (ArbDHP-3) details the tribunal's review of contentions and claims. Reasons given in this pattern should adequately show the arbitrator's analyses and reasoning, while reviewing and summarizing the parties' respective positions. It analyses both the facts and the law by assessing the evidence, and at the same time discussing the range of factual and legal issues involved. This pattern also addresses the context of the award and sets forth specifically relevant legal considerations. The dates of hearing are given and the witnesses may be listed. Besides, goods or samples, land, buildings or plants and machinery may also be reviewed or inspected, so the relevant dates are also given. However, as to whether the parties' cases are dealt with issue by issue or by each party's case as a whole, there is no definite procedure. It all depends on an individual arbitrator's preference. In addition, the review need not give excessive details but will highlight the essentials of the contentions and claims. ArbDHP-3 is composed of two steps:

ArbDHP-3-S1: Analyses
ArbDHP-3-S2: Decisions on the disputed facts and decisions on law

3.4.1. Analyses

In its turn, the step *Analyses* (ArbDHP-3-S1) is composed of three sub-steps:

ArbDHP-3-S1a: Factual analysis (evidence)
ArbDHP-3-S1b: Legal analysis (agreements)
ArbDHP-3-S1c: General principles of good faith (Optional)

Factual analysis (evidence) (ArbDHP-3-S1a) - ArbDHP-3-S1a begins with a consideration of the facts of the award and any evidence offered. Each party provides proof of the facts and presents its case, including relevant documents and testimony which can establish and prove their claim or counterclaim. However, since the tribunal acts as an inquisitor to ascertain the facts, it considers the evidence that the parties offer and decides how that evidence should be weighed when reaching a decision. Both parties present their submissions and evidence. All the facts and the related information relevant to the case are arranged in a logical order, be it the chronological sequence in which they occurred or any other established criteria. The facts are weighed with an assessment of the evidence, and key facts which appear to be crucial to the outcome of the award are identified. It is also essential to disclose the evidence to the parties, so that they have an opportunity to make submissions regarding the evidence or rebut the evidence if appropriate.

While the representative of the other party usually cross-examines the witnesses in order to bring out any inconsistencies or shortcomings in the witness's evidence, the representative of the party may re-examine the witness in order to clarify any matter raised in the cross-examination. The parties' respective expert witnesses or an independent expert may also be called upon in arbitration. A copy of the expert's report will also be delivered to each party so that they can have an opportunity to challenge any part of the report.

Although In ArbDHP-3-S1a, all the documents and information identified and included are specific and relevant to the issue of dispute, it is interesting that the evidence submitted is not analyzed or discussed in great detail. However, opinions are given. The following is a typical example:

(16) The Tribunal examined and evaluated the following evidence submitted by the [Seller]:

a. The fourteen contracts of sale, exports customs declarations, exports foreign currencies exchange declarations, bills of lading and textile products export certificate, commercial invoices, etc;

b. The Audit Confirmation produced by Hong Kong Wang Zheng Bang Accounting Firm on behalf of Company C;

c. Company C's letter dated on 22 November 2001 to the [Seller] demanding the outstanding payment;

d. Communications between parties on the issue of outstanding payments since 6 July 2000;

e. A fax informing that the amount of US $29,700.00 payable to the [Buyer] under Contract No. 21041A was withheld by the [Seller];

f. Other evidence.

In this particular case the Tribunal found that the evidence was objective, relevant, valid and consistent, thus making it acceptable. Even though the Buyer did not submit any evidence nor raise any defence, this did not affect the decision of the Tribunal on the evidence available.

Legal analysis (agreements) (ArbDHP-3-S1b) - ArbDHP-3-S1b follows ArbDHP-3-S1a. This pattern involves the identification of legal issues presented. These issues are then contested and the Tribunal, constituting ArbDHP-3-S1b, determines what law governs the issues based upon the factual scenario. Also considered is how the law that governs the legal issue applies to the facts, and often legal articles are cited, as can be seen below:

(17) The Tribunal accepted that the [Seller] fulfilled its contractual obligations under the fourteen contracts of sales while the [Buyer] took the contractual goods without paying the contract price on time. Therefore, according to Article 25 and Article 53 of the CISG, the [Buyer] is in breach of the contracts.

General principles of good faith (*Optional*) (*ArbDHP-3-S1c*) - ArbDHP-3-S1c involves a principle of contract law, the Good Faith principle, a concept of fair dealing that is sometimes considered in arbitral decisions, which is acknowledged by the CISG and referred to as the Principles of Good Faith. This concept is accepted as being an important rule in international contracts. The interpretation of the good faith concept as a uniform international law text was made plain by Article 7[1] of the CSIG and was interpreted as "the observance of good faith in international trade. The fact that Article 7[1] of the Principles of Good Faith is frequently referred to in arbitral decisions was pointed out by Barnes (2006), who further specified that in most cases the Principles are not the binding legal rules of the contract but are merely referred to or invoked by the tribunals or the parties as an aide in the decision-making process." Article 1.7 of the UNIDROIT Principles of International Commercial Contracts states:

> 1. Each party must act in accordance with good faith and fair dealing in international trade.
> 2. The parties may not exclude or limit this duty.

The sentiments incorporated in the above Article serve to emphasise that the concept of good faith is strongly connected with social and cultural needs. This concept, seen in the light of mutual confidence, correctness, co-operation and tolerance thus forms the basis of every human relationship, including business relationships.

Generally "good faith" involves "being honest in one's purpose and sincere in one's speech as well as the expectation of such qualities in others" (Pound 1922: 188). Even more pertinent is Simpson and Weiner's definition of "good faith" in *The Oxford English Dictionary* (1989: vol. 2, 379), as "freedom from intent to deceive". Mitchell (2006) further comments that while honesty is the touchstone of good faith from the standpoint of a subjective state of mind, this principle can also be viewed objectively incorporating the notions of fairness and reasonableness concerning an objective state of affairs.

While Civil law lawyers have tended to regard the concepts of good faith and fair dealing as essential to their legal systems, common law lawyers view them as recent innovations. Amazingly, of all the common law systems only the United States has taken this doctrine of good faith and fair dealing with regard to the performance of contracts and developed it relatively well to the benefit of all concerned.

A definition of the principles of good faith in arbitration rules is given below:

(18) Moreover, a general principle of good faith prevents a party from taking undue advantage of the remedies provided in case of breach of the other parties' obligations.

> [71] It would certainly be contrary to a general principle of good faith (and to Art. 80 of the CISG) to allow respondent to take advantage of the elapsing of the additional time granted to claimant while claimant was prevented to perform because of respondent's late response to a request for information necessary for performance. …
> [74] Finally, a general principle of good faith (also recalled in Art. 7 of the CISG) prevents a party from taking undue advantage of the

remedies provided in case of breach of the other party's obligations.... An email from Mr. R ... also shows that respondent had decided to terminate the Agreement even before the expiration of the additional period of time granted to for performance, and that its real scope was to use termination to renegotiate new contract terms, which is contrary to the principle of good faith and fair dealing in international trade. (ICC)

3.4.2. Conclusions of factual analysis and conclusions of legal analysis (ArbDHP-3-S2)

After the factual and legal analyses in ArbDHP-3-S1, ArbDHP-3-S2 spells out, as a record of decisions, the conclusions of factual analysis and the conclusions of legal analysis. Thus, a statement of findings of fact is necessary to an award. The clause *I find/found* or *the Tribunal found* is used when stating conclusions of fact analysis, for instance, *the Tribunal found the evidence objective and should be accepted or the prima facie established*. Then the conclusions of legal analysis are also stated, for example, according to relevant provisions, *the respondent is in breach of the contract and the claimant is entitled to the outstanding payments and interest*. It is noteworthy that in an award the law is not discussed in as much detail as it is in a common-law judgment for the reason that in court it is viewed as more essential that each decision of law be illustrated in sufficient detail. Based on the factual and legal analyses, the tribunal further express their view of the dispute, for example, whether they decide for the claimant and support the claimant's claim. In order to do this, the tribunal may also provide reasons to support their views. Certain expressions are used in this pattern, for instance, *Given the fact that, I accept Mr. C... C...'s evidence, I was also impressed by the evidence, I am satisfied that, I therefore conclude that.* The analyses and decisions on certain facts and law provided in this discursive pattern are important for making the final decision on the dispute and the dispute resolution in ArbDHP4 (the award). Examples are provided below:

(19) The Tribunal found that this evidence is objective, relevant, valid and consistent, thus should be accepted. ... The Tribunal accepted that the [Seller] fulfilled its contractual obligations under the fourteen contracts of sales while the [Buyer] took the contractual goods without paying the contract price on time. Therefore, according to Article 25 and Article 53 of the CISG, the [Buyer] is in breach of the contracts. Further, the [Seller] is entitled to the outstanding payments and interest pursuant to Article 74 and Article 78 of the CISG.

and,

(20) I accept Mr. C... C...'s evidence that ... I was also impressed by the evidence that the alleged effect of temperature drift could have been avoided quite easily by [Buyer] ... I am satisfied that no fundamental breach has been established in this case... I therefore conclude that [Buyer] did copy [Seller]'s confidential information and that this was a breach of the agreement entitling [Seller] to relief. (*Sweden*)

3.5. Closure: The Award (ArbDHP-4)

ArbDHP-3 (Reviews of contentions and claims) is followed by ArbDHP-4, which is the closing section of an arbitration award, and in fact contains the award proper which provides a resolution to the dispute. It could include the following steps:

ArbDHP-4-S1: Final decision of the dispute facts and law
ArbDHP-4-S2: Dispute resolution (the award) & Calculation exercise
ArbDHP-4-S3: Operative directions

3.5.1. Final conclusion of the dispute (ArbDHP-4-S1)

After the reasoning and reviewing of contentions and claims in ArbDHP3, the tribunal makes the final conclusion of the dispute in ArbDHP-4-S1 (Final conclusion of the dispute), stating whether one of the two parties is liable for the costs of the arbitration proceedings, or both parties had breached the contractual provisions, with reference to the rules of applicable law. Certain expressions are typically used such as *The Tribunal decides that, the Tribunal finds that, the Tribunal considers that*.... As in the following examples:

(21) The Tribunal decides that the [Buyer] should be liable for all the costs of the arbitration proceedings. (*China*)

Or

(22) Considering the aforesaid and taking into account that both parties had breached both the contractual provisions and the rules of applicable law ... (_2000_02_russian_reduce damage)

3.5.2. Dispute resolution (the Award) and calculation exercise (ArbDHP-4-S2)

ArbDHP-4-S2 immediately follows ArbDHP-4-S1 providing a resolution to the dispute involved, that is, the arbitration award proper. To sum up or conclude the preceding established facts and analyses, recurrent expressions are used. For instance, *Taking the above into consideration / Taking into the account the information of the [party]'s representatives.../ In such circumstance / On the above facts and analysis, the Tribunal rules that / renders the following Award.* ArbDHP-4-S2 explicitly spells out whether the claimant's claims are or are not (fully) granted or denied with justifications. The Award could include the claimant's claims, the arbitration costs, arbitration fees and other relevant expenses such as the incurred costs, the amount of damages as well as the interest on the amount due by claimant and by respondent. There follow some examples:

(23) In such circumstances, the Tribunal finds it proper to apply the principle of joint liability as set forth in article 404(1) of the Russian Federation Civil Code. The Tribunal finds it reasonable to place two third of the [Buyer]'s claims on the [Seller]. The rest of the [Buyer]'s claims of damages should be dismissed.

3.5 [Arbitration fees and expenses]. Since the [Buyer]'s claims are not fully granted, p 6(2) of the Regulation pursuant to Articles on arbitration fees and expenses, the [Seller] should pay such fees and expenses in proportion to the claims granted.

3.6 [Legal expenses]. Pursuant to Article 9 of the Regulations on arbitration fees and expenses, a winning party may demand that the other party reimburse reasonable expenses incurred in connection with the arbitration and, in particular, legal expenses. However, the [Buyer] did not present evidence of his legal expenses. Therefore, the Tribunal denies such claim.

Or

(24) The Decision

On the above facts and analysis, the Tribunal rules:

1. The [Buyer] shall pay the [Seller] the outstanding payments of US $205,280.77;

2. The [Buyer] shall pay the interest in the amount of US $12,109.73.

3. The cost of this arbitration, renminbi [RMB] 73,973 is ordered against the [Buyer]. The [Seller] has paid the arbitration fee of RMB 73,973 in advance to the Arbitration Commission, therefore, the [Buyer] shall reimburse RMB 73,973 to the [Seller];

4. The execution of the above decision shall be completed within 45 days from the day on which this award becomes effective. This decision is final. (*China*)

ArbDHP-4-S2 also involves the calculation exercise by analysing the amount awarded on the claim which includes the principal sums, the cost of damages, the loss profit or expenses incurred and the interest awarded. However, reasons for the award of cost and for any discretion exercised judicially should be explicitly spelt out in order to show that the matter has been dealt with. The whole calculation exercise is done with great care and precision, as in the following example.

(25) (i) Arbitrators typically use the same fee calculation methods as the courts. See Porziqv. Dresdner, Kleinwert, Benson, North America, 2007 W.L. 2241592, at *5 (2nd Cir. Aug. 7, 2007) ("[I]n ascertaining the amount of reasonable attorney's fees to which a successful claimant is entitled, arbitration panels use the same fee calculation methods as the courts -- generally the "lodestar analysis"). Here, the situs of the arbitration is New York. The standard that New York courts use in determining attorney fee awards is one of reasonableness, based on the specific facts of the case. See Downes v. Aran, 273 AD.2d 435, 436, 710 N.Y.S,2d381, 382 (2d Dep't 2000); Santemma v. Chasco Co., 261 A.d.2d 408, 408, 689 N.Y.S.2d 220, 221 (2d Dep't 1999); Colangelo v. Colangelo, 176 Misc. 2d 837, 840, 673 N.Y.S.2d 897, 899 (Oneida Co, 1998); and Antidote Intern. Films, Inc. v. Bloomsbury Pub., PLC, 2007 WL 2175906, at *1 (SD.N.Y, July 30, 2007). "Relevant factors to be considered in determining reasonableness include the time required, the difficulties involved, the nature of the services provided, the amounts involved, the professional standing and ability of counsel, contingency or certainty of compensation, and the results obtained." See In re Estate of Drossos, 26 AD.3d 602, 603, 808 N.Y.2d 837,838 (3d Dep't 2006); Gaffney v. Village of Mamaroneck, 21 AD.3d 1032, 1032, 801 N.Y.S.2d 400, 401 (2d Dep't 2005); and Norwest Financial, Inc. v. Fernandez, 121 F. Supp. 2d 258, 262 (S.D,N.Y. 2000).

3.5.3. Operative directions (ArbDHP-4-S3)

After careful calculation of the amount awarded on the claim, awards then proceed to ArbDHP-4-S3 (Operative directions). This pattern records the decisions of the tribunal and the directions for disposing the costs of arbitration. It is especially useful when later dealing with the liability for recoverable costs. The direction must be specific, unambiguous and can be performed by the party against whom it is directed and no conditions or requirements should be included which make the award impracticable to enforce. The operative directions specify the deadline for completing the execution of the decision about the award. Here is a typical example.

(26) C. Within thirty (30) days of the date of issuance of this FINAL AWARD, Respondent shall take all necessary steps to ensure that the following aggregate sums are paid to Claimant.

(1) $608,323, representing the principal amount of the Interim Award;
(2) $38,689.34 representing pre-judgment interest.
(3) $152,080 representing legal fees.
(4) $28,519.47 representing non-AAA related costs as follows.
$12,600.00 Professor [...]
$4,000.00 Hotel, per diem and transportation
$2,520.00 Airfare
$9,399.41 Nicolletti Office Disbursements
$28,519.47
(5) The administrative fees and expenses of the American Arbitration Association totaling $8,500.00 shall be borne entirely by Respondent, and the compensation and expenses of the arbitrator totaling $71,748.77 shall be borne entirely by Respondent.
Therefore, Respondent shall reimburse Claimant the sum of $48,698.77 representing that portion of said fees and expenses in excess of the apportioned costs previously incurred by Claimant.
(6) Therefore, within thirty (30) days of issuance of this FINAL AWARD, Respondent shall pay to Claimant the total sum of $876,310.58.

D. Post-judgment interest shall be at the rate of the weekly one-year constant maturity (nominal) Treasury yield, as published by the Federal Reserve System, for the calendar week preceding the date of the Final Award. It shall be due per annum beginning thirty (30) days after the date of issue of this FINAL AWARD, until the judgment is paid or otherwise satisfied.

E. Except as expressly set forth above, this FINAL AWARD is in full settlement of all claims and counterclaims submitted to this arbitration.

This FINAL AWARD may be executed in any number of counterparts, each of which shall be deemed an original, and all of which shall constitute together one and the same instrument. SO ORDERED

[...]

(American-Arbitration-Association)

4. Conclusion

This chapter has proposed a categorization of hierarchical discursive patterns in arbitration awards with a view to uncovering regularities in discourse construction. The analysis reveals that arbitration awards tend to favour a typical discursive hierarchical pattern consisting of four individual patterns: ArbDHP-1 Recitals (Background), ArbDHP-2 Details of the disputes, ArbDHP-3 Reviews of contentions and claims, and ArbDHP-4 Closure (The award). These patterns, to a certain extent, may be attributed to the nature and communicative functions of arbitration awards. As discussed earlier in the chapter, in terms of its nature and functions, arbitration is a consensual private dispute resolution process and is consensual in that parties agree to submit their disputes to be resolved by an arbitral tribunal, whereby the resulting award is considered as final and binding. For example, ArbDHP-1 Recitals (Background) sets out the sequence of events leading to the appointment of the arbitrator, and establishes the competence of the tribunal as well as the applicable law. In ArbDHP-2 (Details of Disputes), submissions, claims, witness testimony and other evidence are presented in a similar manner to that of a court of law. Also, relevant laws or rules are referred to, with facts and legal analyses required in both arbitration and in a judicial system. However, the focus of arbitration is to give the reasons for supporting and justifying the claims made, the kind of award that a claimant would like to seek from arbitrators, or the relief sought by the parties. ArbDHP-3 (Reviews of contentions and claims) addresses the context of the award and sets forth specifically legal considerations. The tribunal express their view based on the factual and legal analyses, and decides whether they support the claimant's claim. However, as there is no definite procedure as to whether the parties' cases are dealt with issue by issue or by each party's case as a whole, it all depends on an individual arbitrator's preference. In addition, the review need not include excessive details but rather highlights the essentials of the contentions and claims. The final section ArbDHP-4 (Closure: The Award) offers a resolution to the dispute, giving it final conclusion and a summation of the previously established facts and analyses. Similar to pronouncing judgment in a court, this pattern explicitly spells out whether the claimant's claims are or are not (fully) granted or denied. Justifications and reasons for the award of cost and for any discretion exercised judicially are then explicitly spelt out in order to show that the matter has been dealt with. Thus, although arbitration does not take place in a court, it is still a legal process leading to a final and legally binding decision similar to a court judgment. As far as awards are concerned, they are equivalent to the decree of a court of law which are to be executed directly. On this ground, together with their highly conventionalized patterns as identified in this chapter, international commercial arbitration awards stand out in their own right as a distinctive genre in legal discourse.

References

Barnes, Jeffrey. 2006. "The continuing debate about 'plain language' legislation: a law reform conundrum". *Statute Law Review* 27, no. 2:, 83–132.

Bhatia, Vijay K. 1982. *An Investigation into the Formal and Functional Characteristics of Qualifications in Legislative Writing and Its Application to English for Academic Legal Purposes*. Ph.D. thesis, University of Aston in Birmingham, U.K.

—. 1993. *Analysing Genre – Language Use in Professional Settings.* London: Longman.

—. 2004. *Worlds of Written Discourse: A Genre-Based View*. London: Continuum.

Lung, Jane. 2008. "Discursive Hierarchical Patterning in Law and Management Cases". *English for Specific Purposes* 27, no. 4: 424-441.

Martin, James R. 1985. "Process and Text: Two Aspects of Semiosis". In James D. Benson and William S. Greaves (eds), *Systemic Perspectives on Discourse*. Vol. 1: Selected Theoretical Papers from the 9th International Systemic Workshop, 248-274. London: Ablex.

Miller, Carolyne R. 1984. "Genre as Social Action". *Quarterly Journal of Speech* 70: 151-167.

Mitchell, Andrew D. 2006. "Good Faith in WTO Dispute Settlement". *Melbourne Journal of International Law* 7, no. 2: 339-371.

Oxford English Dictionary 2nd Edition. 1989. Oxford: Clarendon Press.

Pound, Roscoe. 1922. *An Introduction to the Philosophy of Law*. New Haven: Yale University Press.

Swales, John M. 1990. *Genre Analysis: English in Academic and Research Settings.* New York: Cambridge University Press.

Turner, Ray. 2005. *Arbitration Awards: A Practical Approach.* Oxford: Blackwell.

CHAPTER FOUR

PERFORMATIVITY AND DEONTIC STRATEGIES IN FRENCH ARBITRATION AWARDS

CHIARA PREITE

1. Aim and scope

In this chapter, I shall analyse a corpus of arbitration awards comprising 13 awards drafted in French and issued by the International Chamber of Commerce (ICC) of Paris, between 1984 and 2003. My purpose is to investigate some pragmatic aspects framing the French arbitration award, namely how performativity and deontic modality are expressed in these texts.

Arbitration awards can be included in the category of *juridical writings* (Bhatia 1983)[1] or, according to Maley (1994), who refines Kurzon's (1989: 283-284) distinction between *language of the law* and *legal language*,[2] in the class of *judicial discourse.*[3] They are drafted as the result of an arbitration proceeding[4] and their structure and regulatory or prescriptive features are broadly similar to courtroom judgments (especially if supranational). Let us add that arbitration awards are hybrid texts that combine not only prescriptive features but also descriptive and narrative ones, sharing normative purposes and dispute description and narration. In fact, this kind of text is generally composed according to a structure that

---

[1] As against *Academic* writings and *Legislative* or *Statutory* writings.

[2] This distinction parallels a similar one, widely accepted among French scholars, between *Discours législatif*, which uses the *langage du droit*, and *Discours juridictionnel*, which uses *langage juridique*. See, among others, Ziembinski (1974); Cornu (2000); Bocquet (2008).

[3] As against *courtroom discourse*, *language of legal documents* and *anguage of legal consultations*.

[4] For an exhaustive systematization of Alternative Dispute Resolution and (International) Commercial Arbitration see Bernardini (2000) and Mustill and Boyd (1989[2]).

mostly overlaps the subdivision fixed for all French judgments since the publication of the *Nouveau Code de procedure Civile* (Artt. 454-455-456), as explained by Schroeder (1978): the modern presentation of judgments has to contain the *en-tête* (the *heading* in the award), the *exposé du litige* (the *procedural history*, including the *parties' positions*), the *motifs* or *motivation* (the *reasons*, including the *discussion*) and the *dispositif* (the *decision*).

If I apply Adam's (1992) textual theory of prototypical sequences to the sections composing a judgment (award included), the combination of descriptive, narrative and prescriptive features is made clear: the heading shows *descriptive* features; the procedural history and the parties' positions are mostly *narrative*; the reason and the discussion are clearly *argumentative*. Finally, the decision corresponds to the *regulative* or *instructive* prototype, described by Werlich (1975).[5]

1.1. Pragmatic features of legal language

In the judicial area, proceedings can be considered as dialogues among the parties and the judges, and the drafted awards keep trace of this interaction in form of reported speech and argumentation in which all other voices are incorporated. As is only natural, the decision does not imply the agreement of the losing party. The judges can pass a condemnation (even only a pecuniary one) without the losing party's agreement because law and justice have the power to compel people to do what they decide, also via argumentation based on equity and verisimilitude.

In this study, I shall make use of the notions elaborated within the framework of *Speech Act Theory* and, more specifically, of the concept of performativity as introduced by Austin (1962) and Benveniste (1966) and subsequently refined by other authors.[6] In particular the taxonomy of illocutionary acts I shall rely on is that put forth by Searle (1969, 1976) reformulating Austin's categories as *assertives*, *directives*, *commissives*, *expressives* and *declaratives*.[7]

---

[5] Adam (1992: 95) does not accept the autonomy of the *regulative* prototype postulated by Werlich and assimilates it to the *description*, even if aimed at the regulation of a behaviour in order to obtain a result. For a detailed presentation of the sequential heterogeneity of the judgments (drafted in French) of the Court of Justice of the European Union, see Preite (2005, 2008).

[6] For an outline and close examinations see among others Grzegorczyk (1974), Sbisà (1995) and Kerbrat-Orecchioni (2001).

[7] Austin's taxonomy comprises instead *Verdictives*, *Exercitives*, *Commissives*, *Behabitives* and *Expositives* (cf. Lecture XII: 148-163).

Here we are more specifically interested in *directives*, which are a kind of illocutionary acts "by means of which the addresser tries to influence the behaviour of the addressee" (Trosborg 1997: 36) and are characterised by *deontic modality*. *Declaratives* instead overlap with *performatives*, as they are used to perform acts or change a state of reality.

2. Performativity and legal language

As regards in particular institutional performatives, another important distinction is that made by Searle (1969: 33-34) between *regulative rules* (regulating an existent form of behaviour) and *constitutive rules* (bringing into being a new form of behaviour) which is parallel to a categorization customarily made in legal studies. Philosopher of law Gaetano Carcaterra (1994: 219ff.) defined *prescriptive rules* – mostly realised by means of deontic modality – as producing an event by exerting pressure on someone's behaviour, while *constitutive rules* produce contextually the effect they predicate, they constitute it by their coming into effect.

A further specification is highlighted by Conte (1994: 248-249) who distinguishes between performatives realizing an act by their utterance and constitutive performatives bringing into being a modification in reality, a new situation in the juridical setting. In order to name these concepts, Conte coined two terms which are not specifically legal and are consequently more suitable for use in linguistic analysis: he replaced *constitutive performative* by *thetic performative*, which not only performs an act but also constitutes a new state of things, and *simple performative* by the negative form *athetic performative.*

As for thetic performatives, Garzone (1996) observes that in a normative text the value of the declarative verb of the main clause, called *performative prefix* (or *super-énoncé performatif enchâssant* by Kerbrat-Orecchioni 2003), also concerns the content of the immediately following subordinate clause. Due to the *transitivity* property of thetic utterances, Garzone's (1996) argument goes on, the enclosed explicit or implicit content is invested by the performative value of the prefix.

2.1 Performativity and judgments

Within the French tradition, the philosopher of law Kalinowski (1974: 65) draws a parallelism between the functions of the legislator's language – generally seen as prototypically performative – and the judge's :

> Le langage performative du juge est semblable au langage du législateur dans la mesure où il sert lui aussi à une spécifique promulgation des normes édictées par le juge, normes singulières, appelées à régler le comportement des parties. [*The judge's performative language is similar to the legislator's language in so far as it is used also for the specific enactment of rules promulgated by the judge, single rules aimed at regulating the behaviour of the parties*].[8]

This amounts to claiming that judicial discourse is compared to normative or legislative discourse, as belonging to regulative legal texts. In describing French judgments, Cornu (2000: 352-354) points to a specification that also applies to arbitration awards:

> Comme le législateur, le juge dispose [...]. L'essentiel est que le dispositif énonce ce qui est obligatoire, au moins pour les parties, ce que le juge leur impose. Le dispositif porte des marques d'autorité comparables aux marques normatives de la règle de droit [...], mais dans une décision individuelle. [...] *Les verbes du dispositif* [...] *sont des prototypes de performatif* [...]. Cette vertu [...] signifie que *l'énoncé des verbes du dispositif suffit à réaliser la modification de l'ordonnancement juridique qui est attaché à la décision* (*emphasis added*). [*Similarly to the legislator, the judge disposes [...]. What is essential is that his decision enounces what is obligatory, at least for the parties, what the judge imposes on them. The decision features some marks of authority similar to the normative marks characterizing normative rules [...], but within the framework of an individual decision. [...]* The verbs in the decision [...] are prototypes of performatives *[...]. This property [...] means that the* enouncement of verbs in the decision suffices to realize the modification of the legal order which the decision involves (emphasis added)].

This parallelism between the judicial decision (containing the dispositions of the tribunal) and the rule of law allows to consider that thetic performativity (typically assigned to the enacting or promulgation formula of laws, statutes, constitutions, etc.) also characterises the prefix introducing the decision, and transfers this value to the whole text. This value enforces the judges' decision and compels the losing parties to abide by the court's authority.

2.2. Performativity and arbitration award decisions

The reflections above remain valid and applicable as far as arbitration awards are concerned.

---

[8] All translations are mine.

The decision (equivalent to the French *dispositif* mentioned by Cornu) settles the dispute between the parties and is usually introduced by a formula connecting it with the other sections of the text, as directly resulting from the prior discussion, such as the recurrent *Par ces motifs* [*for these reasons*] (cf. Example 1 below)[9] (which is the expression dedicated to the introduction of decisions in the French judicial tradition), or other longer and more explicit reformulations, e.g. *Vu les faits exposés ci-dessus et les considérants qui précèdent* [*in view of the above facts and the foregoing recitals*] (cf. Example 2 below), or the sum of the two as *Par ces motifs: Le Tribunal arbitral, après avoir entendu les avocats des parties et avoir délibéré à Paris le 9 novembre 1990* [*For the foregoing reasons, the arbitral tribunal, after having heard the parties' lawyers and having deliberated in Paris, on the 9th November 1990*] (cf. Example 3 below).

The decision is composed by a main clause containing the performative prefix (with the same value as the enacting formula of law, as mentioned above) and one sentence or a set of sentences representing the propositional content of the decision and comprising other performative verbs, as in examples (1), (2) and (3).

(1) *Par ces motifs*:
Le tribunal arbitral **décide**:
La convention relative au siège de l'arbitrage, incorporée dans la clause d'arbitrage, **lie** toujours les parties.

For the foregoing reasons:
*The arbitral tribunal **decides**:*
*The convention concerning the venue of the arbitration, incorporated into the arbitration clause, **is** always **binding** on the parties.*[10]

(2) *Vu les faits exposés ci-dessus et les considérants qui précèdent*, le Tribunal arbitral ***rend*** la sentence finale suivante:
9.1 **Il est pris acte** du désistement des Parties de leurs demandes respectives.
9.2 La Demanderesse **supporte** la totalité des frais d'arbitrage fixés [...].
9.3 La Demanderesse **doit payer** à la Défenderesse [...].

*In view of the above facts and the foregoing recitals, the arbitral tribunal **renders** its final award as follows:*

[9] Bold and italics in the examples are mine.
[10] The translation of all examples is mine

9.1 The withdrawal of the Parties' respective claims is recorded.
9.2. The claimant ***bears*** *the totality of the fixed costs of the arbitration [...].*
9.3. The claimant ***shall pay*** *to the respondent [...].*

(3) *Par ces motifs*:
Prononce
La clause arbitrale conclue à l'article 22 du contrat passé entre les parties le 24 janvier 1988 (valable dès le 1er janvier 1988) **est résolue**.

For the foregoing reasons:
Pronounces
The arbitral clause included in article 22 of the contract signed by the parties on the 24th of January 1988 (valid since the 1st of January 1988) ***is resolved****.*

In (1), (2) and (3), the verbs in the main clause (in bold types) are explicit performatives that mark the speech act as a declarative and establish the illocutionary force of the whole text. As we can see from the examples, the arbitrators choose declarative (performative) verbs like *décider*, *prononcer*, *rendre*, *déliberer*, *dire*... The transitivity attached to the decisions by means of verbs carrying thetic performativity also involves the propositional content (cf. Garzone 1996),[11] which, in its turn, is strengthened by the presence of multiple performative verbs.

The performativity of the utterance is also ensured by the heading *Sentence* ("award") or *Sentence partielle*, by the signatures of the judges (the subjects of the performative speech acts)[12] that close the text, and by what Amossy, Maingueneau and Haddad (1999) call a *pre-discursive ethos* assigned to the arbitrators and to arbitration as an institution.[13] The

[11] When the performative prefix is absent, performativity is only to be found in the propositional content. To put it with Garzone (1996), although the performative prefix is omitted, the thetic performative value remains intact because it applies to the whole sentence and therefore still brings about a new state of affairs. As pointed out by Laviola: "In such cases, the force of the utterances is ensured by the institutional or conventional context in which they are produced. As a consequence, the force of the utterance is to be found in the subject producing it" (2009: 41).

[12] "The saying of the words, the enactment formula, performs the institutional act of enacting. [...] the substance of the formula specifies one part of the appropriate contextual conditions for its successful performance, that is, the appropriate participants" (Maley 1994: 20).

[13] Since arbitrations are consensual, the parties accept to submit to the authority of the appointed tribunal, whereby the award becomes binding: "Toute sentence

subject passing the award – *le tribunal arbitral* – is generally expressed in the prefix of the decision.

When the performative verb is omitted in the prefix that introduces the decision, the expression of performativity is in the body of the decision. The same subject (*le tribunal arbitral*) is used to ensure authority. As compared to the expression of performativity in the prefix, however, we find a relatively more varied range of verbs, a preference for active versus passive voice (bold used in the examples for the active voice). Contrast, in this respect, examples (4)-(7) and example (2) above, which illustrates the less frequent case of an impersonal verb in the decision:

> (4) *Par ces motifs*, Le ***Tribunal arbitral***, après avoir entendu les avocats des parties et avoir délibéré à Paris le 9 novembre 1990:
> **Se déclare** compétent pour statuer sur les demandes [...],
> **Accueille** en partie la requête de Cambior,
> **Rejette** la demande de Cambior tendant à ce que le Tribunal ordonne [...],
> **Rejette** les demandes de Cambior tendant à ce que [...], le Tribunal arbitral déclare irrecevables les réclamations [...],
> **Ordonne** à chaque partie de constituer en faveur de l'autre une garantie bancaire [...],
> **Dit** qu'il lui en sera référé en cas de difficultés,
> **Ordonne** la poursuite de l'arbitrage,
> **Réserve** sa décision sur les frais de l'arbitrage jusqu'à la sentence finale.
>
> *For the foregoing reasons, the* ***arbitral tribunal****, after having heard the parties' lawyers end having deliberated in Paris, on the 9th November 1990:*
> ***Declares itself*** *competent to decide on the claims in the dispute [...],*
> ***Accedes*** *partially to Cambior's request,*
> ***Dismisses*** *Cambior's claim asking the tribunal to order [...],*
> ***Dismisses*** *Cambior's claim asking the arbitral tribunal to declare the grievances as inadmissible [...],*
> ***Requires*** *each party to provide a bank guarantee in favour of the other party [...],*
> *States that the parties should make reference to the tribunal in case of difficulty,*

---

arbitrale revêt un caractère obligatoire pour les parties. Par la soumission de leur différend au présent Règlement, les parties s'engagent à exécuter sans délai la sentence à intervenir, et sont réputées avoir renoncé à toutes voies de recours auxquelles elles peuvent valablement renoncer" (ICC Règlement d'arbitrage, Art. 28/6). [*All arbitration awards are binding on the parties. By submitting the dispute to arbitration under these Rules, the parties undertake to carry out any Award without delay and shall be deemed to have waived their right to any form of recourse insofar as such waiver can validly be made. Art. 28/6).*

Orders *the continuation of the arbitration,*
Suspends *its decision about the costs of the arbitration until the final award.*

(5)*Par ces motifs*,
Statuant par voie de sentence partielle, le ***Tribunal arbitral***, après en avoir délibéré:
1. **Condamne** Y SA à rembourser à X COMPANY la somme de US$ 40.000 […].
2. **Met à la charge** de la défenderesse Y SA les frais de la procédure […].

For the foregoing reasons,
Deciding by way of a partial award, the ***arbitral tribunal****, after having considered all relevant reasons:*
1. ***Orders*** *Y SA to refund to X Company the sum of US$ 40.000 […].*
2. ***Awards*** *against the respondent Y SA the costs of the proceedings […].*

(6) *Par ces motifs*, le ***tribunal arbitral*** au complet et à l'unanimité:
I. **Se déclare** compétent pour statuer sur les conclusions prises […].
II. **Déclare** sans objet la procédure arbitrale à l'égard de l'entreprise […].
III. **Condamne** le défendeur X à payer à la demanderesse, société Y, la somme de […].
IV. **Dit** que les frais de l'arbitrage ayant été arrêtés à la somme globale de US $ 58.620, le défendeur prénommé **remboursera** à la demanderesse les trois quarts des frais d'arbitrage, soit US $ 43 965, et lui **versera** en outre la somme de US $ 30 000 […].
V. **Libère** la défenderesse X et **condamne** la demanderesse à lui verser la somme de US $ 5.000 […].
VI. **Rejette** toutes autres ou plus amples conclusions.

For the foregoing reasons,
the ***arbitral tribunal*** *unanimously:*
I. ***Declares itself*** *competent to decide on the submissions […].*
II. ***Declares*** *irrelevant the arbitral proceeding concerning the firm […].*
III. ***Orders*** *the respondent X to refund to the claimant, Y company, the sum of […].*
IV. ***States*** *that, having the arbitral costs been determined in the total sum of US $ 58.620, the respondent shall refund three quarters of total arbitration costs, namely US $ 43 965, to the claimant and shall pay in addition the sum of US $ 30 000 […].*
V. ***Releases*** *the respondent X and orders the claimant to refund the sum of US $ 5.000 […].*
VI. ***Dismisses*** *every other or broader submission..*

(7) *Par ces motifs*, Le ***Tribunal***:
1. **Se déclare** compétent à l'égard de toutes les parties défenderesses;
2. **Rejette** les autres exceptions soulevées par les parties défenderesses;
3. **Dit** n'y avoir lieu à sursis;
4. **Prononce** l'ouverture de la procédure sur le fond de la demande [...];
5. **Dit** n'y avoir lieu, en l'état, à statuer sur les frais et honoraires.

*For the foregoing reasons, the **tribunal**:*
*1. **Declares** itself competent with regard to every respondent;*
*2. **Dismisses** the other respondent's claims;*
*3. **States** that there is no need of a suspension;*
*4. **Pronounces** the opening of the proceeding on the substance of the claim [...];*
*5. **States** that there is no need, as things are, to decide on costs and legal fees.*

As can be seen, the arbitral Tribunal is the subject, and all verbs – both the ones in the prefix introducing the decision and the ones in the body of the decision – are in the 3rd person singular of the present active indicative. This is one of the verb forms recognized as appropriate for the expression of performativity by Austin (1976: 57) and Benveniste (1966: 272), who view the 3rd person singular of the present indicative as a transposition of the 1st person singular, the prototypical grammatical form of performativity (Austin 1976: 5).

3. Deontic modality in legal language

Modality can be seen as the expression of the speaker's attitude towards what s/he says.[14] Of all the types of modality listed in Cervoni (1987) – alethic, epistemic and deontic modality – this chapter will only concentrate on deontic modality (included in Searle's (1969) directive speech acts) and on its prescriptive or regulative function in particular. The main reason for this choice lies in the special role that deontic modality plays in legal language:

> Les langages du législateur et du juge sont performatifs et métalinguistiques. Ils sont aussi normatifs (déontiques) [...], parce que tous les deux servent, le premier exclusivement, le second partiellement, à promulguer des

[14] In Le Querler's (1996: 61) words, irrespective of the typology adopted, modality can be defined as "l'expression de l'attitude du locuteur par rapport au contenu propositionnel de son énoncé" [*the expression of the locutor's attitude towards his/her utterance*].

> normes: le langage du juge a en outre une portée normative (déontique) dans la mesure où il est employé pour la formation des énoncés performatifs maintenant ou modifiant le statut juridique des parties (Kalinowski 1974: 73-74) [*The languages of the legislator and of the judge are performative and metalinguistic. They are also normative (deontic) [...], as they both – the former exclusively, the latter partially – have the function of enacting rules: furthermore the judges' language has a normative (deontic) import in so far as it is used for the formation of performative utterances maintaining or modifying the parties' legal status*] (Kalinowski 1974: 73-74).

Unlike thetic and athetic performativity, deontic normativity is used in order to get something done. However, deontic utterances do not by themselves bring about their own realization. In this connection, Carcaterra (1994: 225) states that prescriptive utterances tend to produce an event by exerting pressure on someone's behaviour, so that the prescribed facts are produced in a mediated way, in two different stages: first prescribing, and then performing.

Cervoni (1987: 97) comes to the same conclusions with respect to French:

> La valeur illocutionnaire des auxiliaires modaux est particulièrement évidente dans leur interprétation déontique: en exprimant une obligation, une permission, une interdiction émanant de lui, prise en charge par lui, le locuteur *agit*, et de plus *agit sur* (sur l'allocutaire). [*The illocutionary force of modal auxiliaries is especially evident in their deontic interpretation: by expressing an obligation, a permission, a prohibition issuing from him, for which he is responsible, the locutor acts and also acts upon (the addressee);* my translation]

This twofold structure entails the reference to something that has to be realized in the future, to an obligation the parties must conform to.

In the French tradition, deontic modality is analysed by reference to the "logical square" (*carré logique*) originally elaborated by Ray (1994 [1926]) to classify the propositions used by the legislator in the Civil Code in order to express the authority of the Law, to confer rights and impose obligations.

This square derives from and is isomorphic to the alethic and epistemic models, and comprises four deontic values, most notably Obligation (*Obligatoire*), Prohibition (*Défendu*), Permission (*Permis*) and Facultivity (*Facultatif*), which are strictly connected to each other by a set of logical links (cf. Ray (1994 [1926].

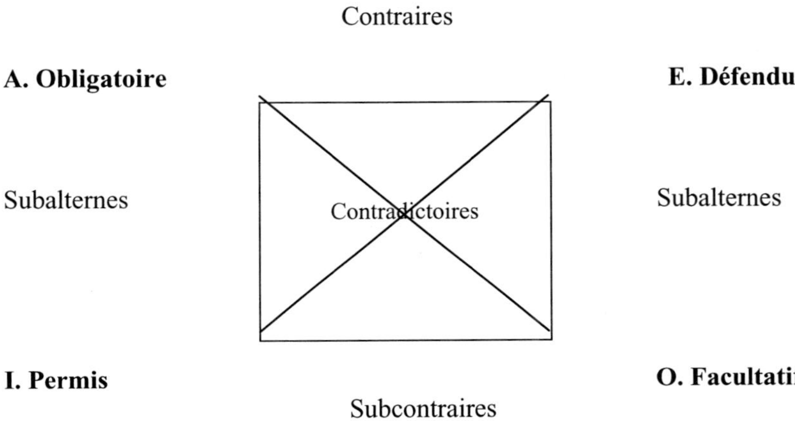

Figure 1. The *carré logique*

3.1. Deontic modality in arbitration award decisions

As far as performativity is concerned, the most relevant portion of the award is definitely the decision, also featuring verbs carrying a deontic value, and in particular Obligation.[15]

The presence of deontic meanings in the decisions can be detected by the use of prototypical modal verbs. Consider, in this respect, this sentence taken from Example (2) above: *La Demanderesse* ***doit payer*** *à la Défenderesse* [*The claimant shall pay to the respondent*].

Obligation, however, can also be expressed by other verb forms. The use of a present simple indicative is one of the strategies used to replace a deontic verb. Example (2) itself, in an identical context, provides evidence for this: *La Demanderesse* ***supporte*** *la totalité des frais d'arbitrage fixés [The claimant bears the totality of the fixed costs of the arbitration].* In this case the present tense takes on a deontic value that can be made explicit by its transformation into the modal *doit supporter*, which retains the same meaning. In Example (1) above, the clause following the prefix (respectively, *Le tribunal arbitral decide* [*the arbitral tribunal decides*], and *La convention relative au siège de l'arbitrage …* ***lie*** *toujours les parties [The convention concerning the venue of the arbitration … incorporated into the arbitration clause,* ***is*** *always* ***binding*** *on the parties])* takes on an assertive force realized by the present tense *lie*, which can be

[15] The following remarks hold for all deontic meanings, but here they refer to Obligation which is the typical value in decisions because of their normativity.

transformed into *doit lier*. Let us add that the present tense can also take on a deontic value in its passive voice (ex. 3: *La clause [...]* ***est résolue*** [*The clause ...* ***is resolved***.]).

Example (6) above shows the use of another tense with a deontic meaning: a future verb form follows a declarative verb:

> Le tribunal arbitral [...] Dit que [...] le défendeur prénommé ***remboursera*** à la demanderesse les trois quarts des frais d'arbitrage [...] et lui ***versera*** en outre la somme de [...] [*The arbitral tribunal states that ... the respondent shall refund three quarters of total arbitration costs ... to the claimant and shall pay in addition the sum of ...*].

The transformation into *doit rembourser* and *doit verser* does not change the meaning of the sentences, and this is evidence of its deontic value.

The choice of a present simple (which is able to convey a future meaning) or a future tense can be explained by the fact that deontic modality generally refers to something related to the future.

In actual fact, when used in decisions, the present and the future tense seem to be able to take on both a deontic and a performative value, as shown with the English modal *shall* (Garzone 1996; 2001).

3.2. Deontic modality across the arbitration award text

Deontic modality is a recurrent feature not only in the decision section of awards, but also in the rest of the text. We therefore move on to identify the variety of modal verbs realizing the four values represented in the 'logical square' in Figure 1 above.

As for Obligation, by which "The addresser [...] instructs the addressee to do X or outlines the obligations to which the addresser must conform" (Trosborg 1997: 45), it is the most frequent value due to the prescriptive purpose of the award and it is preferably conveyed by the prototypical verb *devoir* (8)-(10), even if different forms can express the same idea in French (11)-(16):

> (8) Le Tribunal arbitral estime **devoir** fixer à € 110.000 le montant que la Demanderesse doit à la Défenderesse [...].
>
> *The arbitral tribunal considers that the sum that the claimant owes to the respondent* ***must*** *be fixed in € 110.000.*
>
> (9) Au vu de ce qui précède, l'arbitre considère que la clause arbitrale liant les parties **doit** être résolue par application de l'article 1184 du Code civil.

*In view of the foregoing reasons, the arbitrator considers that the arbitration clause which binds the parties **must** be resolved by the application of article 1184 of the Civil Code.*

(10) Ces documents **doivent** être tenus à la disposition des autorités, la confidentialité et le secret des affaires étant limités par la loi FCPA.

*These documents **must** be kept at the authorities disposal, because the confidentiality and the secrecy of the action are limited by the FCPA law.*

(11) Cependant, **il faut** relever que le Tribunal fédéral n'a, à notre connaissance, jamais eu l'occasion encore de se pencher sur une affaire de trafic d'influence.

*Nevertheless, it **has to** be noticed that, to our knowledge, the federal tribunal has never had the occasion to examine an action of influence peddling yet.*

(12) [...] le jugement plaçant une société en gestion contrôlée **impose** qu'il soit sursis à tous actes ultérieurs d'exécution.

*[...] the judgment placing a company into receivership **imposes** the suspension of any further act of execution.*

(13) L'**obligation** de documentation imposée par la loi FCPA a notamment pour but d'éviter que des paiements illicites soient effectués.

The obligation to present documentation imposed by the FCPA aims to prevent that illegal payments are made.

(14) La *lex concursus* présente alors tous les caractères d'une loi de police que le Tribunal arbitral s'estime **tenu de** prendre en considération, en raison des "liens étroits" qu'elle présente avec le litige et des "intérêts légitimes" qu'elle entend sauvegarder. [16]

The lex concursus then has all the characteristics of a mandatory rule that the arbitral tribunal considers itself obliged to take into consideration, because of the "close links" it has with the dispute and the "legitimate interests" it aims to safeguard.

(15) Enfin, **il incombe** au Tribunal arbitral de veiller à ce que sa sentence "soit susceptible de sanction légale".

---

[16] As proved by some examples, the deontic meanings can also be referred to the Tribunal itself, which is in turn subject to Law.

*Finally, **it devolves** on the arbitral tribunal to ensure that its award "is enforceable by law".*

(16) **Il appartient** à chaque partie et à ses conseils de déterminer l'ampleur des recherches qu'elle considère **nécessaires** et utiles pour la préparation de sa défense.

***It is** for each party and its counsels to determine the extent of the investigations it considers **necessary** and useful for the preparation of its defence.*

This recognition clearly demonstrates the established relationship between modality and negation. When an order is expressed in a negative form, Obligation turns into Prohibition: "The regulation of behaviour can take place by issuing prohibitions" (Trosborg 1997: 47). In fact, in compliance with Ray's scheme, Prohibition and Obligation are opposite – their encounter would cause incompatibilities[17] or antinomies[18]– and Prohibition and Permission are contradictory. So, Prohibition can be conveyed by some typical lexemes (as in (17) and (18) below) or by the negative forms of *savoir*, *pouvoir*, *devoir*, *permettre* (examples (19) to (22)), *être loisible* (example (23)), etc.:

(17) […] l'article 47 devait être interprété comme **interdisant** […] l'engagement d'une procédure arbitrale tendant à la simple fixation d'une créance […].

*[...] article 47 should be interpreted as **forbidding** [...] the undertaking of an arbitral proceeding aimed at simply fixing a claim [...].*

(18) […] il importe néanmoins de souligner que cette loi a pour but de **prohiber** tous trafics d'influences […].

*[...] nevertheless it is important to underline that the aim of this law is to **prohibit** any influence peddling [...]*

---

[17] Two rules are incompatible when they are contradictory, that is when one binds to adopt a behaviour which is forbidden by the other; when they qualify the same behaviour as permitted or forbidden, or as obligatory or optional (Mortara Garavelli 2001: 66-67).

[18] It is possible to speak of legal antinomies "si des conséquences juridiques incompatibles peuvent être tirées de textes d'un même ordre juridique dans une situation particulière" (Perelman 1970: 144). *If incompatible legal consequences can be drawn from texts belonging to the same legal order in a specific situation.*"

(19) La force obligatoire de la clause compromissoire **ne saurait être dissociée** de celle des engagements contractuels de fond.

*The binding force of the arbitration clause **may not be dissociated** from the force of the contract agreement.*
(20) [...] ceux-ci [les tribunaux étatiques] **ne peuvent** entrer en matière tant que subsiste la clause arbitrale.

*[...][the state tribunals] **may not** enter the subject until the arbitration clause is valid.*

(21) Les arbitres **ne doivent pas** rendre de décision qui violerait les principes fondamentaux considérés par le juge de l'exequatur comme d'ordre public international.

*The arbitrators **shall not** render an award which violates the basic principles, under consideration by the judge as to the enforcement of international public order.*

(22) Doctrine et jurisprudence arbitrale sont, à cet égard, nuancées et démontrent que ce terme, à lui seul, n'est pas significatif et **ne permet pas** d'exclure la compétence des institutions locales d'arbitrage.

*Arbitral jurisprudence and doctrine are, in this regard, nuanced and show that this term alone is not significant and **does not allow** to exclude the jurisdiction of local institutions for arbitration.*

(23) En outre et surtout, si, comme le Tribunal arbitral vient de l'exposer, la décision attendue est, par sa nature, une sentence, **il ne lui est pas loisible** de lui donner la forme d'une ordonnance procédurale.

*In addition and especially if, as the arbitral tribunal has just set forth, the expected deliberation is, by its nature, an award, **it is not possible** to give it the form of a procedural order.*

Permission[19] is in a contradictory relation with Prohibition (which can also be expressed by the negation of Permission, as in (22)-(23)) and it is subaltern to Obligation. It establishes a right and issues from the same authority (in this case *le tribunal arbitral*) but, unlike Obligation, it does not order the addressee to do something, it only grants the possibility that

[19] Ray's studies (1994 [1926]) prove that in the French civil Code the expression of Permission is very frequent, because the legislator, apart from influencing our actions by certain obligations or limiting them by some prohibitions, can also grant permissions and allow possibilities.

a certain act be performed. The modal verb expressing Permission is *pouvoir* (24)-(25), but there are also other synonymical forms, such as *permettre* (26)-(27), *admettre* (28), *accorder* (29), the negative forms of Prohibition (30), etc.:

(24) […] la clause arbitrale […] **peut** être résolue aux conditions de l'article 1184 du Code civil si les conditions en sont remplies.

[...] the arbitration clause [...] ***may*** *be resolved according to the terms of article 1184 of the Civil Code if the conditions are met.*

(25) […] les parties **peuvent** s'adresser au juge étatique dans ce cas […].

[...] in this case the parties ***may*** *address to the State Court [...].*

(26) L'article 133 du Code des obligations yougoslave […] **permet** d'invalider le contrat dans la mesure où il concerne le choix du siège du tribunal arbitral.

Article 133 of the Yugoslav Code of Obligations [...] ***allows*** *to invalidate the contract as far as it concerns the choice of the arbitral tribunal venue.*

(27) […] l'assistance **est permise** à certaines conditions spécifiées par l'art. 21 de la même loi.

[...] the assistance ***is allowed*** *under certain conditions specified by art. 21 of the same law.*

(28) La pratique arbitrale de la Chambre de commerce de Zurich est d'**admettre** la compétence de cette institution […].

The arbitral practice of the Zurich's Chamber of commerce is ***to accept*** *the jurisdiction of this institution [...].*

(29) […] en matière d'arbitrage, une caution **ne doit être accordée qu'**à titre exceptionnel.

[...] in case of arbitration, a guarantee deposit ***shall be granted*** *only in exceptional cases.*

(30) L'article 19 de la LDIP […] **n'interdirait pas** au Tribunal arbitral de le faire.

Article 19 of the LDIP [...] ***does not prevent*** *the arbitral tribunal to do it.*

As stated by Ray (1994 [1926]), like Obligation, also Permission has its negative meaning, that is the permission not to do something. For this reason Facultivity – which does not appear to be present in the corpus – is often expressed by negative forms such as *ne pas être tenu de*, *ne pas être nécessaire*, *être dispense de*, etc.

4. Conclusions

This chapter has analysed the arbitration award from the point of view of its strictly prescriptive function, which remains evident even if the award is not a typically/prevalently normative text, but rather belongs to the category of judicial discourse: in fact, like other kinds of judgments, it is binding on the parties. Its normativity is displayed and conveyed by means of thetic and athetic performativity (equivalent to declarative speech acts) and by deontic modality (belonging to directive speech acts). If performativity appears to be highly relevant in decisions, occurrences of deontic verbs can be found across the whole text in the form of Obligation, Permission, Prohibition and, to a lesser extent, Facultivity. In light of the foregoing considerations, it can be stated that both performativity and deontic modality are expressed by a wide range of more or less explicit markers – modal verbs, para-synonymical forms, periphrastic expressions, simple present and future tense – entertaining mutual relationships. This variety of realizations seems to be a feature of French legal language in that it characterizes not only arbitration awards but also judgments passed by the Court of Justice of the European Union, as discussed in Preite (2010).[20] This brings us to the conclusion that although judgments and awards are drafted following a privileged standard structure that ensures its normative value, they do not have to comply strictly with any fixed or formulaic formal requisites. As a result, the linguistic choices conveying performative and deontic values can be said to mirror to some extent the individual style and preferences of the arbitrators drafting the texts.

[20] This study, carried out from a comparative point of view, also shows that Italian judgments are as rich as French ones in terms of deontic expressions. It can be added that in a recent study Bondi and Diani argued, in the context of a comparative investigatoin of contracts, that Italian is richer in deontic markers than English (cf. Bondi and Diani 2010)

References

Adam, Jean-Michel. 1992. *Les textes: types et prototypes*. Paris: Nathan.

Amossy, Ruth, Galit Haddad, and Dominique Maingueneau. 1999. *Images de soi dans le discours. La construction de l'ethos*. Genève: Delachaux et Niestlé.

Austin, John L. 1962. *How to Do Things with Words*. Oxford: Oxford University Press.

Benveniste, Émile. 1966. "La philosophie analytique et le langage". In *Problèmes de linguistique générale*, 267-276. Paris: Gallimard.

Bernardini, Piero. 2000. *L'arbitrato commerciale internazionale*. Milano: Giuffré.

Bhatia, Vijay K. 1983. *Applied Discourse Analysis of English Legislative Writing*. Birmingham: University of Aston.

Bondi, Marina, and Giuliana Diani. 2010. "Conveying deontic values in English and Italian contracts: a cross-cultural analysis". Paper presented at the Conference *Diritto, Linguaggio, Cultura*, Modena, 27 September 2010.

Bocquet, Claude. 2008. *La traduction juridique. Fondement et méthode*. Paris: DeBoeck-Duculot.

Carcaterra, Gaetano. 1994. "Norme costitutive". In *Il linguaggio del diritto*, edited by Uberto Scarpelli and Paolo Di Lucia, 219-231. Milano: LED.

Cervoni, Jean. 1987. *L'énonciation*. Paris: PUF.

Conte, Amedeo G. 1994. Performativo vs normativo. In *Il linguaggio del diritto*, edited by Uberto Scarpelli and Paolo Di Lucia, 247-263. Milano: LED.

Cornu, Gérard. 2000. *Linguistique juridique*. Paris: Montchrestien.

Garzone, Giuliana. 1996. *Performatività e linguaggio giuridico. Una proposta di classificazione. Con osservazioni contrastive inglese-italiano*. Milano: Centro Linguistico Università Bocconi.

—. 2001. "Deontic Modality and Performativity in English Legal Texts". In *Modality in Specialized Texts*, edited by Maurizio Gotti and Marina Dossena, 153-174. Bern: Peter Lang.

Grzegorczyk, Christophe. 1974. "Le rôle du performatif dans le langage du droit." *Archives de Philosophie du droit* 19: 229-41.

ICC Règlement d'arbitrage <http://www.iccwbo.org/court/arbitration-/index.html?id=4199>.

Kalinowski, Georges. 1974. "Sur les langages respectifs du législateur, du juge et de la loi." *Archives de Philosophie du droit* 19, 63-74.

Kerbrat-Orecchioni, Cathrine. 2001. *Les actes de langage dans le discours. Théorie et fonctionnement*. Paris: Nathan/VUEF.
—. 2003. "Les énoncés du législateur: normativité ou performativité ?", In Actes du séminaire SHS/ECLIPS, *Normes, règles, régularités*, du 22 mai 2003 (www.univ-lyon.2fr/article.php3?id article=365)
Kurzon, Dennis. 1989. "Language of the Law and Legal Language". In *Special language: From Humans Thinking to Thinking Machines*, edited by Laurén Christer and Marianne Nordman, 283-90. Clevedon/Philadelphia: Multilingual Matters.
Laviola, Maria. 2009. *Performativity and Legal Discourse. The Case of Arbitration Awards*. Bari: Digilabs.
Le Querler, Nicole. 1996. *Typologie des modalités*. Caen: Presses Universitaires de Caen.
Maley, Yon. 1994. "The Language of the Law". In *Language and the Law*, edited by John Gibbons, 11-50. London: Longman.
Mortara Garavelli, Bice. 2001. *Le parole e la giustizia*. Torino: Einaudi.
Mustill, Michael J. and Stewart C. Boyd. 1989. *Commercial Arbitration*. London: Butterworth.
Perelman, Chaïm. 1970. *Le champ de l'argumentation*. Bordeaux: Presses Universitaires de Bordeaux.
Preite, Chiara. 2005. *Langage du droit et linguistique. Étude de l'organisation textuelle, énonciative et argumentative des arrêts de la Cour (et du Tribunal) de Justice des Communautés européennes*. Roma: Aracne.
—. 2008. "La sentenza della Corte di Giustizia delle Comunità europee: eterogeneità sequenziale ed enunciativa". In *Il linguaggio giuridico. Prospettive interdisciplinari*, edited by Giuliana Garzone and Francesca Santulli, 263-283. Milano: Giuffré.
—. 2010. L'expression de la normativité dans les arrêts de la Cour de Justice des Communautés européennes: une analyse contrastive français-italien. Paper presented at the Conference *La traduction juridique, points de vue didactiques et linguistiques*, Lyon 24-25 mars 2010.
Ray, Jean. 1994. "La struttura logica del codice civile francese". In *Il linguaggio del diritto*, edited by Uberto Scarpelli and Paolo Di Lucia, 281-290. Milano: LED.
Sbisà, Marina. 1995. *Gli atti linguistici. Aspetti e problemi di filosofia del linguaggio*. Milano: Feltrinelli.
Schroeder, François-Michel. 1978. *Le nouveau style judiciaire*. Paris: Dalloz.

Searle, John R. 1969. *Speech Acts: An Essay in the Philosophy of Language*. Cambridge: Cambridge University Press.
Searle, John R. 1976. "The classification of illocutionary acts". *Language in Society* 5: 1-24.
Trosborg, Anna. 1997. *Rhetorical Strategies in Legal Language. Discourse Analysis of Statutes and Contracts*. Tubingen: Narr.
Werlich, Egon. 1975. *Typologie der Texte*. Heidelberg: Quelle & Meyer.
Ziembinsky, Zygmunt 1974. "Le langage du droit et le langage juridique: critères de leur discernement". *Archives de Philosophie du droit* 19: 25-32.

CHAPTER FIVE

DIALOGISM IN ARBITRATION AWARDS: FOCUS ON CONCESSIVE CONSTRUCTIONS

GIULIANA GARZONE*

1. Aim and method

This chapter explores internal dialogism as an aspect of polyphony in arbitration awards. More specifically, it draws on the notion of polyphony to examine arbitration awards as argumentative texts in which arbitrators construct their arguments giving account of the views of the parties and making reference to relevant texts, and in so doing they also respond to all possible objections and anticipate counterarguments by incorporating them in their decisions.

This study is a continuation of a previous work on polyphony in arbitration awards (Garzone and Degano 2012) where, given the complexity of this phenomenon in deliberative texts, attention was concentrated exclusively on reported language as the most manifest form of polyphony. Results confirmed the pervasiveness of reported voices in the textual construction of awards, and identified regularities in the deployment of syntactic structures and in the choice of reporting verbs/nouns as a function of various textual and contextual variables, e.g. participants involved, argumentation type, argumentative use of quotations, etc.

While the form of polyphony discussed in Garzone and Degano (2012) consists in the openly signalled embedding of excerpts of 'alien' texts in discourse, the phenomena that will be explored in this chapter are part of a less manifest form of polyphony which has been denominated 'internal dialogism' because at the syntactic level it takes the form of an internal dialogue (Bakhtin 1952/1979/1984: 102), i.e. a 'virtual' dialogue integrally

* The research on which this chapter is based contributes to the National Research Programme "Tension and Change in English Domain-specific Genres" (prot. 2007JCY9Y9), funded by the Italian Ministry of University.

enacted by the locutor him/herself and mostly implied rather than stated. In this case, utterances are inherently dialogic as they respond to other utterances which are not openly formulated but only implied. Thus the dialogue does not take the form of subsequent turns, but rather of an inherent enunciative duality: two utterances in one single and same syntactic unit ("la dualité énonciative: *le deux dans l'un*": Authier-Revuz 1995, emphasis in the original) (cf. Bres and Nowakowska 2005: 140).

In particular, the analysis will be limited to some aspects of what has been named '*dialogisme interlocutif*' or "interlocutive dialogism', in which "the locutor addresses an interlocutor and never ceases to anticipate his/her understanding/response" (Bres and Nowakowsa 2005: 139).[1] Interlocutive dialogism is mostly realized at the micro-levels of linguistic encoding, with 'ghost' utterances deeply buried in discourse, their textual *enfouissement* (Bres and Nowakowsa 2005: 139) being so profound that they are often not immediately identifiable as separate from the main utterance.

1.1. Lexicogrammatical features associated with dialogism: analytical frameworks

However, the fact that the devices realizing interlocutive dialogism are hidden in the deep folds of discourse does not mean that in interlocutive dialogism there are no lexicogrammatical clues to signal the presence of two or more enunciative instances or points of view.[2]

In the works of scholars who have studied dialogism in discourse such "weak" indicators mostly figure in comprehensive lists together with more manifest forms. This is the case with the categorization put forth by Bres and Novakowska (Bres 1999; Bres/Nowakowska 2005; Nowakowska 2005), which is thus summarized in Dendale (2006): irony, negation

---

[1] The other type of dialogism categorised by Bres and Nowakowsa (2005) is interdiscursive dialogism' ('*dialogisme interdicursif*) which includes the interference of 'discourses made previously by others, with which one can only interact', and affects the macrolevels of discourse, being mostly realized explicitly (as is the case with language reporting).

[2] Dendale (2006: 5ff) points out that Ducrot's (1984) definition of polyphony is general and in its application Ducrot does not use the term 'voice' univocally, neither do the ScaPoLine scholars. Both propose a complex classification of '*sujets parlants'* (speaking subjects), but for the purposes of this study Dendale's simplified generalisation will suffice: "polyphony can be looked upon as the co-presence of at least *two discursive entities*, two entities that do no share the same point of view and/or that do not represent the same person" (Dendale 2006: 9).

(including '*renchérissment*', i.e. rectification: '… not only … but also…'), confirmation, concession and opposition, presupposition, interrogation, comparison, cleft sentences, extraposition (i.e. right- or left-dislocation), use and alteration of proverbs, the French *conditionnel* with hearsay value, echo-utterances, autonymical modalisation and reported speech.

Some of these same discursive traits – speech reportage (or 'language representations'), presupposition, negation, irony – figure in the list of indicators of "manifest intertextuality" given by Fairclough (1992: 117-118), who does not use the notion of polyphony, but prefers to include these dialogic phenomena within the general category of intertextuality.

It can be observed that both Bres and Novakowska's and Fairclough's lists appear rather non homogeneous in terms of the degree of explicitness or manifestness of the features included. For instance, they include reported speech, in which the presence of a voice other than that of the locutor in the text is clearly signalled on the surface of discourse, often with the indication of the boundaries between the interlocutor's discourse and alien discourses, but also patterns – such as negation and irony – in which the presence of another voice integrated in the text is not openly indicated, and the recipient is not made explicitly aware of the dialogism inherent in the utterance. Another problem with the categorizations above is that there seems to be a tendency to broaden so much the criteria for inclusion in the list and the number of textual clues associated with polyphony and dialogism that in the end the heuristic effectiveness of these notions risks going lost.[3]

In light of the foregoing observations, this study will concentrate on a limited number of linguistic patterns whose nature is dialogic beyond all reasonable doubt. In this respect some interesting indications come from research on polyphony in academic discourse – an area where these aspects have certainly been investigated more extensively[4] than in research

---

[3] It is worth noticing that, in spite of the considerable number of items they include in their inventory of dialogical markers, Bres and Nowakowska express awareness of this danger, closing one of their studies of dialogism with a question they leave unanswered: "De sorte de ce qui fait la force de la notion de dialogisme, fait put-être également sa faiblesse. Puissante, trop puissante: à tout pouvoir expliquer, ne court-elle pas le risque de ne plus expliquer grand-chose, de devenir un hochet ou un sésame qui n'ouvre que sur des évidence?" (Bres and Nowakowska 2005: 152). To support this view, they also make reference to Todorov (1981/1984: 60), who describes dialogism as "loaded with such an embarassing multiplicity of meanings".

[4] Various forms of polyphony and dialogism in academic discourse are dealt with in Thompson's works (cf. Thompson and Yiyun 1991; Thompson 1994, 1996, 2001); also all the studies of the ScaPoLine group explore polyphony in academic

on legal discourse,[5] so it seems reasonable to rely at least partially on results obtained in investigations in that sector.

Especially useful for the sake of this discussion are the patterns identified by Thompson as typically dialogic in a study aimed at "highlighting the ways in which writers can bring the underlying dialogue to the surface" (Thompson 2001: 59). According to Thompson, such patterns of discourse are Hypothetical-Real and concessive, which qualify as "two of the main discourse contexts in which the reader-in-text is given a voice" (2001: 65). In actual fact, however, Thompson does not look at these patterns extensively, but prefers to examine only the "signals of dialogism" that he sees as associated with them, which are: (a) modal verbs expressing possibility, which modalize propositions that are more or less implicitly attributed to the reader-in-the-text (especially 'may' and 'might'), and (b) modal disjuncts such as 'of course' and 'certainly', as well as comment clauses such as 'it is true/certain that',[6] which enable the writer to incorporate readers' "questions and reactions in the text" (Thompson 2001: 59).

An accurate analysis of the examples given to illustrate the use of these lexicogrammatical features (cf. Thompson 2001: 63, 68-71) indicates that in actual fact virtually all modal verbs, modal disjuncts and comment clauses generally used dialogically have a concessive value. This is amply justified if one considers that concessive constructions at all syntactic levels (noun phrase, clause complex, sentence complex) have the function of bringing in a proposition that is contrary to the proposition actually asserted by the encoder. This is also highlighted by Thompson and Zhou in their study of evaluative disjuncts (cf. Thompson and Zhou 2000) in which they argue that the concessive relation often takes on an interpersonal import, in addition to its traditionally recognised text-cohesive function, thus assuming a rhetorical/argumentative function[7] as it

---

discourse (cf. among others, Fløttum and Rastier (eds) 2003; Nølke, Fløttum and Norén 2004: Fløttum 2005; Fløttum, Dahl and Kinn 2006).

[5] As regards legal discourse, to my knowledge the notion of polyphony has rarely and only recently been used as a research tool, and mostly not as the main focus but rather as part of a diversified methodological framework; cf. e.g. Mazzi (2007a), (2007b) on judicial argumentation, Azuelos-Atias (2010) on proofs of criminal intent, and Yovel (2010) on lay litigants' submissions. On polyphony in arbitration awards cf. Garzone and Degano (2012).

[6] Thompson (2001: 65) sees modal disjuncts/modal comment clauses as instances of 'high value objective modalization' and modals expressing possibility as instances of 'low-value subjective modalization'.

[7] In Thompson and Zhou's original model this is shown only for sentences containing an attitudinal disjunct, but it has been subsequently extended to

makes it possible to anticipate objections to the writer's contentions and incorporate them in the text.

In light of these considerations, this work will focus on the signals of dialogism listed in (a) and (b) above, originally proposed in Thompson (2001) for academic discourse, but they will be treated as specific cases of the dialogic use of concessive constructions in awards.

It is to be noted that all these features – (a) and (b), and concessive constructions in general – are classified by Martin and White (2005) as resources for intersubjective positioning that realize the writer's 'engagement', a broad category of meanings "which in various ways construe for the text a heteroglossic backdrop of prior utterances, alternative viewpoints and anticipated responses" (Martin and White 2005: 97). The focus here will be especially on anticipated responses which can be put to use for rhetorical purposes mainly to construe an 'envisaged' addressee in the text, anticipating his/her views and objections and dealing with them.

In this work, I shall first explore the properties of concessive constructions in general, giving special attention to how they are exploited for dialogic purposes. I shall then look at how dialogism is realized in awards by means of concessive clauses, conjuncts, and other devices potentially endowed with a dialogic import – modals, disjuncts and comment clauses. Finally, it will be shown how the different discourse patterns considered are actually used.

1.2. Materials

This study is based on the analysis of a corpus ('the Awards corpus') of 74 awards of the Paris International Chamber of Commerce (ICC) rendered between 1984 and 2003, extracted from the Kluwer Bank <http://www.kluwerarbitration.com>,[8] for a total amount of about 445,000 words, as shown in the following Table:

Files	74.00
tokens used for word list	445,383.00
types (distinct words)	19,372.00
standardised TTR	34.48

Table 1. Awards Corpus characteristics.

concessive constructions in general, in all of their possible grammatical forms (cf. Garzone 2005).

[8] Unless otherwise indicated, all websites were accessed on 1 November 2010.

A qualitative analysis of the corpus is carried out in a discourse-analytical framework, as illustrated in §1.1 above. Recourse is also made to corpus linguistic tools – and specifically to Wordsmith Tools 4.0 (Scott 2004), one of the most widely used text interrogation software suites – in order to obtain confirmation of qualitative insights, especially by means of concordancing, and possibly indications for further analysis.

Besides, in order to evaluate the significance of the resulting data and their conformity with or divergence from discursive patterns deployed in court judgments, an institutional genre that is usually considered to be akin to awards, they are also compared with those obtained from the analysis of a corpus of Judgments of the House of Lords (the 'Judgments Corpus') containing decisions issued in the same period as those in the Awards corpus (1984-2003)[9] with a parallel distribution over time, totalling a similar number of words (446,648 vs 436,035), as shown in Table 2:

Files	38.00
tokens used for word list	444,868.00
types (distinct words)	11,780.00
standardised TTR	34.43

Table 2. Lords' Judgments Corpus characteristics.

As can be seen from Table 2, care has been taken that the corpus used for comparison has a size similar to that of the main corpus so that not only percentages but the raw data too can be easily compared, thus making it possible to evaluate also the relative incidence of lemmas with a frequency of less than 0.01.

2. Concessive structures in arbitration awards

Table 3 shows a comparison of the incidence of linguistic features associated with concessive structures in the Awards corpus, and the Lords' Judgments corpus. As already noted, the two corpora are approximately the same size, so the raw data are comparable. For items that do not always have concessive or hypothetical meaning, only the frequency of occurrences with a concessive/hypothetical meaning has been included.[10]

---

[9] For a more detailed description of the Corpus, cf. Garzone and Degano 2012.

[10] For *while* and *yet* that can carry different meanings only the occurrences that clearly have concessive meaning have been selected by looking at the concordance lines and, whenever necessary, also at the source texts. *But* is sometimes included

Concession	Awards		Lords' Judgments	
Conjunctions / conjuncts		%		%
Albeit	3	<0.01	31	<0.01
Although	154	0.03	199	0.04
Even if	143	0.03	54	0.01
However	521	0.11	417	0.09
Nevertheless	60	0.01	59	0.01
Notwithstanding	38	<0.01	35	<0.01
Though	69	0.02	105	0.02
While (concessive)	96	0.02	66	0.01
Yet (concessive)	11	<0.01	15	<0.01
Modalizers (dialogic use)				
Admittedly	6	<0.01	3	<0.01
Be true that[11]	26	0.01	19	
Certainly	22	0.01	10	0.01
Obviously	14	<0.01	5	<0.01
Of course	9	<0.01	24	<0.01
True (attitudinal disjunct)	1	0.01	1	<0.01

Table 3. Comparison of indicators of concession in the two corpora.

In line with the now generally accepted view of arbitration as increasingly judicialized (Nariman 2000: 262; Marriott 2004: 354), in the two corpora the overall frequency of concessive conjunctions, conjuncts and disjuncts is similar, although there are slight divergences: Lords' judgments have higher scores for *albeit, although* and *though*, which may indicate a preference for more formal stylistic choices and for hypotaxis, while awards show higher frequencies for *even if* and *while*, certainly associated with a less elaborate style, and *however* which is used in paratactic constructions. Another factor which may have some impact is that differently from Lords' judgments, ICC awards are not always drafted by native speakers of English.

---

among concessive conjunctions, but here it has been excluded from the analysis, on account of its special status as a 'nearly pure' coordinator (cf. Quirk *et al.* 1972: 552-560; 564-565) and of its prevalently contrastive meaning with which concessive meaning mostly co-exists.

11 Here the pattern is indicated as "be true that" although actual occurrences often contain adverbial expressions like *also*, *particularly, of course,* e.g. "it is also true that…", "

In Section §2.1 the dialogic relevance of concessive constructions will be illustrated, and the main patterns realizing concession at clause and sentence level will be discussed. Then, the use of some of the linguistic indicators of dialogism identified in Thompson (2001) will be examined in detail, limiting the analysis to concession-associated modals, modalizers and comment clauses.

2.1. Concessive constructions

It is noteworthy that the frequency of concessive conjunctions and conjuncts (*although, though, however, nevertheless, notwithstanding*) is similar in the arbitration Awards corpus and in the Lords' Judgments corpus, although in the aggregate data obtained by summing up all concessive conjunctions/conjuncts in each corpus, 1,095 for Awards and 991 for Judgments, there is a slight difference in favour of Awards.

In Martin and White's model, concessive constructions are included in a sub-category of 'engagement' which they denominate 'disclaim' as 'they invoke a contrary position which is then said not to hold' (Martin and White 2005: 120) and in this way they 'counter' it.

As regards the ways in which concessive constructions realize dialogism, they have peculiar syntactic, semantic and pragmatic characteristics which make them a case apart amongst adverbial clauses (cf. König 1986, 1988, 1989). First and foremost they do not encode conceptual meaning (i.e. mental representations), but rather procedural meaning (i.e. computations performed on representations) (cf. Blakemore 1987, 1989; Iten 1998).[12]

In other words, differently from other adverbials (e.g. causal, conditional, temporal), concessive clause-complexes[13] do not express a two-term relation, but a possible *use* of a sentence or a clause (cf. König 1989: 149). What is important for the sake of this discussion is that – as was already pointed out by Grice (1961/1989) and by Frege before him (1892/1994) –

---

[12] For distinguishing expressions encoding procedural meaning from those that encode concepts, Wilson and Sperber (1993) and Rouchota (1998), who apply Relevance Theory to concessive construction, list criteria belonging to three different areas: cognition, truth-evaluability and compositionality (cf. Iten 1998: 9-10). It can be observed that the Relevant Theoretic interpretation has not been free from criticisms by scholars of other schools of thought. Cf. among others Rieber (1997).

[13] It is to be noted that for the sake of a focalized discussion, here only clause-complex and sentence-complex level constructions will be considered, leaving out concessive noun phrases (i.e. those introduced by *despite* and *in spite of*).

concessives carry with them a conventional implicature, i.e. a proposition which is "implied as distinct from being stated" (Grice 1961/1989: 127) that has no bearing on the truth or falsity of what is said, and is generally in opposition or contrast with the main proposition in the utterance.

Indicating the asserted proposition as Q and the conceded proposition as P, this can be schematized as follows, for hypotactic clause complexes:

(i) Q although P (consequence^concession)
(ii) Although P, Q (concession^consequence) (cf. Halliday 1994: 236).

and for paratactic clause complexes:

(iii) True, P. But Q.
(iv) Q. However, P.

In both cases, the propositional content of the sentence can be schematized as follows:

(v) P & Q.

The presentation of propositional content within a concessive clause complex signals a relation of contrast, incompatibility or unexpectedness between the conceded proposition P and the asserted proposition Q. The implicature generated could be formulated as follows:

(viii) Normally, if P then not Q.

or
(ix) Normally, P causes not Q.

But it is in the rationale underlying concessive constructions that, more or less unexpectedly, P is presented to be less valid than Q.

Thus, thanks to the implicature the writer can accommodate other people's views in his/her own discourse, and present them as overridden by the main proposition which expresses his/her own stance.

See the following example from one of the awards:

(1) Although the notice was sent in Italian to the New York office of the claimant, not expressly addressed to the President or managing director,

> the sole arbitrator felt that these circumstances did not deprive the notification of its effectiveness. (2003_1: 150)

The proposition in the subordinate clause, anticipating a possible objection to the arbitrator's stance, licences the implicature "normally, when a notice is sent in an inappropriate language and not expressly addressed to the person to whom it is supposed to be addressed, it is ineffective". Of course, this implicature can be understood and works only if the reader shares with the writer the conviction that notices should be written in the appropriate language and addressed to the correct recipient. In other words, the use of a concessive construction projects on to the reader a particular axiological paradigm and construes him/her sharing this axiological paradigm with the writer (cf. Martin and White 2005: 121),[14] a fact which in other circumstances may also have an ideological import (cf. Garzone 2005: 139-140). The conceded proposition and its implicature is there to be contradicted, as it sets the stage for a statement to the contrary that is made in the main clause, in which the arbitrator rejects the conceded objection by presenting it as opposite to his/her own point of view (in this case, his/her conviction of the effectiveness of the notification), and dismisses it. Thus, by making recourse to a concessive construction, the arbitrator anticipates a possible objection to his/her stance and rules it out.

In paratactic concessive clause complexes some similar mechanisms are at work, with the important difference that the conceded proposition must always precede the consequential proposition, and thus in most cases its concessive value comes, as it were, unannounced. The following example featuring the concessive conjunct 'however' illustrates this point:

> (2) In order to determine the meaning of this choice of law clause, it is necessary to ascertain the intent of the parties according to the provisions of Art. 8 CISG,(47),(48) in so far as such intent may be found. *In the instant case, such intent is hardly ascertainable.* However, *the arbitrator is of the view that it is appropriate to apply the presumption formulated by one of the leading legal scholars*: …. (2000_2: 125)[15]

In this excerpt, the arbitrator is going to illustrate his/her decision about the controversial problem of the law to be applied to the case, but before doing so in the second sentence of excerpt (2) s/he anticipates the

---

[14] Martin and White (2005) borrow and slightly modify the notion of 'axiological paradigm' from Pagano (1994).

[15] In all examples emphasis is added.

possible objection that in actual fact in the case at hand the intent of the parties cannot be ascertained. Since that sentence is free from any indicator that may betray its conceded nature, the reader may initially take it as an assertive statement, but when s/he gets to read the third sentence, introduced by 'however', s/he becomes aware that that proposition is stated only to be contradicted.

It is to be noted that this pattern is by far the preferred form of concessive discourse in the corpus, as 'however', with 521 occurrences, is more than twice as frequent as the subordinators 'although' and 'though' together (223 occurrences), a trend that can be found also in the Judgments Corpus, although less marked (417 occurrences against 204 for 'although' and 'though' together). In addition, one should consider that in the Awards Corpus there are also 60 occurrences of 'nevertheless' (29 in the Judgments Corpus) which is used in the same type of discourse pattern, as in the following example:

> (3) Under French law, one must resort to the courts in order to terminate a contract based on a breach of such contract. It is, nevertheless, possible for the contract to override this principle and provide that either party may put an end to the contract if the other party does not perform its obligations under the contract. (1995_2: 118)

Here the arbitrator is going to argue that it is possible for a contract to provide that in case of non-fulfilment of contractual obligations by one of the parties the other party may terminate the agreement without going to court. Since this goes against a basic principle of French law, set out in the first sentence, before putting forth his/her opinion s/he acknowledges the existence of such a principle and anticipates the possible objection that it should be applied, before going on to assert that in the case at hand the principle can be overridden.

As will be seen shortly, in paratactic constructions the writer sometimes avoids leaving the conceded sentence without an indication of its real concessive character and prefers to make it immediately manifest by resorting to one of the signals of dialogism listed above (modal disjuncts, comment clauses or modals: cf. Thompson 2001). In Martin and White's (2005: 122-126) model these signals of dialogism are seen as forms of 'proclaim' whereby the writer overtly announces that s/he temporarily agrees with the projected dialogic partner about certain notions or knowledge, but this concurring concession is then followed by a counter, realizing a 'concur + counter' pairing.

Patterns realizing these 'concur + counter' pairings will be discussed in the next few sections (§2.2, §2.3, §2.4) which will focus respectively on modals expressing possibility, disjuncts and comment clauses.

2.2. May and might

The modals expressing possibility to be analysed here are 'may' and 'might', i.e. those that are by far most frequently used with a dialogic import. For 'may' a possible concessive value has also been explicitly hypothesized in grammar books (cf. Palmer 1979/1990: 52-53), although the values traditionally attributed to it are essentially deontic (root) and epistemic. In my view the dialogic/concessive value of 'may' is an extension of epistemic possibility and encodes a proposition that is presented as possible (cf. e.g. Palmer 1979/1990: 52-53), the truth-value of which is unquestionable, but is discursively indicated to be less valid than that encoded in the following part of the utterance. Therefore, in this chapter, I shall just postulate that in the modal 'may', as well as in the 'tentative' form 'might', in addition to their traditionally recognized basic meanings in certain contexts it is possible to identify a dialogic/concessive component, which I see as an extension of their epistemic meaning.[16]

In particular, 'may'/'might' takes on a dialogic/concessive value when it is followed by a sentence opened by a concessive or adversative conjunct like 'however', 'nevertheless' or 'but', or when it appears in a concessive clause (e.g. "although the plaintiff may be convinced ...."). But, as we shall see, there are contexts where 'may'/'might' is dialogic even if it is not followed by such devices. This typically occurs when it is used in the expression of unattributed mental and verbal processes to explicitly anticipate counterarguments and objections ("one *may* observe ...", "the argument *may* be advanced ...", "it *might* be expected that...") (cf. Thompson 2001: 65-67)

An analysis of the Wordlist for the Awards Corpus and of concordance lines for *may* and *might* has made it possible to determine the real value of modal verb forms in each case, distinguishing those with a deontic, epistemic and concessive meaning respectively. The results are shown in Table 4.

[16] I use the verb 'postulate' because this point is controversial, and debated among scholars, but here it is not possible to discuss the problem in detail. Cf. e.g. Souesme (2004).

	Awards Corpus			Lords' Judgments Corpus		
	Total	Dialogic	%	Total	Dialogic	%
'may'	762	73	9.5%	966	53	5.5%
'might'	135	16	11.8%	350	13	3.7%

Table 4. Dialogic use of *may/might* in Awards and Lords' Judgments corpora.

In the Awards Corpus *may* is used dialogically in 73 of its 762 occurrences (9,5% of all cases), against 53 out of a total of 966 occurrences (i.e. 5,5%) in the Lords' Judgment corpus. In the Awards corpus *might* is used dialogically in 16 instances out of 135, i.e. in 11.8% of the cases, while in the Lords' Judgments Corpus in 13 occurrences out of a total of 350 (3.7%).[17] It can be observed that while the raw data about the dialogic use of these modals are very similar for the two corpora, percentage data instead are lower for Lords' judgments as the total frequency of *may/might* is considerably higher than in awards.

The discussion of a few examples will serve to illustrate the dialogic use of 'may' and 'might' in arbitration awards. In the following example the dialogic/concessive value of the modal is highlighted by the presence of 'but' to introduce the clause that follows:

> (4) Taken at its face value this argument *may have* some weight, *but* one should also consider:
> (i) that the modification in the assortments could be a consequence of the reduction in the production of the raw material due to the drought;
> […] (2000_1: 21)

In (4) the modal is used to admit discursively the possible validity of an argument, but this validity is shown to be partial or nil in light of other arguments to be also considered.

In this type of use *may* is often accompanied by *well* as an emphasizer (cf. Quirk *et al.* 1972: 442-443):

[17] These data are in line with those found by Mazzi (2008) in a similar research on the dialogic use of *may* and *might* in a corpus composed of judgments from various courts: *may* was used dialogically in House of Lords judgments (14.8% for total occurrences of *may* and 5.6% for *might*), Supreme Court of Ireland judgments (8.6% for *may* and 4.6% for *might*) and in European Court of Justice judgments (1.2% for *may* and 0 for *might;* cf. Mazzi 2008: 250).

> (5) The fact that D's operational department submitted each year to the legal department a list of contracts in force, including the 1954 Contract, does not refute this observation. *It may well be* that D was under the impression that the 1954 Contract was still in force. *However*, this impression was not conveyed to S, which, for its part, appears to have been under the impression that the 1971/1972 Contracts governed its contractual relationship with D. (1998_2: 64)

In the following passage the arbitrator anticipates the possible objection that rules that are not explicitly contained in a statute may nevertheless be implicitly part of the lawmaker's purpose:

> (6) The Tribunal notes that Sect. 1962(a) does not require expressly that the 'enterprise' in which the proceeds are invested be distinct from the person (legal or natural) who earned the income through a pattern of racketeering activity [...]. *It might be that* such features follow from the lawmaker's purpose, *but* they are in any event not clearly expressed in the provision itself. To the contrary, it is reasonable to construe Sect. 1962(c) as implying a distinction between the person who committed the racketeering activity and the enterprise which that person is 'conducting', [...]. (1992_3: 105)

Here the anticipated objection introduced by 'it might be' is dismissed on account of the absence of an explicit formulation in the text under discussion, and the rejection is reinforced in the next sentence, introduced by 'to the contrary', where an opposite stance is taken. It is clear here that the writer, rather than denying squarely the possibility that in the folds of the statute text there may be an implicit intention to overlook the distinction between the person and the enterprise, prefers to show that s/he has actually given due consideration to the idea and rejected it, before going on to set forth his/her view.

Excerpt (7) shows a typical example of dialogic use of 'might' with an unattributed verbal process ('It might be argued …'):

> (7) Claimant claims the costs associated with the inspection of the rejected goods during the arbitration, including the costs of obtaining the samples by the tribunal's experts. *It might be argued that* these constitute `expenses reasonably incurred in inspection, receipt, transportation and care and custody of goods rightfully rejected'. *However*, the tribunal is of the opinion that almost all such costs were incurred for the purposes of this arbitration and in particular for the defence by claimant of its interests and as such, will be dealt with at the same time as the costs of arbitration… (1993_1: 138)

The proposition introduced by 'however' is presented as the response to an objection regarding the attribution of costs anticipated in the previous sentence introduced by 'it might be argued' which the arbitrator acknowledges, but then puts forth an idea that counters it, thus undermining its validity.

In the following example, the reasoning is more complex, as the refutation of the soundness of the objection introduced by 'it may be observed' is not signalled by a disjunct, but formulated as a hypothetical:

> (8) In this context *it may be observed* that the insertion of an arbitration clause in a contract may be considered to permit the inference that the parties have submitted their contract to the law of the country in which the arbitration is to take place. If one bases the reasoning on this hypothesis, it does still not clarify whether the parties meant the substantive law or the conflict of law of such place. (2001_2: 51)

The arbitrator, who is dealing with the problem of the applicable law in a dispute between a commodities trading company and a shipping company, anticipates a possible suggestion that the presence of an arbitration clause in the contract is in itself indicative that the parties accept the law of the country in which the arbitration is to take place as the applicable law. This idea is conceded, and then declared non conclusive for the final solution of the dispute.

Similarly, in the following excerpt, the conceded proposition is expanded by a number of considerations:

> (9) *One may then wonder* if a party is acting in conformity with the rules of good faith, a principle which dominates all Swiss law, when it invokes as the commencement of the running of the statute of limitations, a date which is indeed that from which the time limit must start to run, being the acceptance of the installation, but which it accepted to indicate on the document establishing this acceptance [dated 30 March, although the definitive acceptance of this part of the installation occurred on 23 March]. *This question does not need to be answered* because the requests of the claimant based on defects affecting the equipment which does not have to do with treating the water in the system are totally unfounded. (1995_6: 14)

The conceded proposition, introduced by 'one may wonder' is expanded by a number of subsequent clauses, and is dismissed only in the following paragraph not on its merits, but because it is seen as part of a line of claims which is considered unfounded.

The latter example shows that there are cases where *may/might* are used dialogically although the utterance does not contain a concessive/contrastive conjunct that explicitly indicates the conceded nature of the proposition they contribute to formulating.

In particular, there are cases where these modals are used with an impersonal subject (*one*) to attribute ideas or stances to a virtual interlocutor, as if they had not been elaborated by the arbitrators themselves, although it is obvious that they reflect the Tribunal's views:

> (10) *One may easily conclude* then that the Sponsor sought to operate as a 'Service Agent' of the type described in that Art. 13. *One may even note* the similarity in the wording of the Scope Clause of the Agreement with the wording of Art. 13 of Law 3/1985. The similarity is striking. *It is therefore reasonable for the Tribunal to assume* that whoever drafted the Agreement must have adopted this Law as a model. (1994_4: 69)

Here the text presents a sort of dialogue between the Tribunal and a potential addressee ("one"), whose proposals are presented in the text not to be overridden or refuted, but rather to be relied on in the conclusions. In this case the dialogic presentation of an argument is purely fictional and can be interpreted as a procedure to avoid taking categorical stances which may seem face threatening for the implied reader.

2.3. Other dialogic devices

This section will examine a group of attitudinal disjuncts (e.g. *certainly, of course, for sure,* etc.; cf. Quirk *et al.* : 508, 511-512; 674-675) that may have two different meanings: in some cases they construe strong commitment to a proposition, while in their dialogic use they imply agreement with an implied partner.

Among the disjuncts with a potentially concessive/dialogic value, the most frequently used in the Awards corpus is *certainly*, which is dialogic 52 times out of 81 (41.31%), while *of course* is used dialogically only 8 times out of 34 (23.52%).

The other lexicogrammatical signals of dialogism to be considered here – disjuncts and comment clauses – mostly appear in the corpus within the context of the 'counter' discourse patterns discussed in the previous section. By making recourse to the 'concur' (or 'concede') + 'counter' pairing, the arbitrator "validates the reader's [expected] contrary viewpoint by acknowledging that it is understandable and has a rational basis" (Martin and White 2005: 125), and then goes on to refute it.

In paratactic concessive clause complexes, disjuncts are often used to signal immediately the conceded nature of the anticipated objection in the first part of paratactic concessive constructions, as in the following examples featuring 'certainly' and 'of course':

(11) The arbitral tribunal *certainly* does not dispute these allegations. *But* whatever first and second defendants may have done in that connection should not obscure what they did not do, i.e., sit at the negotiation table with claimant, talk, and, if possible, settle. (1994_7: 105)

(12) *Of course*, this does not exclude the debtor from being a 'third party', as he certainly is. *However*, the risk that the transfer of the credit may give rise to an actual or potential prejudice to the third party's rights (and so therefore to the debtor's rights whenever the debtor is the third party in question), appears to be the main concern of the Legislator when setting the provisions of Art. 1690. 2001_1: 31)

(13) It was, *of course*, open to A to refuse these new conditions. *However*, it did not do so. (1995_3: 145)

(14) There is *obviously* a division of authorities on that issue. *However*, the Tribunal does not have to rule on this question. (1992_3: 89)

In these instances the presence of the disjunct prevents the conceded value of the first sentence from passing unsignalled until the reader comes across the conjunct introducing the asserted proposition that follows.

In many cases, instead, disjuncts are used in combination with other concessive markers thus emphasizing the dialogic character of the utterance. In example (15) below the disjunct is used in a subordinate concessive clause:

(15) *Although* both parties *certainly* seem to have contemplated that A-Europe would perform part of its obligations through A, the benefit and burden of the Agreement was to have been A-Europe's alone.(1995_3: 141)

In Excerpt (16), instead, *certainly* is used in combination with a verb form indicating a verbal process with 'might':

(16) As far as the debtor is concerned, *it might certainly object* that the transferor could not transfer more rights than those belonging to him, if and when we should enter into the discussion of the substance of the claim. *However,* such an objection would possibly affect the quantum claimed. It would not affect the title to claim. (2001_1: 33)

In (17) *to be sure*, which right from the very onset signals the conceded character of the proposition, is followed by three parallel clauses introduced by concessive 'may', and at the end of the sequence the asserted proposition is opened by 'but':

> (17) *To be sure*, *it may be that* by asserting these claims as it did, claimant was in gross error, both legally and factually; *it may be that* the legal basis thereof is incorrect, because claimant failed to properly characterize it; *it also may be* that the tentative amounts are unrealistic, because claimant, as claimants often do, may have exaggerated them. *But* these are clearly matters for the arbitral tribunal to decide, after having given all due weight to the arguments of the parties. (1994_7: 87)

When used in initial position, disjuncts (*certainly, to be sure, obviously, of course*) do not need to be accompanied by concessive *may* or *might*, but are sufficient in themselves to indicate the conceded character of the proposition:

> (18) *Certainly*, claimant did not at that time have access to all of defendant's internal documents, and defendant's knowledge was superior to that to claimant's, but claimant was a knowledgeable corporation, advised by international specialists, not ignorant of questions that were debated in international meetings it attended. (1993_3: 85)

This applies more specifically to 'true' when used as an attitudinal disjunct, given that in semantic terms it is the most clearly dialogic of the markers examined here:

> (19) *True*, the March 1991 letter refers to a previous telex of May 1990. However, the claimant did not submit the telex to the Arbitral Tribunal. (1993_2: 46)

'True', which is also the adjective typically used in dialogic comment clauses, occurs 86 times in the Awards corpus and in 26 of them (i.e. 22.36%) is clearly dialogic, as in the following example, where it is repeated twice:

> (20) *It is true that* this clause would seem to address the case of partial non-performance, rather than total non-performance […]. *It is also true that* [a clause] of the Contract, which governs the damages that one party may request, does not exclude damages for lost profits. *Nevertheless*, the Arbitral Tribunal considers that [this] language ... is too general to be restricted to a certain type of situation and that it does not allow the

granting of damages for the lost profits as claimed by claimant. (1995_2: 119)

In the corpus there appear various variations of this basic pattern ('it is true that ...'). In some cases, the dialogic strength of the structure is reinforced by combining it with 'may':

(21) *It may be true that* the processing of the goods has changed its condition within the literal meaning of UCC Sect. 2-608(2). A literal reading, *however*, is not a sound reading. (1993_1: 120)

or by using it in a concessive clause introduced by 'though':

(22) But *though it is true* that drought is not specifically mentioned, Art. 7(1) refers to 'natural catastrophes' and also to 'other circumstances outside control', terms under which one is entitled to include drought. (2000_1: 20)

3. Conclusion

This study has presented an analysis of lexicogrammatical elements and structures associated with concession and dialogism in a corpus of international arbitration awards. Findings confirm the complexity and stratification of the system of 'voices' in this text genre and contributes to highlighting the high degree of polyphony characterising it.

As far as linguistic devices generating concessive meaning are concerned, they appear to be particularly important in arbitration awards as they make it possible for arbitrators to cast their arguments and opinions in overtly interpersonal terms "simultaneously accepting the truth of the [conceded] proposition and in a way calling it into question in relation to the (following) dominant assertion" (Thompson and Zhou 2000: 130). This is essential as arbitrators do not have the absolute authority and authoritativeness that characterizes judges as a result of their position in the judiciary. Rather, arbitrators are delegated their authority by the parties themselves, so it is only natural that they should try to justify their decisions extensively, demonstrating that all the arguments put forth by both parties – also those of the party to which the award is unfavourable – have been acknowledged and taken into due account, all the more so as awards – although formally binding – may always be disregarded in favour of litigation, or appealed to in court.

In strictly rhetorical terms, recourse to concessive constructions as well as to modals and disjuncts with a concessive/dialogic value enables the arbitrator to meet his/her interlocutors on their own ground, acknowledging in each case not only a possible objection – set out in the conceded proposition – but also the pragmatic inference, or implicature, it licences (Toulmin's 'warrant': cf. Toulmin 1958: 98ff.), thus incorporating their point of view in the text.

In itself this formal acknowledgement of the interlocutor's point of view, albeit obviously vitiated by the determination to refute it, represents in textual terms the ostensible attempt to find objects of agreement (Perelman and Olbrechts-Tyteca 1958/1969) which may serve as premises for argumentation.

Recourse to concession in some cases also responds to another rhetorical exigency; through the use of 'may'/'might' with unattributed verbal/mental processes it also enables arbitrators to present their own views as if they derived from someone else's contribution, rather than averring them openly as their own, thus organizing their arguments dialectically and avoiding categorical face-threatening assertions. This is in line with the results of a previous study by this author (Garzone and Degano 2012) which demonstrated the pervasiveness of language reporting in awards.

Of course, these findings contribute positively to shedding light on the realization of polyphony in arbitration awards as a text genre, but the results are by definition limited and partial, on account of the multiplicity and complexity of the phenomena to be investigated. There are still many aspects to be explored before being able to draw a satisfactory and comprehensive account of polyphony and dialogism in this text genre.

References

Authier-Revuz J. 1995. *Ces mots qui ne vont pas de soi*. Paris: Larousse.

Azuelos-Atias, Sol. 2010. *A Pragmatic Analysis of Legal Proofs of Criminal Intent*. Amsterdam/Philadelphia: John Benjamins Publishing Co.

Bakhtin, Mikhail. 1952/1979/1984. "Les genres du discours". In *Esthétique de la création verbale*, 265-308. Paris: Gallimard.

Blakemore, Diane. 1987. *Semantic Constraints on Relevanc*e. Oxford: Blackwells.

—. 1989. "Denial and Contrast: A Relevance Theoretic Account of *but*." *Linguistics and Philosophy* 12: 15-37.

Bres, Jacques. 1999. "'Vous les entendez?' Analyse du discourse et dialogisme". *Modèles linguistiques* 20: 71-86.

Bres, Jacques and Alexandra Nowakowska. 2005. "Dis moi avec qui tu 'dialogues', je te dirai qui tu est … De la pertinence de la notion de dialogisme pour l'analyse due discours". *Marges Linguistiques* 9: 137-153. Online at <www.marges-linguistiques.com>.

Dendale, Patrick. 2006. "Three Linguistic Theories of Polyphony /Dialogism: An External Point of View and Comparison". *Sprogli Polyphony Arbeitspapiren* 5. Februar 2006. Roskilde: Institut for Sprog og Kultur, Roskilde Universitetscenter, online at <http://webh01.ua.ac.be/dendaleArticles/Dendale2006PolyphonyRoskilde.pdf>.

Ducrot, Oswald. 1984. *Le dire et le dit.* Paris: Les Éditions de Minut.

Fairclough, Norman. 1992. *Discourse and Social Change*. Oxford: Polity Press.

Fløttum, Kjersti. 2005. "The Self and the Others – Polyphonic Visibility in Research Articles". *International Journal of Applied Linguistics* 15: 29-44.

Fløttum, Kjersti, Trine Dahl and Torodd Kinn. 2006. *Academic Voices*. Amsterdam: John Benjamins.

Fløttum, Kjersti and François Rastier (eds). 2003. *Academic Discourse. Multidisciplinary Approaches*. Oslo: Novus.

Frege, Friedrich L. G. 1892/1994. "On Sense and Reference". In *Basic Topics in the Philosophy of Language,* edited by Robert M. Harnish, 142-160. Englewood Cliffs, N.J.: Prentice-Hall.

Garzone, Giuliana. 2005. "Pragmatic and Discoursal Features of Annual Executive Letters: Observations on the Rhetorical and Evaluative Function of Concessive Constructions". In *Cross-Cultural Encounters. Linguistic Perspectives*, edited by Marina Bondi and Nick Maxwell 130-141. Rome: Officina.

Garzone, Giuliana and Chiara Degano. 2012. "Voices in Arbitration Awards: Polyphony and Language Reports." In *Discourse and Practice in International Commercial Arbitration. Issues, Challenges and Prospects,* edited by Vijay K. Bhatia, Christopher N. Candlin, and Maurizio Gotti, 179-207. London: Ashgate.

Grice, Paul 1961/1989. *Studies in the Way of Words*. Cambridge Mass. & London: Harvard University Press.

Halliday, Michael A. K. 1994. *An Introduction to Functional Grammar.* London: Edward Arnold.

Iten, Corinne. 1998. "The Meaning of *although*: a Relevance Theoretic Account". *UCL Working Papers in Linguistics*, 10.

König, Ekkehard. 1986. "Conditionals, Concessive Conditionals and Concessives: Areas of Contrast, Overlap and Neutralization". In *On*

Conditionals, edited by Elisabeth Closs Traugott, Alice Ter Meulen, Judy Snitzer Reilly and Charles A. Ferguson, 229-246. Cambridge: Cambridge University Press.

—. 1988. "Concessive Connectives and Concessive Sentences: Cross-Linguistic Regularities and Pragmatic Principles." In *Explaining Language Universals*, edited by John A. Hawkins, 145-166. Oxford: Blackwell.

—. 1989. "Concessive Relations as the Dual of Causal Relations". In *Semantic Universals and Universal Semantics*, edited by Deitmar Zaefferer, 190-209. Dordrecht: Foris.

Marriott, Arthur. 2004. "Less is More: Directing Arbitration Procedures". *Arbitration International* 16, no. 3: 353-56.

Martin, James R., and Peter R.R. White. 2005. *The Language of Evaluation. Appraisal in English*. London: Palgrave Macmillan.

Mazzi, Davide 2007a. *The Linguistic Study of Judicial Argumentation. Theoretical Perspectives Analytical Insights.* Modena: Edizioni Il Fiorino.

—. 2007b. "Reporting Verbs: A tool for a Polyphonic Analysis of Judgments". *Studien zur Rechtscommunikation,* edited by Konrad Echlich and Dorothée Heller, 31-55. Bern: Peter Lang.

—. 2008. "La sentenza come genere argomentativo: una riflessione linguistica". In *Il linguaggio giuridico. Prospettive interdisciplinari,* edited by Giuliana Garzone and Francesca Santulli, 239-262. Milano: Giuffré Editore.

Nariman, Fali S. 2000. "The Spirit of Arbitration: The Tenth Annual Goff Lecture". *Arbitration International* 16, no. 3: 261-278.

Nølke, Henning, Kjersti Fløttum and Coco Norén. 2004. *ScaPoLine. La théorie Scandinave de la polyphonie linguistique*. Paris: Editions Kimé.

Nowakowska, Alexandra 2005. "Dialogisme, polyphonie: des textes russes de M. Bakhtine à la linguistique contemporaine". In *Dialogisme, polyphonie: approches linguistiques*, edited by Jacques Bres *et al.*, 19-32. Louvain-la-Neuve: De Boek Duculot.

Pagano, Adriana. 1994. Negatives in Written Text. In *Advances in Written Text Analysis*, edited by Malcom Coulthard, 250-265. London: Routledge.

Palmer, Frank Robert. 1979/1990. *Modality and the English Modals*. London: Longman.

Perelman, Chaïm and Lucie Olbrechts-Tyteca. 1958/1969. *The New Rhetoric: A Treatise on Argumentation* (*Traité de l'argumentation - la nouvelle rhétorique*, translated by John Wilkinson and Purcell Weaver). Notre Dame: University of Notre Dame Press.

Quirk, Randolph, Sidney Greenbaum, Geoffrey Leech and Jan Svartvik. 1985. *A Comprehensive Grammar of the English Language.* London: Longman.

Rieber, Steven 1997. "Conventional Implicatures as Tacit Performatives". *Linguistics and Philosophy* 20: 51-72.

Rouchota, Villy. 1998. "Procedural Meaning and Parenthetical Discourse Markers". *Discourse Markers. Descriptions and Theories*, edited by Andreas Jucker and Yael Ziv, 97-126. Amsterdam: John Benjamin.

Scott, Mike 2004. *Wordsmith Tools 4.0.* Oxford University Press.

Souesme, Jean-Claude. 2004. "MAY in concessive contexts". <http://portail.unice.fr/jahia/webdav/site/myjahiasite/users/souesme/public/souesme/may.pdf>.

Thompson, Geoff. 1994. *Reporting.* Collins COBUILD English Guides 5. Birmingham: Collins COBUILD.

—. 1996. "Voices in Text: Discourse Perspectives on Language Reports". *Applied Linguistics* 17, no. 4: 501-530.

—. 2001. "Interaction in Academic Writing: Learning to Argue with the Reader." *Applied Linguistics* 22, no.1: 58-78.

Thompson, Geoff and Ye Yiyun. 1991. "Evaluation in the Reporting Verbs Used in Academic Papers." *Applied Linguistics* 12, no. 4: 365-382.

Thompson, Geoff and Jinglin Zhou 2000. "Structuring Role of Evaluative Disjuncts". In *Evaluation in Text. Authorial Stance and the Construction of Discourse*, edited by Susan Hunston and Geoff Thompson, 121-141. Oxford: Oxford University Press.

Todorov, Tzvetan. 1981/1984. *Mikhail Bakhtin. The Dialogic Principle.* Transl. by Wlad Godzich. Manchester: Manchester University Press.

Toulmin, Stephen. 1958. *The Uses of Argument.* Cambridge: Cambridge University Press.

Wilson, Dan and Deirdre Sperber. 1993. "Linguistic Form and Relevance". *Lingua* 90, no. 1/2: 1-25.

Yovel, Jonathan. 2010. "Language and Power in a Place of Contingencies: Law and The Polyphony of Lay Argumentation." Yale Law School Faculty Scholarship Series. Paper 32. Online at <http://digitalcommons.law. yale.edu/fss_papers/32>.

Awards quoted

2003_1. Final award in case no. 11849 of 2003. *Yearbook Commercial Arbitration*, A.J. van den Berg (ed.), Vol. XXXI (2006), pp. 148 – 171.

2000_1. Final Award in Case No. 8790 of 2000. *Yearbook Commercial Arbitration*, A.J. van den Berg (ed.), Vol. XXIX (2004), pp. 13 – 25.

2000_2. Final Award in Case No. 10329 of 2000. *Yearbook Commercial Arbitration*, A.J. van den Berg (ed.), Vol. XXIX (2004), pp. 108 – 132.

2001_1. Final Award in Case No. 9762 of 2001. *Yearbook Commercial Arbitration*, A.J. van den Berg (ed.), Vol. XXIX (2004), pp. 26 – 45.

2001_2. Final Award in Case No. 9771 of 2001. *Yearbook Commercial Arbitration*, A.J. van den Berg (ed.), Vol. XXIX (2004), pp. 46 – 65.

1995_2. Final award in case no. 8032 of 1995. *Yearbook Commercial Arbitration*, A.J. van den Berg (ed.), Vol. XXI (1996), pp. 113 – 122.

1995_3. Final award in case no. 7626 of 1995. *Yearbook Commercial Arbitration*, A.J. van den Berg (ed.), Vol. XXII (1997), pp. 132 – 148.

1998_2 Final award in case no. 9302 of 1998. *Yearbook Commercial Arbitration*, A.J. van den Berg (ed.), Vol. XXVIII (2003), pp. 54 – 67

1995_6 Final award in case no. 6197 of 1995. *Yearbook Commercial Arbitration*, A.J. van den Berg (ed.), Vol. XXIII (1998), pp. 13 – 29

1994_4 Final award in case no. 7639 of 1994. *Yearbook Commercial Arbitration*, A.J. van den Berg (ed.), Vol. XXIII (1998), pp. 66 – 79.

1994_7 Final award in cases nos. 6515 and 6516 of 1994. *Yearbook Commercial Arbitration*, A.J. van den Berg (ed.), Vol. XXIVa (1999), pp. 80 – 106.

1993_1 Final award in case no. 6955 of 1993. *Yearbook Commercial Arbitration*, A.J. van den Berg (ed.), Vol. XXIVa (1999), pp. 107 – 140

1993_2 Final award in case no. 7301 of 1993. *Yearbook Commercial Arbitration*, A.J. van den Berg (ed.), Vol. XXIII (1998), pp. 42 – 48

1993_3 Final award in case no. 7063 of 1993. *Yearbook Commercial Arbitration*, A.J. van den Berg (ed.), Vol. XXII (1997), pp. 87 – 91.

1992_3 Final Award in case no. 6320 of 1992. *Yearbook Commercial Arbitration*, A.J. van den Berg (ed.), Vol. XX (1995), pp. 62 – 109.

CHAPTER SIX

ARBITRATION AWARDS IN ITALY: SOME ARGUMENTATIVE FEATURES IN THE DISCOURSE ANALYTICAL PERSPECTIVE

DONELLA ANTELMI
AND FRANCESCA SANTULLI

1. Study design

The aim of this chapter is to examine arbitration awards produced in Italy, in order to single out some of their most relevant features and to show in which aspects they differ from judgments. The discussion will be focused on the various forms of dialogism, a discursive feature widely exploited in these texts as a means of introducing different 'voices' – mainly the parties and legislation – whose claims are then examined in order to be, partially or totally, accepted or refuted.

The analysis of texts will be preceded by a brief survey of the approach to arbitration in Italy, which, though strongly conditioned by a long-established conflict between litigation and 'private justice', has undergone significant changes in recent years. This conflict, combined with the existence of explicit legislative norms, has conditioned the forms adopted for the production of written texts, influencing their global structure as well as some more specific aspects. In particular, the main elements of enunciation – combined with argumentative strategies – generate some characteristics that seem to be typical of awards.

Therefore, the legislative background will be sketched, giving special attention to the changes introduced in 2006; the structure of judgments – with its legislative rationale – will then be examined and compared with that of the awards.

Having considered these preliminary and general aspects, the study will tackle discursive problems, starting from a synthetic presentation of the theoretical approach chosen, which combines the typical features of Discourse Analysis with more genuinely argumentative insights.

Under this research perspective, which makes qualitative analysis more appropriate for the specific aims of this study, about 35 arbitration awards in Italian have been examined: this sample includes all the texts published in the *Archivio giuridico delle opere pubbliche* (2006) n. 71-72 as well as some texts available on the Internet.

Among other characteristics, dialogism will be examined focusing, on the one hand, on the different forms described by Bres and Nowakowska (2006: auto-dialogism, interdiscursive dialogism and interlocutive dialogism; cf. also Bakhtin 1978) and, on the other, on the different possibilities of expressing it, namely quotations, hedging and concessive structures.

2. Historical background

In Italy arbitration has traditionally been a controversial institution. Actually, the very possibility of establishing a special procedure to settle a controversy that may arise between private parties implies that the administration of justice is not a matter exclusive of the State. The opposition between a rigidly state-oriented approach and the idea that legislation should allow negotiatory forms of resolution of disputes has led to different interpretations of the institution itself. Arbitration has been considered a form of litigation or, vice versa, as a private trial. Moreover, law scholars, jurists and experts of the legal professions have expressed different opinions concerning the opportunity of accepting, expanding and/or regulating the practice of arbitration, above all when the Public Administration is involved in the process.

The expression of caution towards the introduction of arbitration norms dates back to 1923, when Mortara in his Commentaries on the Civil Code of Procedure (*codice di procedura civile* or *c.p.c.*) emphasised the risk that arbitration practice may violate state sovereignty. As a way to limit this risk and make arbitration institutionally acceptable, Mortara gave special attention to the formal aspects of the procedure, as strict regulation was considered to be the only viable option to guarantee a fair judgment. In other words, arbitration could be accepted only insofar as it was controlled by the state.[1]

In the modern perspective, this theoretical position may be considered unusual and rather contradictory. A seminal work by Chiovenda (1933-34)

---

[1] For an interesting discussion of these problems in the historical perspective, cf. Montedoro 2004.

shows an evolution in the approach to arbitration, which is accepted by the author as a form of negotiation. The whole arbitration procedure stems from the arbitration clause, which is the result of the agreement of the parties who signed the contract: this is why arbitration can only be considered as the expression of the common will of the parties. However, the final result of the process – the award – is enacted by a public jurisdictional institution (through the so-called *exequatur*), and has therefore full public value: according to Chiovenda, despite the negotiatory nature of arbitration, the decisions taken by arbitrators are parallel to those adopted by 'ordinary' judges.

More recently the private nature of arbitration has been widely recognised, and the value of the decision stemming from the procedure has been accepted. This changing attitude is confirmed by the recent approval of legislation that deals with the matter comprehensively. The provisions enacted in 2006 (D.L. 02.02.2006) reflect a more rational approach to the whole matter, and include norms concerning different aspects of the question.

The most relevant points can be synthesised as follows (Montalenti 2007):

- international arbitration is no longer recognised a special status, and is regulated by the same norms applying to home-based controversies. As for the language to be adopted for the procedure, the parties have freedom of choice;[2]
- the traditional distinction between the so-called 'irritual' (non-standard) arbitration procedure and 'ritual' (standard) arbitration is *de facto* eliminated, with the prevalence of the latter (it must be considered that only ritual arbitration allows the enactment of awards and is recognised at the international level);
- arbitration awards are recognised the same effectiveness as judgments;
- excessively formal rules that had traditionally governed the writing of awards were eliminated;
- the possibilities of appeal have been limited: challenge is allowed only when the arbitration clause, or legislation, explicitly provides for this possibility.

[2] On this point, cf. Frigo (this volume).

3. Judgments and awards

Judgments are a typical example of *juridical* texts: in the classification of the different instances of language of the law, Bhatia (1987) distinguishes them from legislative texts on the one side, and specialized publishing on the other. The taxonomy, slightly modified by Garzone (1997), actually stems from the fundamental contraposition, dating back to the work of Oppenheim (1944), of *sentences of law* vs *statements about sentences of law*, which underlines the difference between the texts that make up the law (legislation, norms, agreements, decisions, etc) on the one hand, and texts commenting on legal provisions on the other: the latter are a form of metalanguage, and include genres that explain, interpret or discuss the law at a more or less specialized level, ranging from papers for academic journals to newspaper articles aimed at popularization. Under this perspective, awards do not differ from judgments, as they both function as a form of interpretation and, above all, application of legislative norms to real cases.

In systems based on civil law (as is the case in Italy) a fundamental feature of judicial decisions is that they have to be *justified*. Historically, crucial innovations in the administration of justice were the separation of powers, the publication of written codes and the principle that a judge is obliged to justify his decision with reference to legislation. According to Perelman (1976) this is the starting point of the modern approach to the problem of equity, a fundamental characteristic that has had direct consequences on the nature and structure of judgments as texts. A judgment must obviously illustrate a decision and contain prescriptions for the parties, but it must also include an argumentative section in which the reasons for the decision are explained.

This general but precise principle is clearly affirmed in the Italian Constitution (art. 111), which provides for the necessity of stating the reasons for the decisions in all judicial pronouncements. More concretely, the general dispositions that precede the Civil Code of Procedure (*disposizioni attutative c.p.c.*) include an article that describes the basic structure of a judgment (art. 118): it imposes the examination of the case (i.e. of the sequence of facts that make up the trial) and the discussion of the reasons for the decision (stemming from the application of legislation to the individual case). Only at the end of this sequence can the judgment proper be pronounced.

The structure of judgments is therefore explicitly codified; besides, there are precise norms that regulate formal, though more marginal, aspects of the text. A judgment is pronounced "on behalf of the Italian people" and must have the indication of the date and the signature of the judge. It starts with an introduction, where the parties and the judge are identified, followed by the illustration of the various stages of the trial (the so-called "facts", or *il fatto*); in the subsequent part, usually described as *diritto* ('law foundations'), the arguments for the application of norms to the case are illustrated; finally there is the pronunciation of the judgment, ritually introduced by the acronym *P.Q.M.* (or *per questi motivi*, 'for these reasons'), consisting of a performative formula with a fixed structure: subject (or the name of the judge taking the decision) + performative verb (third person singular of the present indicative), as for example "il Tribunale accoglie l'istanza del ricorrente" ('the Tribunal accepts the requests of the plaintiff') (cf. Santulli 2008).

In comparison with this rigid and legally regulated structure, in theory arbitration awards can display more flexible characteristics. However, despite the absence of explicit legislative provisions, they are generally organised with a similar sequence, whose main steps are: the description of the procedure and the reasons for the decision. Typically an award also includes a preliminary discussion of the admissibility of the procedure and the choice of arbitrators.

Considering the similarities in the general principles underlying the structure of the texts, the crucial difference between judgments and awards stems from the different legal status of the institutions pronouncing them, and is the bare consequence of the relative position of litigation and arbitration, which, apart from actual legal differences, are also assigned different decisional value.

For all these reasons the analysis of language and textual features cannot lead to significant results unless it takes into consideration the characteristics of the participants involved in communication. Argumentative moves have to be examined against the background of the global pragmatic context (Adam 2008). This chapter will therefore privilege the discourse analytical point of view,[3] a theoretical and methodological approach which focuses on enunciation (Benveniste 1974) and considers its social, historical and institutional context. As a matter of fact, this brief survey of arbitration awards will try to show that in these texts enunciation

[3] Though it cannot be considered an autonomous field of studies, Discourse Analysis has been accepted worldwide, and includes different theoretical approaches. Among the various lines of research, the most relevant are the 'French school', based on research dating back to the 1960s-1970s (Charaudeau 1983, Maingueneau 1991, Maingueneau 1995), and the 'Anglo-Saxon' school, drawing on critical linguistics and on the studies carried out in the English-speaking world (Fairclough 1995, van Dijk 1993, 2001).

affects argumentation, and modulates its tone as a consequence of external factors, linked to the institutional status of the locutors and, in turn, of the texts they produce.

4. Theoretical background: discourse analysis and argumentation theory

In recent years argumentation has aroused growing interest in the area of language studies: the link between argumentation and rhetoric has been widely recognised and has opened up totally new perspectives, as shown by the seminal work by Perelman and Olbrechts-Tyteca (1958) or, a few decades after the publication of *La nouvelle rhétorique*, by the fortune of the pragma-dialectical approach (cf. for example, van Eemeren and Grootendorst 1992). Researchers have re-discovered the contribution of ancient rhetoricians and philosophers to the debate on the persuasive function of language, and have further considered the relationship between rhetoric and argumentation proper. Less attention has been devoted to the possibility of integrating argumentation theory with discourse analytical principles. Only recently has this field been explored (*Semen 17*/2004; Amossy 2006, 2009), and research has emphasised evident similarities, but it has also revealed the presence of different methods and sometimes incompatible theoretical approaches (Doury and Moirand 2004).

As a matter of fact, it cannot be denied that any instance of discourse includes an argumentative component – and this circumstance makes argumentation a privileged area of study for discourse analysts. On the other hand, however, recent theories aim to make argumentation an autonomous and self-contained area of research (Anscombre and Ducrot 1988; Toulmin 1958; van Eemeren and Grootendorst 2004), where the attention is focused either on discourse genres (political, legal, etc; Charaudeau 2005) or on language structures (Ducrot 1984).

One of the reasons why argumentation theory and discourse analysis have had difficulties in communicating lies in the choice of the objects of their analysis. While argumentation theory pays attention to genres considered inherently argumentative, discourse analysis takes into consideration texts belonging to any genre, and with the most diversified characteristics. The discourse analytical approach can be systematically integrated by the study of argumentative aspects of discourse, so that argumentation itself becomes a component of *any* form of discourse, and is no longer limited to a set of genres traditionally investigated by means of rhetorical analytical tools. As a consequence, a text can be classified as argumentative, even if it is not openly aimed at persuasion.

It is however possible to avoid a sharp distinction between argumentative and non-argumentative texts, and adopt the hypothesis of gradual differentiation, so that there exist prototypical argumentative genres of discourse (deliberative, judicial, etc), which have an explicit persuasive goal, but there are also less evident forms of argumentation, which do not imply the adoption of explicit and/or stringent schemes.

Grize (1990: 41), for example, defines argumentation as a set of discursive strategies through which a speaker addresses a hearer in order to modify his/her judgment on a situation. Under this perspective, argumentation is functional to a form of exchange rather than being an instrument for persuasion: "l'argumentation considère l'interlocuteur non comme un objet à manipuler mais comme un *alter ego* auquel il s'agira de faire partager sa vision". Grize develops a theory of argumentation as a discursive activity: in this theoretical approach the dialogic nature of discourse, which is emphasised by the importance of polyphony and intertextuality both in written and oral texts, plays a crucial role. On the one hand, it is possible to recognise an argumentative component in any type of discourse, as stated by Plantin:

> Toute parole est nécessairement argumentative. C'est un résultat concret de l'enoncé en situation. Tout enoncé vise à agir sur son destinataire, sur autrui, et à transformer son système de pensée [All words are by necessity argumentative. This materially results from the enunciation in situation. Every enunciation aims at acting upon its addressee, upon another person, and transform his/her thought system; *our translation*] (Plantin 1996: 18).

On the other hand, it can be noted that it is the dialogic nature of discourse that implies a certain degree of argumentative force, even when there is no explicit persuasive goal or the interlocutors do not interact *in presentia*. Any statement can be considered as a reply to another statement previously uttered in an "interdiscursive space", as underlined by Bakhtin:

> L'orientation dialogique est, bien entendu, un phénomène caractéristique de tout discours [...] Le discours rencontre le discours d'autrui sur tous les chemins qui mènent vers son objet, et il ne peut pas ne pas entrer avec lui en interaction vive et intense [The dialogic orientation is a phenomenon characterising all discourse [...] Discourse encounters other people' discourse along all the paths that lead to its goal, and cannot but start a lively and intense interaction with it; *our translation*] (Bakhtin, cit. in Todorov 1981: 98).

The gradual notion of argumentativeness illustrated above makes it possible to apply the principles of argumentative analysis to any kind of text, from everyday conversation to literature, from news to legal texts. The adoption of a discourse analytical approach in argumentation research implies that argumentation should be considered a linguistic activity performed in the actual context of communication rather than the mere production of propositions in a logical sequence. As a consequence linguistic analysis should take into account the role and the characteristics of the addressee, as well as the pragmatic function of texts, considering that subjects, topics and arguments are displayed in a text that belongs to a specific genre, and is therefore organised in accordance to its rhetoric, structural and linguistic rules (Maingueneau 2002).

In other words, it is always possible to discover an argumentative component in texts, even if they do not have an explicit persuasive goal, but simply aim to reinforce an opinion or stimulate reflection and discussion (Amossy 2009: 32).

5. Analysis of texts

The analysis of arbitration awards immediately reveals some regularly occurring features, which this text genre shares with judgments. However, more specific characteristics emerge, depending on the specificity of arbitration as opposed to litigation.

In arbitration awards, argumentative discourse, though displaying its typical structure, includes a more constant dialogic interaction with the parties on the one hand, and, on the other, a different attitude of the enunciator towards his/her own verbal action.

Therefore, here argumentative connectors will be considered only briefly, and the study will focus on other aspects that seem to be more typical of awards – namely the argumentative value of the different voices as well as the role of dialogism.

5.1. The lexicon of argumentation

As anticipated above, the texts examined for this study show some formal and stylistic features that are typical also of judgments. Both judgments and awards include argumentative sections (cf. § 3 above), but their respective writers have different institutional roles: in awards, for example, the enunciator must preliminarily legitimate the choice of the arbitrators (and therefore his/her own right to decide). The very position of arbitration in the legal system as a whole induces writers to prefer more blurred argumentative structures. Considering this special feature of awards, it is possible to extend the approach adopted by Mazzi (2007) in his research on judicial argumentation to arbitration.

For example, in the sample connectors and argumentative lexicon[4] are the same as those occurring in judgments: *ne consegue, ciò comporta, si desume, deriva che risulta che* etc [it follows that, this implies, it can be inferred, it derives that, it results that] – all marking a progressive form of reasoning, which makes the cause/effect nexus explicit. Similar observations emerge from Sala's analysis (this volume), who notes that in the typical argumentative structure adopted in Italian arbitration awards the causes are introduced before the effects. Sala's observations, corroborated by quantitative data, confirm that the logical movement of progressive reasoning can be considered the most adequate to lead gradually from premises to conclusion – and so to the final decision.

5.2. Dialogism

In a discourse analytical perspective, dialogism can be considered to be inherently present in any kind of discourse: even if there is no physically present interlocutor, the enunciator however has his/her actual or potential audience in mind. Argumentatively speaking, dialogism has its counterpart in the notion of audience, as described by Perelman and Olbrechts-Tyteca (1958), who – given the intention of the speaker to influence somebody else with his/her arguments – emphasise the importance of being perfectly aware of the characteristics of the addressees: the audience is therefore "a thought-construction of the arguer" (van Eemeren *et al.* 1996: 97).

The actual composition of the audience can vary: in the case of arbitration awards, arbitrators obviously address the parties, and it is important to convince them that both the procedure and the decision are correct, and therefore difficult to challenge. Moreover, in the case of an appeal, the reasoning must stand to scrutiny, and so, in a wider perspective, reinforce the conviction that arbitration is an effective and lawful method to settle disputes.

Although an award is a written document produced by one single locutor or a unitary group of locutors, it includes different voices and arguments, introduced either as quotations or as presupposed opinions (which are then refuted).

To express dialogism, different linguistic strategies can be adopted: reported speech is used to introduce other people's voices; mitigation and hedges reveal the speaker's stance towards his/her own words; it is

[4] For these aspects s. Mortara Garavelli 2001; Santulli 2006.

moreover possible to accept or refute alternative opinions or, finally, appeal simply to common sense (or *doxa*).

Quotations generally function as a form of argument of authority, as they generally introduce legislative provisions. The other forms of dialogism can be divided into three groups:

- auto-dialogism, which refers to the enunciator's attitude towards his/her own words;[5]
- interdiscursive dialogism, which includes pieces of previous discourse concerning the same topic;
- interlocutive dialogism, which shows the attitude of the enunciator towards his/her co-enunciators, whose positions are anticipated and/or contrasted.

5.3. Quotations and arguments

In the case of quotations, the different voices are a form of guarantee. Verbatim quotations or explicit references to legal norms can be considered a rhetorical technique functional to confirming the objective value of a certain point of view; they can also be an argument of authority or a way to reduce the enunciator's responsibility.

In arbitration awards, argumentation performs three main functions: arbitrators must support their decision discursively, but argumentation is not limited to the illustration of their conclusions; it concerns at least two other questions, namely the legitimacy of the procedure itself and the evaluation of the documents and the pleadings produced by the parties. The way arguments are introduced changes according to the function.

5.3.1. Legitimacy of the arbitrators to discuss the case

At a macro-structural level, the text generally starts with the conclusion, expressed with a formulaic statement, which is then followed by the exposition of the grounds for the decision, normally justified by the arbitration clause (which is however rarely quoted *in extenso*). The arbitration clause is therefore the authoritative voice that legitimates the procedure:

> (1) L'eccezione è infondata e deve essere respinta. La clausola arbitrale non demanda infatti alle parti la nomina degli arbitri [The claim is

---

[5] The distinction between *enunciator* and *locutor* (based on Ducrot 1984) is accepted here, though other researchers prefer to use the terms as interchangeable.

ungrounded and must be rejected. The arbitration clause does not provide for the parties to appoint arbitrators].

5.3.2. Interpretation of norms to be applied to the case

Arbitrators must provide reasons for their decision, giving arguments to support their interpretation of legislation and explaining why they apply a certain rule to the case discussed. Usually, in Italy they refer to legislative texts with a mere indication of their number and date (elements that are evidently sufficient for the addressees to identify them). However, when they refer to the contract from which the procedure arises, they normally quote the relevant passages:

(2) [...] condizioni imposte dall'art. 17 comma 1 del Capitolato speciale di appalto, per cui "*l'appaltatore risponderà della funzionalità ed efficienza delle opere realizzate assumendosi ogni responsabilità in merito al funzionamento...*" [these conditions are imposed by art.17, paragraph 1, of the Specifications of the contract, according to which "the contractor is responsible for the effectiveness and the efficiency of the works as well as for their functioning..."]

5.3.3 Evaluation of documents and pleadings produced by the parties

Arbitration awards, like judgments, refer to a written record of facts – which may include the minutes of hearings and examinations of experts and/or witnesses – so that the final decision not only stems from the application of legislation and contract norms, but is also the direct consequence of a series of discursive moves of the parties. In the text, the whole case is re-examined, and this 'narrative' part displays a feature that is more frequent in awards than in judgments: the writer does not synthesise the facts, but prefers to quote from the statements produced by the parties. Letting "the parties speak" arbitrators give a more transparent status to their decision, and, at the same time, do not take the responsibility to ascertain whether the facts told by the parties are actually true or not.

(3) L'eccezione di decadenza è stata sollevata dalla difesa dell'azienda in occasione del deposito dell'atto di costituzione là dove si legge: "*In particolare, rileva fin d'ora, che tutte le riserve iscritte dalla società YYY sono tardive, inammissibili, inefficaci e, comunque, infondate*". [The defendant claimed forfeiture in its act of response, writing: "In particular, it can be noticed that all claims made by company YYY are late, inadmissible, ineffective and in any case ungrounded"].

Three different voices are therefore systematically exploited, and each of them is functional to expressing the specific aim of single parts of the award: arbitration clause, legislation and observations of the parties. These are introduced in different ways, which are in tune with the expectations of the implied addressees and the different degree of enunciator's commitment towards his/her own discourse. The three corresponding functions can be described as follows:

- justification of one's own role, which stems from explicit reference to the arbitration clause and is affirmed with a formulaic statement – the enunciator expresses the highest level of responsibility without any form of modulation, as the point is crucial to legitimise the action of arbitrators itself;
- interpretation of legislation, for which arbitrators are responsible – in these sections the style is similar to the style adopted in judgments; the addressees are "peers" who will be able to understand the typical (and often cryptic) legal expressions;
- argumentation for the decision: in these parts of the award, the text is highly transparent, and includes verbatim quotations from the parties' statements. The main addressees are the parties themselves, whose words are inserted into a global representation of facts, in which arbitrators are not included, and therefore are not responsible for the authenticity of the narrative.

5.4. Auto-dialogism: hedging and *doxa*

Although arbitration awards – as clearly stated in recent Italian legislation – display their effects not differently from judgments, the institutional status of arbitrators cannot be compared to that of judges. This can explain the presence of a high number of hedges (*a parere/avviso del Collegio, il Collegio ritiene, i più del Collegio manifestano l'avviso...* [according to the Court/in the Court's opinion/the majority of the Court's members believe…]), which are functional to modulating the enunciator's statements, thus producing a mitigation effect.

Moreover, arbitrators often introduce the concept that their decision stems from a sort of 'necessity': this strategy makes it possible for them to avoid taking a stance. The impersonal form (*pare incontestabile/è indubitabile/non vi è dubbio* [there is no doubt/it cannot be denied]) is frequently used to express an idea of necessity, so that arbitrators can avoid taking a personal position towards the parties.

Both strategies can be considered a form of auto-dialogism, which concerns the attitude of the enunciator towards his/her own words. Quantitative data concerning this form of dialogism can be found in the chapter by Sala (in this volume) mentioned above.

It can be added that this category also includes references to common sense, or – in rhetorical terms – *doxa*. As opposed to *episteme*, or true knowledge, *doxa* concerns probable truth, ideas that can be accepted on the basis of reasoning by any audience composed of sensible human beings. Statements can be acceptable either because they reflect the point of view of the majority, or because they are based on the opinion of experts and/or authorities. In the latter case *doxa* is legitimated by the authority itself.

In arbitration awards the effort to find a fair solution to the controversy is testified by frequent reference to common sense, or to current interpretations of legislation or of general principles of law:

(4) Il Collegio ritiene di aderire alla tesi (che appare dominante) secondo cui ... [The Court thinks it is possible to accept the opinion (which appears to be predominant), according to which...]

(5) Giova rammentare, sul punto, che la filosofia di fondo di tutta la vigente normativa sui lavori pubblici.... [In this respect, it is worth mentioning that the basic principles in legislation concerning public works...]

5.5. Interdiscursive/interlocutive dialogism

Concession is one of the most evident strategies adopted to introduce voices from outside into the discourse: concessive structures mark linguistically the opening of a dialogic perspective, and for this reason they have been frequently studied form the discourse analytical point of view (König 1989, Stati 1998, Garzone 2005, Antelmi and Santulli 2009).

Thanks to concession, it is possible for the enunciator to accept a thesis temporarily, thus creating an initial form of agreement with the addressee, which would expectedly lead to a conclusion in tune with the addressee's point of view: the conclusion is however rejected and replaced by a new one, which reflects the opinion of the enunciator. Schematically, the logic form of a concessive structure is the following: [6]

THOUGH P, Q (normally P entails non-Q, but the expectation is frustrated)

---

[6] For a more extensive discussion of recourse to concessive discourse as a form of polyphony in arbitration awards, cf. Garzone, Chapter Five (this volume).

In judicial argumentation, and above all in judgments, the dialogic perspective implies that the discourse includes the voices of the other participants in the trial, whose statements influence or at least may influence the reasoning of the writer. The latter, however, finally formulates, and accepts, a contrasting statement.

In arbitration awards this form of dialogism seems to be introduced to comply with the principle that all possible interpretations have to be taken into consideration, thus guaranteeing that the arbitrators tackle the case carefully and impartially:

> (6) Tra le due domande v'è differenza sia di *petitum* che di *causa pretendi*, pur essendovi degli elementi comuni, costituiti dal riferimento all'anomalo andamento dell'appalto ... [The two claims show a difference both in *petitum* and in *causa petendi*, although there are some common elements referring to the unusual procedure adopted for the contract ...]

There are also many (if not more) examples of interlocutive dialogism, which refers to the enunciatee, whose moves and/or objections are often anticipated by the arbitrators. In the latter case counterfactual concessive structures are often used, where the contrast between the subordinate and the main clause combines with the non-truth condition of the subordinate. This circumstance gives more strength to the statement contained in the main clause.

As a matter of fact, counterfactual concessives, rather than expressing a temporary agreement, anticipate possible objections of the enunciatee, and reject them. Not surprisingly, these structures mostly occur in the sections of the award where the objections of the parties are discussed, and the sequence of arguments is coherently and concisely introduced:

> (7) Comunque, anche se questa condizione si fosse verificata, non poteva certamente farsi valere in sede arbitrale.... [However, even if this had been the case, it could not be relevant for the arbitration procedure...].

6. Concluding remarks

Arbitration awards as a text genre are similar to judgments, but display a larger number of elements and structures that express the different enunciative stance of arbitrators. Within its globally rigid formal structure and in presence of a reasoning process that links arguments using the typical connectors of judicial discourse, the award contains other elements that indicate the presence of dialogism – namely hedges and concessive structures. Concession indicates that a different point of view is recognised a certain degree of validity and, even in those cases when it is finally rejected, the presence of concession marks the enunciator's willingness to negotiate and find an agreement.

The different types of dialogism present in the sample – auto-dialogism, interdiscursive and interlocutive dialogism – are used with reference to the different enunciators encoded in the text. They have different functions and are closely linked to the positioning of awards in the legal system as a whole and to the validity and value attributed to them.

The linguistic texture of awards, with its more or less blurred argumentative structures, is a clear consequence of the juridical debate on the nature and validity of arbitration, which has been a constant in the Italian academic and forensic tradition. The writer of an award must reduce the risk of challenge, but at the same time he/she must discursively create his/her own credibility, objectivity and impartiality.

In the light of these considerations the study of argumentation cannot be isolated from different approaches that analyse awards as an instance of discourse: the structure of the enunciation and the arguments are influenced not only by generic norms – which are basically similar to those typical of judgments – but also by the institutional framework (tasks and powers of chambers of arbitration) and by the respective status of participants (arbitrators, parties, legislation and jurisprudence).

References

Adam, Jean-Michel. 2008. *La linguistique textuelle. Introduction à l'analyse textuelle des discours*. Paris: Armand Colin.

Amossy, Ruth. 2006. *L'argumentation dans le discours*. Paris: Armand Colin.

—. 2009. "The New Rhetoric's Inheritance. Argumentation and Discourse Analysis". *Argumentation* 23, no. 3: 313-324.

Anscombre, Jean-Claude and Oswald Ducrot. 1988. *L'argumentation dans la langue*. Liège: Mardaga.

Antelmi, Donella and Francesca Santulli. 2009. "Effetti pragmatici della relazione concessiva: forme e funzioni in generi argomentativi diversi". In *Sintassi storica e sincronica dell'italiano. Subordinazione, coordinazione, giustapposizione*. Atti del X Congresso SILFI, edited by Angela Ferrari, 905-926. Firenze: Franco Cesati Editore.

Bakhtin, Mikhail. 1978. *Ésthetique et Théorie du Roman*. Paris: Gallimard.

Benveniste, Émile. 1974. *Problèmes de linguistique générale II*. Paris: Gallimard.

Bhatia, Vijay K. 1987. "Language of the Law". *Language Teaching* 20: 227-234.

Bres, Jacques and Aleksandra Nowakowska. 2006. "Dialogismo: du principe à la matérialité discursive". In *Le sens et ses voix. Dialogisme et polyphonie en langue et en discours. Recherches Linguistiques,* vol. 28, edited by Laurent Perrin, 21-48.

Charaudeau, Patrick. 1983. *Langage et Discours*. Paris: Hachette.

—. 2005. *Le Discours politique. Les masques du pouvoir*. Paris: Vuibert.

Chiovenda, Giuseppe. 1933-1934. *Istituzioni di diritto processuale civile I.* Napoli: Jovene.

Doury, Marianne and Sophie Moirand. 2004. *L'Argumentation aujourd'hui*. Paris: Presses Sorbonne Nouvelle.

Ducrot, Oswald. 1984. *Le dire et le dit*. Paris: Éd. De Minuit.

Fairclough, Norman. 1995. *Critical Discourse Analysis: The Critical Study of Language*. London: Longman.

Garzone, Giuliana. 1997. "Inglese giuridico e generi testuali nella prospettiva didattica". In *La lingua del diritto*, edited by Leo Schena, 207-234. Roma: CISU.

—. 2005. "Pragmatic and Discoursal Features of Annual Executive Letters: Observations on the Rhetorical and Evaluative Function of Concessive Constructions". In *Cross-Cultural Encounters: Linguistic Perspectives*, edited by Marina Bondi and Nick Maxwell, 130-143. Roma: Officina Edizioni.

Grize, Jean-Blaize. 1990. *Logique et langage*. Paris: Ophrys.

König, Ekkehard. 1989. "Conditionals, Concessive Conditionals and Concessives: Areas of Contrast, Overlap and Neutralization". In *On Conditionals*, edited by Elisabeth Closs Traugott, Alice Ter Meulen, Judy Snitzer Reilly and Charles Ferguson, 229-246. Cambridge: Cambridge University Press.

Maingueneau, Dominique. 1991. *L'Analyse du discours, introduction aux lectures de l'archive*. Paris: Hachette.

— (ed.). 1995. "Les Analyses du Discours en France". *Langages,* numéro special 117.

—. 2002. "Discourse genres". *Discourse Studies* 4, no. 3: 319-342. <http://pagesperso-range.fr/dominique.maingueneau/intro_topic.html).

Mazzi, Davide. 2007. *The Linguistic Study of Judicial Argumentation: Theoretical Perspectives Analytical Insights*. Modena: Edizioni Il Fiorino.

Montalenti, Paolo. 2007. "La riforma dell'arbitrato: primi appunti". *Giurisprudenza italiana* 2: 501-504.

Montedoro, Giancarlo. 2004. "L'arbitrato: un istituto alla ricerca di certezze". *Urbanistica e appalti* 5: 504-511.

Mortara, Lodovico. 1923. *Commentario del codice e delle leggi di procedura civile*. Milano: Giuffrè.

Mortara Garavelli, Bice 2001. *Le parole e la giustizia*. Torino: Einaudi.

Oppenheim, Felix E. 1944. "Outlines of a logical analysis of law". *Philosophy of Science* 11: 142-170.

Perelman, Chaïm. 1976. *Logique juridique. Nouvelle rhétorique*. Paris: Dalloz.

Perelman, Chaïm, and Lucie Olbrechts-Tyteca. 1958. *Traité de l'argumentation. La Nouvelle Réthorique*. Bruxelles: Éditions de l'Université de Bruxelles.

Plantin, Christian. 1996. *L'argumentation*. Paris: Seuil "Mémo".

Santulli, Francesca. 2006. "Strutture argomentative e scelte lessicali nel linguaggio della giurisprudenza". In *Prospettive nello studio del lessico italiano. Atti SILFI 2006*, edited by Emanuela Cresti, 461-469. Firenze: Firenze University Press.

—. 2008. "La sentenza come genere testuale: narrazione, argomentazione, performatività". In *Il linguaggio giuridico. Prospettive interdisciplinari*, edited by Giuliana Garzone and Francesca Santulli, 207-238. Milano: Giuffrè.

Semen 2004. Numéro special 17. *Argumentation et prise de position: pratique discursives,* edited by Ruth Amossy and Roselyne Koren.

Stati, Sorin. 1998. "La concession: syntaxe, logique et argumentation". *La linguistique* 34, no. 2: 119-122.

Todorov, Tzvetan. 1981. *Mikhail Bakhtine. Le principe dialogique*. Paris: Minuit.

Toulmin, Stephen. 1958. *The Uses of Argument*. Cambridge: Cambridge University Press.

van Dijk, Teun A. 1993. "Principles of Critical Discourse Analysis". *Discourse and Society,* special issue 4, no. 2: 249-283.

—. 2001. "Critical Discourse Analysis". In *Discourse Analysis,* edited by Deborah Schiffrin, Deborah Tannen and Heidi Hamilton, 352-371. Oxford: Blackwell.

van Eemeren, Frans H. and Rob Grootendorst. 1992. *Argumentation, Communication and Fallacies. A Pragma-dialectical Perspective.* Hillsdale (N.J.): Lawrence Erlbaum Associates.

—. 2004. *A Systematic Theory of Argumentation. The Pragma-Dialectical Approach*. Cambridge: Cambridge University Press.

van Eemeren, Frans H., Rob Grootendorst and Francisca S. Henkemans. 1996. *Fundamentals of Argumentation Theory*. Mahwah, New Jersey: Lawrence Erlbaum Ass.

CHAPTER SEVEN

CANADIAN ARBITRATION AWARDS: A GENRE-ORIENTED LINGUISTIC DESCRIPTION OF PROFESSIONAL DISCURSIVE PRACTICES

GIROLAMO TESSUTO

1. Introduction

Various studies focusing on linguistic and discoursal features of international arbitration documents have recently appeared in published volumes (Bhatia, Candlin and Engberg 2008; Bhatia, Candlin and Gotti 2010; Salmi-Tolonen, Tukiainen and Foley 2011; Bhatia, Candlin and Gotti 2012), offering interesting sources for analyses and perspectives on legal communication practices in this complex area of law. Evidence in many such studies points not only to variation in professional practices of arbitration across different *loci* of law but also to the increasing influence of litigation over arbitration. The resulting mixture of discourses from arbitration and litigation therefore provides a strong case for the role and function of "interdiscursivity" in professional genres (Bhatia 2010, 2011).

Yet, the dramatically expanded role of out-of-court arbitration process (as opposed to in-court litigation process) across legal jurisdictions and cultures is not immune from legal scholars and practitioners' concerns about its developments. As one of several kinds of ADR, arbitration is in fact an established means of finally resolving disputes in a wide range of areas of commercial and other activities, be they insurance or securities, antitrust matters or employment discrimination claims. The list is lengthy. And while each area of activity tends to be rooted in its own jurisdictional and cultural traditions, the arbitrator's final and binding 'decision' on the contentious issues between the parties (the 'award') has its own peculiarities in the professional communication practices.

In an attempt to contribute to the above discourse analytical studies, this chapter investigates genre-based discursive and professional practices in arbitration awards produced in the Canadian jurisdiction of law. Drawing on (meta)discourse and genre analytical literature (Bhatia 1993; 2004, 2010, 2011; Bhatia and Gotti, 2006; Bhatia, Candlin and Engberg 2008; Hyland 2005), this study reports on a small-size corpus of Canadian awards selected for quantity-qualitative analytical data.

In the following sections, I will first introduce the corpus and present the method by which this investigation was conducted. I will then discuss the results by looking first at the content of the awards and, secondly, by examining the generic-move (macro) structure in light of the communicative purpose and context of the awards under scrutiny. Thirdly, I will examine the linguistic (micro) resources used by arbitrators to encode their identity and authoritativeness in the organizational, rhetorical patterns of the genre, shedding light on potential analogies with the discursive and professional practices used in the legal judgment genre.

This study provides a descriptive and interpretive analysis of legal discourse in the chosen genre and highlights the intergeneric relationship between arbitration awards and legal judgments, shaped by the respective roles of genre writers within their professional and organizational practices of legal discourse.

2. Materials and Methods

2.1. The Corpus

The comparable investigation on which this chapter is based relied on ten *reasoned* awards produced in the Canadian locus of arbitration law, and selected randomly from the official website archive of Canadian Railway Office of Arbitration & Dispute Resolution, referred to as the "Office of Arbitration" or "CROA&DR" under the relative Memorandum of Agreement <http://www.arbitrations.tk/>.[1] This Memorandum spells out the nature of cases referred to arbitrators and the type of relationship between the disputing parties (point 6):

> The jurisdiction of the arbitrators shall extend and be limited to the arbitration, at the instance in each case of a railway, being a signatory hereto, or of one or more of its employees represented by a bargaining agent, being a signatory hereto, of;

[1] All websites referred to in this chapter were last accessed and further checked on 25 October 2010.

> (A) disputes respecting the meaning or alleged violation of any one or more of the provisions of a valid and subsisting collective agreement between such railway and bargaining agent, including any claims, related to such provisions, that an employee has been unjustly disciplined or discharged; and
> (B) other disputes that, under a provision of a valid and subsisting collective agreement between such railway and bargaining agent, are required to be referred to the Canadian Railway Office of Arbitration & Dispute Resolution for final and binding settlement by arbitration;
> but such jurisdiction shall be conditioned always upon the submission of the dispute to the Office of Arbitration in strict accordance with the terms of this agreement.

Given the composition of the arbitral authority in Montreal (the seat of the CROA), where the hearing of the cases principally took place during 2008-2009, CROA awards were decided upon by two different arbitrators, although mostly by one single arbitrator. The latter was designated as the "Chief Arbitrator" under the Memorandum of Agreement Establishing CROA&DR (point 4).

In terms of the relevant law, CROA awards benefit from the formulation of international legislative instruments establishing the court's deference in enforcement matters – namely, the Model Law on International Commercial Arbitration (Model Law) and the New York Convention on the Recognition and Enforcement of Foreign Arbitral Awards (New York Convention), as well as the recently enacted Canadian arbitration legislation incorporating the Model Law, i.e. the International Commercial Arbitration Act 1996. In particular, the Canada Labour Code intervenes to settle disputes arising from collective agreements by arbitration.

In terms of authorship, the awards selected for the corpus appear in their full text form and include arbitrators' signatures and dates when the awards were made. The awards selected for this analysis were all drafted in the English language, reflecting the policy of the Arbitration Office that Canadian arbitrators can deal with arbitration hearings and write their awards in either and/or both Canada's official languages.

The data source for this study is a 11,458 word corpus of electronically published awards, with stored data being searched automatically via computer for specific linguistic items and frequency. These items were analyzed through a manual (non-automated) textual reading. Table 1 shows the composition of the corpus; each award is listed by means of the Case number, the date, and the name of the arbitrator, as well as the word count for each award. The bottom line indicates the number of words included in the whole corpus.

The first important feature worth noting in Table 1 is that it indicates that the length of each award is proportionally at variance throughout the corpus, being dependent upon the kind of remedy sought by the griever:

CROA&DR–Canadian Railway Office of Arbitration&Dispute Resolution Awards <http://www.arbitrations.tk/>	**Tokens**
3666 – 12 April 2008 – Picher	1,381
3669 – 14 April 2008 – Moreau	818
3670 – 14 April 2008 – Picher	1,044
3700 – 20 October 2008 – Picher	707
3701 – 20 October 2008 – Picher	1,005
3716 – 15 December 2008 – Picher	768
3727 – 20 February 2009 – Moreau	2,105
3728 – 17 February 2009 – Moreau	1,097
3731 – 17 March 2009 – Picher	1,446
3733 – 16 March 2009 – Picher	1,087
TOTAL: 10	11,458

Table 1. Source and length of arbitration awards.

2.2. Methodological procedure

Drawing on the literature on specialized discourse and genre studies (Bhatia 1993, 2004, 2010, 2011; Bhatia and Gotti, 2006; Bhatia, Candlin and Engberg 2008), the methodological procedure adopted here is based on the multi-perspective model for the analysis of written discourse (Bhatia 2004). The procedure analyzed and interpreted CROA awards not only as textual and genre-specific products, but also as reflections of professional practice and culture within a social communicative purpose.

In addition, the focus on "discursive procedures" (Bhatia 2004: 128-130) provided the framework for an answer to the following question:
"Who [has] the authority to contribute what to the construction of specific genres?" (Bhatia 2004: 129). In the awards under discussion, this authority is to be found in the Office of Arbitration which acts as an independent, professional community to provide for the operation of arbitration processes and procedures in Canada. These processes and procedures are further prompted by a mission statement originating in the Memorandum of Agreement Establishing the CROA&DR, which in itself allows for "a distinctly rich intertextual and interdiscursive patterning" (Bhatia 2004: 129) in the construction and use of awards.

The method for analysing and interpreting discursive procedures displayed in the awards, i.e. Bhatia's (2004) textual perspective, was integrated with the tools for the analysis of metadiscourse (Hyland 2005) and other interpersonal and evaluative aspects (Hyland and Tse 2005) in professional discourse. By relying also on the interdiscursive relations with other text genres (i.e. judgments), the overview of the content and structure of the genre examined provided the background for an analysis of the interpersonal and evaluative resources deployed in the overtly visible argumentative section, the ARGUING section, and the role these resources play in stancetaking. This role was examined by selecting different linguistic tools of writer manifestation in the text – namely, personal forms in identity-marking schemes, evaluative *that*-clauses and the types of verbs controlled by personal forms, in conjunction with the syntax of personal and impersonal constructions. In this study, the parties' names in the relevant cases were kept anonymous as ///.

3. Results and Discussion

3.1. CROA awards: identifying contents

First, the essential contents of arbitral awards are examined as they result from the conduct of arbitration processes and procedures established under the Memorandum.

As noted before about the nature of disputes, a reading of this text (Memorandum) shows that the contents are determined by the nature of the so-called *requests for arbitration of grievances*, which deal with such issues as those arising from 'the meaning or alleged violation of provisions of a collective agreement between a railway signatory and bargaining agent', including any claims made by an 'employee' in regard to his being 'unjustly disciplined or discharged'. Implicitly, the contents also identify the kind of remedy being sought in the process. Thus, in a context where a distinction has been made in legal literature (Carrell and Heavrin 2004) between Labour Arbitration (settling industrial disputes among labour unions, employers and employees) and Commercial Arbitration (settling disputes arising from business and consumer transactions), the *request for arbitration* in the awards under scrutiny – as reflected indeed by the topic of the dispute – is necessarily a matter for Labour Arbitration rather than Commercial Arbitration to deal with. Within Labour Arbitration, in addition, a useful distinction is made in legal literature (Carrell and Heavrin, 2004) between "interest arbitration" (when disputes arise from existing collective-bargaining agreements) and "rights arbitration" (when there is no agreement underlying such disputes), which helps us to better determine the essential contents of the current awards.

3.1.2. Identifying Content by Key Terms

As a result of the dividing line between interest arbitration and rights arbitration, then, key legal terms are used in the specific legal branch in focus, namely Labour (Arbitration) Law. In that sense, terms used commonly in labour relations occur in the awards, such as *wage rate*, *working hours* and *collective bargaining*, denoting conflicts of interest over the conditions of employment (interest arbitration), or *grievance* to denote the subject of complaint filed by an employee with an employer in regard to a violated right of the collective agreement, involving the *discipline* and *discharge* of an employee with *just cause* (rights arbitration). These terms are significant lexical features that functionally identify the topic of the dispute in both categories of Labour Arbitration. Of these topic-specific terms, *grievance* and its noun agent *grievor* (i.e. an employee who files a complaint with an employer) are especially frequent in the current awards, where they are used instead of the most typical terms *claim* and *claimant* utilized under similar circumstances in which relief of some kind is sought. As a result of these lexical features, therefore, the surface realizations of awards constantly inform us about the arbitrators' task which is to rule whether the *discharge* was consistent with *just cause* and, if so, *to entitle the grievor to be reinstated to his job*.

3.2. CROA awards: identifying basic structure

Through its Memorandum (points 7-16), the Office also spells out the formal requirements and procedures that must be complied with by the arbitrator when handing down a final and binding reasoned award:

> "The Arbitrator's decision shall be rendered in writing, together with written reasons therefor, to the parties concerned ..." (point 14); and
>
> "Each decision of an arbitrator ... shall be final and binding upon the Railway, the bargaining agent and all the employees concerned." (point 15)

In this framework, a six-part organizational structure, as proposed here, is identified in CROA *reasoned* awards. For the sake of clarity and comprehensiveness, this structure is outlined in Table 2, where the various sections/parts define the "staged and goal-oriented" organization of the genre (Martin 1984, 1992, 1998; Eggins 1994) or similarly, in the SFL perspective, the rhetorical moves and their associated "communicative purposes" (Bhatia 1993, 2004) achieved in the conventionalized and standardized rhetorical structure. The various stages or moves through which the awards unfold in certain, generally predictable sequences allow the arbitrators to accomplish the overall communicative purpose of the award: to hand down the *final and binding Decision* on the contentious matters, and to notify the parties of such Decision by publication of the award. As such, rhetorical stages or moves respond to effective ways of getting things done in the professional genre, whose identifiable structural identity, or what Bhatia (2004) calls "generic integrity", enables the arbitrator to arrive at an informed Decision as to what is the correct 'justice' in the case, while also responding to the social purpose of the genre.

Yet, reliance on conventionalized communicative contexts in terms of move sequences or genre staging yields useful comparison with other legal genres. In broad terms, the move sequences, or rhetorical contexts, as identified of CROA awards, tend to be analogous to, or otherwise overlap with, those of appeal judgments in ordinary judicial writing although, as will be discussed shortly, noticeable variation exists as to how they are constructed in the two genres. In view of such *inter*generic analogy, the rhetorical move sequences outlined in Table 2 may be functionally associated to Bhatia's (1993) generic Move-structure model of the judgment genre. This Table reports the genuinely published profile of awards where the major sequences appear under the (bold-typed) labels **Dispute**, **Joint Statement of Issue** and **Award**, which in themselves are self-explanatory and readily recognizable by their specific function and content, and therefore describe distinct communicative purposes or functional foci in the whole body of the texts.

As noted, the move sequences identified in the structural model description must be taken flexibly in that, by common knowledge, they are differently positioned and labelled in judgments. Such is the case with Dispute (Move 2), which in judgments is normally encompassed in the elements of Establishing Facts (Move 2), and with the *Giving a history of the case* sub-move, as part of the *Arguing the case* Move 3 (Bhatia 1993) in judgments, which is totally missing in Awards (Move 4) but is dealt with only summarily in *Joint Statement of Issue* (Move 3). Allied with such differences is the reduced length of the current awards, where the rhetorical contexts of the moves are far more succinctly set out than are normally expected of judgments under similar circumstances. And while, intuitively, this succinctness is one that immediately leads the reader through to the arbitrator's conclusion, the overall effect is that such sequential moves read like a concise report.

CROA *reasoned* awards		
Move-Generic Structure	**Rhetorical function**	*Judgment* Move structure (Bhatia 1993)
Move 1 Heading	Identifying the case, place, date of the hearing, opposing parties	Move 1 Identifying the Case
Move 2 Dispute	Outlining the contentious matter in a snapshot	
Move 3 Joint Statement of Issue	Summarising contentions, procedures and application, including appearances	Move 2 Establishing Facts
Move 4 AWARD	Presenting arguments of parties and of arbitrator, together with reasons for the arbitrator's decision as to individual issues of fact and law, by repeating contentions, procedures and applications already previewed in Joint Statement of Issue ARGUING	Move 3 Arguing the Case
Move 5 Decision	Giving effect to the award by specifying conditions or terms in question	Move 4 Pronouncing Decision
Move 6 Formalities	Providing date of award and signature of arbitrator	Closing

Table 2. Six-move rhetorical structure of awards and associated functions.

To illustrate briefly the function of the move sequences, a bound-in list of case identifying elements in **Heading** (Move 1) proceeds towards information about the **Dispute** (Move 2), which sketches out the contested issue in ways that it reflects the rationale of being eye catching and quickly read by the interested reader, whether parties or future judges:

CANADIAN RAILWAY OFFICE OF ARBITRATION
& DISPUTE RESOLUTION
CASE NO. 3700
Heard in Montreal Tuesday, 14 October 2008
Concerning
CANADIAN NATIONAL RAILWAY COMPANY
and
TEAMSTERS CANADA RAIL CONFERENCE

DISPUTE:
Appeal discharge of Locomotive Engineer (///) of Toronto, Ontario for Conduct Unbecoming on November 19, 2007.
(///). Name: anonymized

The **Joint Statement** (Move 3), preparing for the next ARGUING section, opens with a very short account of the facts of the case prior to the *request for arbitration*, by reporting such facts in narrative form based on an average half a dozen sentences with verb forms in the past tense. It then goes on with a further short account of these facts using reporting verbs with present tense finite *that*-clauses that summarise each of the party's claims leading up to the award. In these clauses the grammatical subjects (the parties) are invariably referred to by specific terms (e.g. The Union *submits that ...* / The Company *disagrees with the Union and maintains that ...*) rather than the usual *claimant* and *respondent*, suggesting that the specific identification of the parties helps in the understanding of the award. The corpus shows that *contend* (18 occ.) and *request* (10 occ.) are the two most frequently used reporting verbs in these types of clauses foregrounding the Award. The following full extract may give a flavour of this:

JOINT STATEMENT OF ISSUE:

On November 19, 2007, Mr. (///) was employed as a locomotive engineer in the terminal of Toronto South. Mr. (///) while in the booking in room at MacMillan Yard encountered (///) a new employee making her initial training trips as a conductor. Mr (///) made a number of comments to the employee which made her feel uncomfortable and she filed a complaint with the Company. Following an investigation of the matter, Locomotive Engineer (///) was discharged effective 19 November 2007 for conduct unbecoming. The Union has appealed the discipline based on the grounds that it was too severe, and request that the discipline be adjusted to a more appropriate level such as a suspension. The Company disagrees with the Union and maintains that the discipline assessed in this situation was warranted and reasonable.

FOR THE UNION:	FOR THE COMPANY:
(SGD.) (///)	**(SGD.) (///)**
GENERAL CHAIRMAN	**MANAGER, LABOUR RELATIONS**

There appeared on behalf of the Company:
(///) – Manager, Labour Relations, Toronto
…….. ……..

(///). Name: anonymized

Next in the sequence is the **Award** section (Move 4), which covers a considerable portion of the whole text. As a manifestly argumentative move, this section provides the reasons for the arbitrator's decision as to the disputed facts, based on the arbitrator's analysis of (substantive) individual issues of law applied to facts, including parties' submissions and evidence. In providing his reasons, however, the arbitrator also evaluates the strengths and weaknesses of the parties' positions and the parties' potential exposure to liability. CROA arbitrators, therefore, effectively present and evaluate materials by providing detailed arguments and reasons for their decisions on the individual issues already previewed in the **Joint Statement**. They do so by functionally guiding the readers to understand how the information is developed on a single topic in the text, achieving paragraph unity in relation to such topic (Arnaudet and Barret 1990; Peck 1991; Langan 2001)[2]. As is typical of texts that analyse and argue, each paragraph thus contains a topic sentence that develops one main idea and helps the arbitrator to stay focused on his objective. The topic sentence controls the rest of the paragraph via supporting sentences (subtopics) that provide details of the law applied to facts. The concluding sentence in the paragraph either returns to the notion set out in the initial topic sentence, or connects to the main idea (topic sentence) presented in the next paragraph. By using a topic sentence to introduce one paragraph and writing support sentences to achieve paragraph unity in relation to the topic sentence through cohesive devices, the natural flow and clarity of the **Award** section is therefore maintained in a sufficiently standardised rhetorical structure for "imagined readers" (Coulthard 1994) to understand their positions in the overall resolutive process of arbitration. These readers are identified here primarily in the parties and their advisers, with the court intervening in the reading of the award in the event of the arbitrator's decision facing judicial scrutiny.[3]

As with the **Joint Statement of Issue**, the **Award** section as well includes critical stages of interaction from earlier narratives of facts and specific hearing procedures prior to award writing itself. In the **Award**, in particular, evidence of the participants' intentions and purposes in

---

[2] However, the focus of this discussion on topic sentence is not the only approach to defining paragraph unity and cohesion. Among discourse analysts, Hoey (1991; 2005) claims that a paragraph, defined as a grammatical unit, is the result of the relationship between blocks of information which can be marked by lexical choices. The choice of lexical items identifies paragraph boundaries.

[3] In fact, under article 36 (iii) of the International Commercial Arbitration Act 1996, it is established that challenges can be made by parties against arbitral awards on several grounds.

arbitration hearings is actually given by the arbitrator referring back to so-called *Questions and Answers* (e.g. "Secondly, the Arbitrator cannot disregard the fact that during the course of investigation Mr Burke did 'come clean' as reflected in *Question and Answer 77*").

The **Decision** (Move 5), provides the 'operative' part of the entire award by disposing of the case on matters of procedural law (e.g. *allowing grievance*) and specifying such conditions or terms (e.g. *reinstatement into employment*) as are necessary to give effect to the decision made. Finally, the **Formalities** section (Move 6) provides attestation of the award content in the concluding lines of the document by carrying the signature of the arbitrator and the date when the award was made.

3.3. CROA awards: the personal tenor in identity-marking scheme

Evidence in the written data shows that, in writing their awards, arbitrators take different orientations in encoding their personal tenor, in spite of the standardised rhetorical structure characterising this genre.

Focusing on the interactional resource of "self-mentions" (Hyland 2005: 52-54), which realize the main metadiscourse function of interactively locating "the writer's perspective towards both the propositional information and readers themselves" (Hyland 2005: 52), the use of self-referential items was observed in the corpus. As shown in Table 3, the first-person pronoun *I* is followed in incidence by the possessive *my* (referring to personal opinion) down to the pronoun *me* (as in the prepositional structure *before me*, exemplifying the writer's institutional presence as a sole tribunal in arbitration). These add to the lexical item *the arbitrator* aimed at "self-representation" (Ivanič 1998, quoted in Hyland 2005: 53).

Table 3 shows the overall incidence of these personal forms in the data examined, amounting to 68 total occurrences in the corpus.

AWARD	*I*	*in my view*	*me*	*the arbitrator*
3666	1	-	-	7
3669	3	-	-	5
3670	3	-	1	4
3700	-	-	-	5
3701	-	-	-	4
3716	3	-	-	6
3727	3	4	-	1
3728	2	2	-	2
3731	1	2	-	3
3733	-	-	-	6
Total: 68	16	8	1	43

Table 3. Items of personal tenor in each text.

In a context where no use of an '*I*-writer' and '*you*-reader' orientation appears in the corpus, as would be the case with lawyer-client letter writing, for instance, personal pronouns and possessive adjectives perform their discourse functions in Move 4 in relation to the analysis of facts and law. By clearly indicating "the degree of explicit author presence in the text" (Hyland 2005: 53), such personal items allow the arbitrators to explain and justify the correctness of their reasoned arguments which will contribute to their final decision, while at the same time persuading the potential readers.

However, as shown in example (1) below containing excerpts taken from one single award, arbitrators tend to represent themselves more frequently by means of the lexical item *The arbitrator* in initial clause positioning, totalling 43 occurrences. Unlike the *I*-orientation, used only for the analysis of reasons, this lexical item is found to occur in the entire sequences of Move 4 and Move 5, where it invariably provides the grounds for the analysis of reasons and the resulting decision:

> (1) ***The Arbitrator*** is satisfied that there was no discrimination or bad faith exhibited by the Company in its decision to close the employment file of Conductor ///. There are, however, certain factors which arise in the evidence which, …(*Analysis of Reasons*)
>
> There is, *in my view*, an element of arbitrariness for the Company to have summarily terminated Mr. /// in these circumstances. When these facts are coupled with the failure to provide him the requisite training, *I* am satisfied that in the unusual circumstances of this case that the Union has discharged the burden of establishing that the grievor's termination was arbitrary, albeit there was some element of fault on the part of the grievor. (*Analysis of Reasons*)

> For the foregoing reasons, the grievance *is allowed*, in part. **The Arbitrator** *directs* that the grievor be reinstated into his employment forthwith, without compensation for wages and benefits lost, and without loss of seniority. The grievor's reinstatement … (Case 3731) (*Decision*)

The higher incidence of the noun phrase *The Arbitrator* provides the source of authority to that which is decided, and is used as a powerful tool for claiming authoritative stance in institutionally situated contexts of discourse. And while this tool is one which permits a more objective, formal tone than a subjective '*I* construction', it is no less significant to recognise that the source of authority encoded in *The Arbitrator* is dependent upon the important conditions of (arbitrator's) appointment agreed upon by the disputants themselves. Clearly, a similar source of authority will also be assigned to an ordinary judge speaking in the first person (*I*), but the consequence of that comparison will be that a judge is government appointed, with no contractual terms between him/her and the parties. Even when both arbitrators and judges render impartial decisions for the parties to a dispute in order to maintain justice, the issue of role-based authority is still significant to understand that an arbitrator will usually determine whichever rules or procedures fit the parties involved by viewing disputes from a more 'commercial perspective', as opposed to a 'more legal perspective' by which judges are bound.

Apart from the resulting diversity of role-based authority in arbitration and judicial practices, the higher incidence in the corpus of the phrase *The Arbitrator* is a useful device which allows the arbitrator to project two different identities into the text: the arbitrator as an 'arguer', or 'evaluator' in the analysis of reasons (Move 4), and the arbitrator as an 'adjudicator' in the final Decision (Move 5).

In the case of the arbitrator as arguer/evaluator, the identity-marking scheme projected by the use of the noun phrase *The Arbitrator* adds to a similar projection by the use of the first person pronoun *I* and the co-occurring verbs in main clauses, reflecting the purpose of any argumentative discourse based on the illocutionary force of justifying by persuasive and consistent reasoning to the opposing parties. Thus, recourse to the first person singular pronoun *I* and to the noun phrase *The Arbitrator* in main clauses (in combination with typically performative verbs) introduces expressions of personal judgments through which arbitrators, as discourse producers in arbitral awards, take up stance in relation to their arguments. The resulting roles or identities are therefore necessary to project the arbitrator's personal responsibility of sieving and weighing the evidence and submissions in order to render an *ad hoc* decision in an arbitration award.[4]

In the case of the arbitrator as adjudicator, who determines questions of fact and law much like a judge, the arbitrator's identity is marked by the lexical item collocating with the directive verb *direct* (used 9 times in the corpus as opposed to the verb *determine* used only once) in active simple present in a *that*-clause structure. Move 5 in (1) above (*The Arbitrator directs that ...*), in fact, is self-explanatory of the arbitrator performing his rhetorical role of adjudicator who presents his own conclusion disposing of the remedy sought. And while the rhetorical role of the Decision marks the cogency, certainty, and finality of the award by promoting 'adjudicatory consistency' as an important generic norm in the award, it also exemplifies the overall communicative purpose resulting from the sum of the moves or stages, as noted before. Adjudicatory consistency of purpose, therefore, becomes necessary to legitimise a decision as to the fairness of the arbitrator's argument for the parties concerned and other professional peers, by showing that it derives from a convincing and sound reasoning in the rhetorical move structure of the genre.

Hence, the arbitrator's authoritative Decision, either allowing or dismissing the grievance, is not that different from the "declaratory and justificatory" interpersonal function of the judge's Decision in the judgment genre (Maley 1994), insofar as the generic roles of arbitrators and judges are kept distinguished on matters of law and procedures as identified above, which will become increasingly clear throughout the analysis below.

3.4. Stancetaking: personal and impersonal constructions

So far my analytical focus has been on the ideas of stance as referring to the arbitrator's textual voice (*I*) or his authoritatively recognized personality (*the Arbitrator*), allowing the arbitrator to present different identities and roles in discourse.

I shall now proceed to examine stancetaking along a continuum of interpersonal linguistic resources available to arbitrators, ranging from evaluative *that*-clauses to epistemic comment verbs and modality patterns. These resources are accounted for by the incidence of personal constructions

[4] As a result of this responsibility, the objectivity projected by *The Arbitrator* individual tenor further strengthens the discourse practice of arbitration as the process of referring a dispute to an 'impartial, neutral' intermediary chosen by the parties who agree in advance to abide by the arbitrator's award issued after a hearing.

(*I* / *the arbitrator*) and impersonal *it* constructions in main clauses that signal the functional development of argumentative discourse prior to concluding via the Decision move. As listed in the Appendix, the total incidence of personal constructions (35), which strategically involve the arbitrator in the text, is reasonably close to that of impersonal constructions (30) throughout the corpus.

3.4.1. Personal constructions

In this section, I shall draw on Hyland and Tse's (2004) description of stance as involving interpretive statements based on subjective judgments, and their discussion of the range of predicates (nominal predicates such as adjectives, as in the present discussion) determining "evaluative *that*-clauses" (Hyland 2005: 124-125). Following on from Hyland and Tse's model, arbitrators, present in first and third persons in the current corpus, tend to express their attitude towards the proposition by the most frequently occurring "super-ordinate clauses" (in the authors' terminology): *The Arbitrator is satisfied* (11), *I am satisfied* (10), *The Arbitrator is persuaded* (3), *I am not persuaded* (1), with the adjective *satisfied* ('convinced') naturally resulting from a lexical convention in legal English contexts, including judgments. By way of example, we read:

> (2) **The Arbitrator is satisfied** *that the tone and choice of words unfortunately used by Mr /// were dismissive and demeaning of GO supervisor, causing her unnecessary embarassment in the face of a group of employees.* **I am also satisfied** *that the grievor's words could reasonably have been interpreted by Ms /// at indicating that the grievor might take steps to have ... .* (Case 3716: 2)

Found in proportionally higher incidence (25 total occ.) than other personal constructions, super-ordinate clauses allow the arbitrators to project their evaluative meaning of certainty in the information presented in *that*-clauses, bringing the parties around to the accuracy and legitimacy of the arbitrators' reasoning.

Next in line are other evaluative options available to arbitrators, as shown in examples (3) and (4) below. Although these options play only a marginal role in the incidence of expressions conveying personal judgments, they contribute to communicating the arbitrator's stance of certainty with the negative modal *cannot* ('theoretically or actually impossible' and, therefore, likely to express epistemic modality – i.e. a truth value), or the arbitrator's stance of "(logical) necessity" and "obligation or compulsion" meanings (Quirk *et al.* 1985: 224-225) with the modal *must*:

(3) Secondly, **the Arbitrator cannot disregard the fact that** *during the course of the investigation Mr. /// did "come clean" as reflected in Question and Answer 77.* (Case 3669: 3)

(4) From the standpoint of aggravation, **the Arbitrator must agree with the Company that** *the incident could have had catastrophic results.* By allowing his movement to proceed some thirty-five feet beyond the ultimate stop signal, ... (Case 3701: 4)

In example (4), in particular, the potential value of the modal *must* is one which results from the arbitrator's attitude as logically entailed by observation of the facts known to him. This value is naturally based on the compelling source of authority who seeks to provide persuasive and convincing reasoning at this stage of the decision-making.

Lastly, other personal constructions are observed in the corpus. These tend to collocate with the epistemic comment verbs *agree*, *consider*, *find*, and *understand* in their flexible role of describing the cognitive process they perform[5] in specific structures introducing *that*-clauses or infinitive constructions. To illustrate this, examples in (5) and (6) show that argumentative stance procedures range from positive and negative evaluations, with the function of the verbs (*not*) *agree* and (*not*) *consider* showing explicit acceptance or rejection of the proposition stated, to other evaluations such as in (7), where the function of the verb *find* is the result of speculation or inquiry in expressing judgment, and is further hedged by the 'difficulty' of evaluating the facts in issue:

(5) **I agree with the Company** *that a proper briefing is essential when the assignment conditions change.* Without a radio, there was no way ... . (Case 3727: 4)

(6) In the context of the relationship between Mr /// and the inspector, **I do not consider** *that he was in fact crossing the line of harassment and bullying.* Boards of arbitration, including this Office, have well recognised the need ... . (Case 3670: 3)

---

[5] In this study, the verbs examined constitute only one group of the three categories of reporting verbs identified by scholars (Thompson and Ye 1991; Hyland 2002) in academic writing, this group being narrowed to Thompson and Ye's "mental verbs" (to refer to mental processes – e.g. *think, believe*) categorised as "cognitive" verbs, in Hyland's terminology.

(7) **The Arbitrator finds this to be** *one of those difficult cases where* a long-term employee with a commendable work record suddenly finds himself being disciplined for what he views as an innocent accident. Applying pressure on an Allen wrench is a manoeuvre undertaken ... .
(Case 3728: 2)

In particular, the example in (7) sheds light on other observable instances (7 occ.) of evaluating arguments based on existing knowledge of the facts at issue, as shown further in (8) below. Drawing on Hyland's (1998: 142-148) system of hedging, this example illustrates that efforts are also made by the arbitrators in the corpus to provide reliable expressions of judgment by hedging the accuracy of existing knowledge which they treat first as 'difficulty' (*The Arbitrator has ...*) and immediately after as 'certainty' (*I am satisfied ...*) when evaluating propositions:

(8) **The Arbitrator has substantial difficulty with the position advanced by the Company** *with respect to the grievor's status insofar as his conversation with the Transport Canada inspector is concerned.* **I am satisfied** *that he was communicating with her solely in his capacity as the Provincial Legislative Representative for Manitoba.*

In the current range of personal constructions, however, exceptions arise in two instances shown in (9) and (10) where forms of the verb *find* are used in different discourse functions:

(9) Most importantly, **I am satisfied** *that the admission made by the grievor in that statement is accurate.* **The Arbitrator expressly finds** *that there was no violation of the requirement to provide a fair and impartial investigation, on the particular facts disclosed. Nor was the handling of item 7 inappropriate in all of the circumstances.* (Case 3669: 2)

(10) In the result, **the Arbitrator must find** that aspect of the grievor's misconduct is simply not made out. **Nor am I satisfied** *that the evidence is sufficient to conclude, on the balance of probabilities, that the grievor ...* .
(Case 3666: 4)

Considering that in (9) the verb *find* appears in the concluding statement of the paragraph (based on analysis of reasons) prior to the final Decision, it can be stated that its value in the *that*-clause statement is typically performative. This allows the arbitrator to take up his stance in relation to the fact at issue by authoritatively encoding the force of his statement in a way which is analogous to a court 'officially declaring something to be the case', thus performing an act or creating a state of affairs by the fact of its being uttered under appropriate circumstances. And this function is reinforced by the use of boosters such as *expressly*, showing the certainty held about the substantive law issue and addressed persuasively to the parties. In a similar vein in example (10), but outside the *that*-clause pattern, the performative function ('officially declaring') of the concluding statement is further enhanced by subjective, imperative-like use of *must* co-occurring with *find*, not least because of the consequential item *In the result*.

3.4.2. Impersonal constructions

As noted above, the incidence of agentless constructions (i.e. anticipatory *it*) in the corpus is only relatively lower than that of personal constructions. The reason for this close incidence lies in the fact that the ARGUING section also revolves around arguments based on party submissions and evidence that are constructed around human grammatical subjects, who are usually identified by their proper names.

Thus, in a context such as this where depersonalisation techniques obscure the self authoritative source of the evaluation in a way which renders the discourse more distanced and objective,[6] depersonalisation with empty subject *it* in the corpus occurs mostly in relation to the issues of fact and law requiring an evaluation. Empty subjects allow the arbitrators to describe and evaluate the strengths and weaknesses of the case being decided upon, whether or not hedging their responsibility towards the propositions, as the context requires.

To illustrate this, there are instances, such as those in examples (11) and (12) below, where a degree of tentativeness is created by what Salager-Meyer (1994) calls "compound hedges", resulting in my data from the combination of two hedges (a modal auxiliary verb and a modal lexical verb with a hedging content, such as *it would seem*) and sometimes three hedges (a modal auxiliary combined with a lexical verb and an adjective in hedging content, such as *it would seem reasonable*) in anticipatory *it* introducing *that*-clauses:

> (11) In fact, **it would seem** *that Locomotive Engineer /// made his brake applications at or about the same locations as he would normally do in better weather conditions, thereby falling to give due allowance to the icy conditions.* (Case 3701: 3)

---

[6] In a similar vein, Gotti (2003: 99-102) argues for objectivity resulting from "depersonalisation" to be a common feature of "specialized discourse".

(12) **It would appear** from the investigation *that the grievor was not, in fact, aware of the channel on which radio transmission for the 14:30 Yard Assignment was to be communicated.* As his road assignment was on a different channel, ... (Case 3666: 3)

The inspiring source for examining the evaluative potential in other clause patterns in the corpus was provided yet again by Hyland and Tse's (2005: 130-136) elaboration of sentences containing evaluative *that*-clauses. By adapting the semantic value conveyed by initial super-ordinate clauses in my data to Hyland and Tse's elaboration, this evaluative potential emerges clearly in the set of examples from (13) to (18):

(13) **It is not disputed** *that Conductor Jim Ellis did engage in unacceptable behaviour.* By his own admission, on June 23 2007, the grievor voiced insulting and provocative remarks to another person ... . (Case 3666: 2)

(14) The grievor, Conductor ///, was discharged for making a false wage claim. **It is significant**, however, *that the wage claim which he made was by a computer entry which, by its very nature, would ensure that his claim would be reviewed by an analyst.* (Case 3669: 2)

(15) **It is common ground** *that the grievor did violate CROR Rule 429 when he operated his GO Train consist past stop signal 397A at Union Station on February 7, 2008.* (Case 3701: 2)

(16) **It is clear** *that that condition was operative on the occasion of the incidence which is the subject of this grievance.* **It should be noted**, however, *that the grievor's medical condition was not communicated to the Company at the time of its disciplinary investigation.* (Case 3700: 3)

(17) What, then, does the evidence disclose? Firstly, **it must be recognized** *that the allegation made against the grievor, to the extent that the Company believes that he was the author of the radio communication which was plainly in the nature of harassment and threats of a serious nature, requires a standard of proof commensurate with the seriousness of the allegation.* (Case 3666: 3)

(18) **It must be concluded** *that the better evidence in that regard is advanced by the Union.* (Case 3670: 4)

Here, we can see arbitrators:

(a) presenting a reference source of the evaluation based on certainty or equally an epistemically accepted view derived from the arbitrators' claims in the contentious matters in the (NOT) DISPUTED, CLEAR and COMMON GROUND clause types; or
(b) presenting their "attitudinal position" as "*affect*" (Hyland and Tse 2005: 129-130; italics in the original) in the NOTED and SIGNIFICANT clause types; or
(c) presenting such position as "*obligation* (what should be done)" (Hyland and Tse 2005, 129-130; italics in the original) in the RECOGNISED and CONCLUDED clause types, thus expressing their evaluative arguments as objectively as possible in all such cases.

In this framework, however, arbitrators do not shy away from attributing the source of their evaluation to the knowledge built by their peers in earlier decisions of CROA awards. This can be seen in the sentences in (19) and (20) containing evaluative *that*-clauses determined by the adjectival predicates SETTLED and ESTABLISHED. These clauses allow the arbitrators to express evaluative meaning of certainty, as seen before, but this time help them to attribute responsibility of their arguments by relying on shared knowledge and consensus among the members of the Office of Arbitration (CROA) in community-situated discourse:

(19) **It is well settled** *that boards of arbitration do not lightly interfere with the decisions of employers with respect to the termination of newly hired employees during the course of a probationary period.* **The governing principles were summarized as follows in CROA 1568:**
It is common ground that the standard of proof required to establish just cause for the termination of a probationary employee is substantially lighter than for a permanent employee. ... (Case 3731: 2)

(20) **It is well established** *that a positive drug test which reveals the presence of antibodies to THC in the body does not establish impairment.* **In Canadian National Railway Company (2000) 95 L.A.C. 4th 341 [SHP 530] at p. 400 the arbitrator commented:**
A positive drug test is not conclusive of impairment when on duty, subject to duty or on call. It does not, therefore, of itself constitute just cause for discipline or discharge. ... (Case 3670: 3)

As seen, the nature of contentious matters in the current awards is one which requires arbitrators to apply the 'relevance test'[7] in rule citation, so as to be able to conduct arbitral proceedings and finally hand down an award. Here, 12 instances, as those in (19) and (20), are recorded in the corpus in which arbitrators acknowledge the legal relevance of their propositions to not only substantiate their reasoning but also to add credibility to their evaluative arguments expressed in *that*-clauses, so as to be able to arrive at an informed Decision. CROA arbitrators, in fact, do so by resorting to "intertextual and interdiscursive elements" (Candlin and Maley 1997: 203), consisting of quotation from, or paraphrase of, other text sources – namely, Canada Labour Code, articles of collective agreements, and previous CROA Decisions (awards). Where, in particular, arbitrators engage with previous awards, they seem to intrinsically generate a notion of 'arbitral precedent' for their final reasoned Decision, which allows them to engage in an explicit discussion of decisional predicates in order to serve a legitimacy-seeking strategy of the award. Comparably, however, this notion is not dissimilar to the practice used by Common Law judges, who typically rely on the hierarchy of judicial sources ('precedent') to arrive at their own Decision. Despite the allowable similarities in citing the relevant sources of law to support their work (award and judgment), key differences remain between arbitrators and judges in terms of their role and practice. CROA arbitrators (as those from other jurisdictions by common knowledge) are not strictly bound by rules of technicality and evidence when handing down their awards, since the 'flexibility and informality' of the arbitration process allow them to be free to decide whichever rules or procedures are appropriate for the parties concerned. Judges, on the other hand, especially those from the Common Law system, are known to be bound by the 'judicial precedent' when handing down their judgments.

Beyond these distinctive features, it seems fair to argue that a body of arbitral precedent and other regulatory predicates confer the award genre the same factually and legally required credibility in the professional discourse practice of arbitrators as the judicial precedent traditionally does in the institutional, professional discourse practice of judges. Reliance on such interacting patterns of intertextuality and interdiscursivity is therefore crucial not only to shape the arguments disputants and arbitrators make for 'cause' but also to accomplish the resolutive purpose assumed for the

[7] To exemplify, the relevance test requires the arbitrators to understand the elements or exceptions that prove a particular rule cited when arguing for or against the party in the award.

arbitrator's role. In the latter sense, the legitimizing function of *reasoned* awards, as examined here, can only be thought of as acquiring an important value in the organizational structure of the profession, where it becomes a measure for the discourse practices of arbitration and, more importantly, the distinct roles of genre producers (arbitrators and judges).

4. Conclusion

In this chapter I have examined discursive practices in the professional genre of Canadian arbitration awards.

The rhetorical-grammatical study has emphasised interacting relationships between two generic constructs, arbitration awards and legal judgments, in terms of rhetorical devices and associated communicative purposes. Analysis of the written data show that awards rely on conventionalized and standardized features although, to the best of this author's knowledge, awards often vary in content and structure within other jurisdictions. This ties in with Bhatia's (2004) theoretical model, where the most important aspect of the (genre-based) view of language is the emphasis on conventionalized as well as dynamic structural features of genres used in academic and professional settings.

The analysis of the move-structure and accomplished purpose(s) in awards points to similarity in a certain limited number of rhetorical and discursive devices between awards and court judgments - limited because such devices in awards are set in more narrowly configured rhetorical contexts of legal action and procedure than in judgments. Such degree of similarity therefore squares fairly well with the phenomenon of "interdiscursivity" based on "appropriation of generic resources" (Bhatia 2004, 2010, 2011), so that the adoption in arbitration awards of rhetorical conventions typical of the judgment genre is conducive to the "colonization of one genre by the other by invading its integrity" (Bhatia 2004, 87). This colonization comes about in such a way that the 'imported' conventions prove to be well-received in the genre examined.

Despite the allowable similarities, however, essential distinctions between the two generic constructs remain, on account of some easily identifiable constraints determined by important external factors of both substance and procedure between litigation and arbitration. First, account should be given to the nature of Common Law appeal judgments in litigation practice (whether or not dealing with arbitral matters and resulting decisions) which usually contain the individual voices of various judges, either with supporting or dissenting opinions. This contrasts with the awards examined which contain only one single voice, although some types of awards may also allow for more than one arbitrator, and thus for more than one voice. Secondly, judges' voices are entirely associated with their status and hierarchy in the court procedure, where their decisions do not lead to any agreement between the disputing parties. Conversely, in the written data examined, the arbitrator's voice is the result of his being neutrally appointed by the parties under the terms of the Memorandum of Agreement Establishing CROA&DR, as well as the relevant collective agreement.

The analysis of internal linguistic resources, based purely on argumentation, has shown that the arbitrators' source of authority in the differently projected personal tenor (*I/the arbitrator*) can be posited as an appropriate condition whereby communicating the arbitral decision is, in pragmatic terms, a dialectic process of representing the self in the authoritative, institutional exercise of the professional discourse of arbitration. While the *I/the arbitrator* orientations provide the arbitrators with useful strategies to encode their own identities and roles in the texts much like the *I/The Court* orientations do for judges in judicial texts, they also carry out the pragmatic function of including the intended reader in the institutional, professional and organizational practices of discourse. The relevance of discourse practices ensures that the different aspects of the matters in arbitration are decided in the interests of the parties, having weighed the evidence and submissions. In this context, the performatively encoded Decision of the arbitrator means that the award does not remain as a 'free-standing document'– that is, leaving the other party to continue with the claim – but stands precisely as a procedural final and binding award. Here, the final directive pronouncement disposing of the matters functions as an institutionally performative utterance, as it does in the legal judgment, and similarly strengthens the discursive realization of the Decision in the award as an operative and performative instrument.

In this process, stancetaking has been viewed in terms of specific linguistic resources, ranging from writer evaluation in *that*-clauses to verb types with an epistemic value, as the most typical interpersonal resources available to arbitrators. Judging from the slightly higher incidence of personal constructions and the function performed by the resulting clause patterns, arbitrators would seem to be more inclined to express their personal responsibility towards evaluative arguments. However, their responsibility is also expressed recursively by obscuring their source of direct evaluation through recourse to *it* subjects. Here, the written data bear qualitative evidence of intertextual/interdiscursive reference to other peer views in cited sources, where the reference to past awards helps arbitrators situate themselves in a 'precedential' community of discourse which contributes authoritativeness to their professional writing.

In light of the internal discursive realisations examined, arbitrators therefore interact effectively with the intended readers by adapting and anticipating their values, interests and expectations. And it is telling that their personal judgment and responsibility are projected in the awards by the important requirement for 'natural justice' with which Canadian arbitrators are invested when writing such documents under their own individual authority. Inference of such a requirement can be seen under the Memorandum, demanding Canadian arbitrators to act in line with the principles of natural justice, such as acting fairly by being certain or uncertain of the party's case and, in the latter option, contradicting the party if it is proper to do so.

References

Arnaudet, Martin L. and Mary E. Barret. 1990. *Paragraph Development: A Guide for Students of English*. Englewood Cliffs, NJ: Prentice Hall.

Bhatia, Vijay K. 1993. *Analysying Genre. Language Use in in Professional Settings*. London: Longman.

—. 2004. *Worlds of Written Discourse: A Genre-Based View*. London: Continuum.

—. 2010. "Interdiscursivity in Professional Communication". *Discourse and Communication* 4, no. 1: 32-50.

—. 2011. "Interdiscursive Colonization of Arbitration Practice". *World Englishes* 30, no. 1: 76-80.

Bhatia, Vijay K. and Maurizio Gotti (eds). 2006. *Explorations in Specialized Genres*. Bern: Peter Lang.

Bhatia, Vijay K., Christopher N. Candlin and Jan Engberg (eds). 2008. *Legal Discourse Across Cultures and Systems*. Hong Kong: Hong Kong University Press.

Bhatia, Vijay K., Christopher N. Candlin and Maurizio Gotti (eds). 2010. *The Discourses of Dispute Resolution*. Bern: Peter Lang.

—. 2012. *Discourse and Practice in International Commercial Arbitration*. Farnham (UK): Ashgate.

Candlin, N. Christopher and Yon Maley. 1997. "Intertextuality and Interdiscursivity in the Discourse of Alternative Dispute Resolution". In *The Construction of Professional Discourse,* edited by Britt-Louise Gunnarsson, Per Linell and Bengt Nordberg, 201-222. London: Longman.

Carrell, Michael and Christine Heavrin. 2004. *Labor Relations and Collective Bargaining*. New Jersey: Prentice Hall.

Coulthard, Malcom (ed). 1994. *Advances in Written Text Analysis*. London: Routledge.

Canada Labour Code R.S.C. 1985, c. L-2. Available at: <http://www.canlii.org/en/ca/laws/stat/rsc-1985-c-l-2/latest/rsc-1985-c-l-2.html>.

Eggins, Suzanne. 1994. *An Introduction to Systemic Functional Linguistics*. London: Pinter.

Gotti, Maurizio. 2003. *Specialized Discourse*. Bern: Peter Lang.

Hoey, Michae.l 1991. *Patterns of Lexis in Text*. Oxford: Oxford University Press.

—. 2005. *Lexical Priming: A New Theory of Words and Language*. London: Routledge.

Hyland, Ken. 1998. *Hedging in Scientific Research Articles*. Amsterdam: John Benjamins.

—. 2002. "Activity and Evaluation: Reporting Practices in Academic Writing". In *Academic Discourse*, edited by John Flowerdew, 115-130. London: Longman.

—. 2005. *Metadiscourse*. London: Continuum.

Hyland, Ken and Polly Tse. 2004. "Metadiscourse in Academic Writing: A Reappraisal". *Applied Linguistics* 25, no. 2: 156-177.

Hyland, Ken and Polly Tse. 2005. "Hooking the Reader: A Corpus Study of Evaluative *that* in Abstracts". *ESP* 24: 123-139.

Ivanič, Roz. 1998. *Writing and Identity. The Discoursal Construction of Identity in Academic Writing*. Amsterdam: John Benjamins.

Langan, John. 2001. *English Skills*. New York: The McGraw Hill Companies.

Maley, Yon. 1994. "The Language of the Law". In *Language and the Law*, edited by John Gibbons, 11-50. London: Longman.

Martin, James, R. 1984. "Genre as Social Action". In *Quarterly Journal of Speech* 7: 151-167.

Martin, James R. 1992. *English Text: System and Structure*. Philadelphia and Amsterdam: John Benjamins.

Martin, James R. 1998. "Linguistics and the Consumer: The Practice of Theory". *Linguistics and Education* 9, no. 4: 411-448.

Peck, Charles W. 1991. "Readability Revisited". *Notes on Linguistics* 55: 19-26.

Quirk, Randolph, Sidney Greenbaum, Geoffrey Leech and Jan Svartvik. 1985. *A Comprehensive Grammar of Contemporary English*. London: Longman.

Salager-Meyer, Françoise. 1994. “Hedges and Textual Communicative Function in Medical English Written Discourse”. *English for Specific Purposes*, 13, no. 2: 149-170.

Salmi-Tolonen, Tarja, Iris Tukiainen and Richard Foley (eds). 2011. *Law and Language in Partnership and Conflict*. A Special Issue of the *Lapland Law Review* 1, n. 1.

Thompson, Geoff and Yiyun Ye. 1991. “Evaluation in the Reporting Verbs used in Academic Papers”. *Applied Linguistics* 12, no. 4: 365-382.

Corpus

Awards available at: <http://www.arbitrations.tk>

Memorandum of Agreement Establishing the CROA&DR: <http://www.croa.com/e-home.html>

Appendix A

Personal constructions (*I* / *the arbitrator* = 35) and impersonal *it* constructions in main clause types (= 30): occurrences in the 'Arguing' section

▪ Personal forms in main clauses

I am satisfied that .... (8 occ. including 2 in negative contexts)
The Arbitrator is satisfied that ... (x 11)
I am not persuaded that ...
The Arbitrator is persuaded that ... (x 3)

▪ Personal forms in modalized main clauses introducing an object complement realised by the *that*-clause

The Arbitrator cannot sustain the position of the Company that ...
Secondly, the Arbitrator cannot disregard the fact that ...
The Arbitrator must agree with the Company that ...

▪ Personal forms in main clauses followed by various structures

I do not consider that...
I agree with the Company that ...
I do not agree with the Company that ...
I do not agree with the Union that ...
The Arbitrator expressly finds that ...
I find this to be a case where ...
I find it difficult to understand ...
Nor do I consider it necessary to determine whether ...
The Arbitrator finds this to be one of those difficult cases where ...
The Arbitrator must find that aspect of the grievor's misconduct is simply not made out.

Total occurrences: 35

▪ *It* impersonal constructions in main clauses

*... it **would seem** that ...*
*... it **appears** that ...* (x 2)
*It **may** be that ...*
*It is **reasonable** that ...*
*It **seems** that ...*

... it is not inappropriate ***to suggest*** *that ...*
It is not disputed that ... (x 9)
It does not ***appear*** *disputed that ...*
Firstly, it is common ground that ... (x 2)
It is clear that ...
It is well settled that ... (x 3)
It is well established that ... (x 2)
It is significant, however, that ...
Firstly, it must be recognised that ...
It should be noted that ... (x 2)
It must be concluded that ...
Total occurrences: 30

PART TWO.

EXPLORING THE HYPOTHESIS OF THE COLONIZATION OF ARBITRATION DISCOURSE BY LITIGATION

CHAPTER EIGHT

ARGUMENTS BY ANALOGY IN ARBITRATION AWARDS

CHIARA DEGANO*

1. Introduction

This chapter aims at verifying whether recourse to reference to prior cases, i.e. recourse to precedent, in international arbitration awards has increased over recent decades, as a possible effect of the influence of common law on arbitration. The assumption that international commercial arbitration (ICA) is not connected with any specific legal system is a fundamental principle of its rationale. However, since ICA does not take place in a vacuum it is often suggested that it may be subject to influences on the part of national legal systems, either as an effect of the legal mentality of arbitrators, a heritage of their education and professional setting (Gotti 2008: 223), or of national laws that in some countries still regulate access to arbitration and establish what subject matters can be resolved through such practice (Lew 2006: 179).

Bhatia *et al.* (2008: 21) point out that economic globalization, a phenomenon that has greatly contributed to the rapid spread of international arbitration, has also created the basis for an influence of common law on arbitration practices, by reason of the dominant position held by the United States in international trade and investment practice. Also language plays a crucial role, and if the status of English as an international language is generally recognized as a vehicle for English-speaking countries' cultural influence, in legal contexts this is even more so. Legal terminology is so culture-bound that it is often impossible to separate a word from its referent, which is also the reason why a

* The research on which this chapter is based contributes to the National Research Programme "Tension and Change in English Domain-specific Genres" (prot. 2007JCY9Y9), funded by the Italian Ministry of University.

satisfactory translation is at times impossible (see Frigo, this volume). For all these reasons, Gotti (2005: 157) argues that "when the language chosen for international commercial arbitration is English, there is a tendency to adopt procedures typical of common law countries".

Another factor that may contribute to the reproduction of case-based logic in arbitration awards is the increasing availability of literature on international awards and of awards themselves (Jolivet 2006). Although arbitral tribunals do not have to follow prior awards when deciding a new case, the possibility to access existing awards published in books, journals and databases with international circulation, together with arbitrators' "sense of obligation" to comply with principles of predictability and consistency that are fundamental tenets of the law (Kaufmann-Kohler 2007) may have the effect of conferring, to some extent, value of precedents on awards.

In light of the considerations above, this chapter aims at verifying whether in the texts actually produced within the arbitration process there is any prevalence of discursive practices associated with common law, focusing in particular on argumentation based on a relation of analogy. As Walton *et al.* remark, argument by analogy is "the foundation of all case-based reasoning", i.e. of law based on the doctrine of precedent – as is the case for Anglo-American law – whereby "if a case has been decided by a court in a certain way, then a new case that is similar to it should be decided in the same way" (Walton *et al.* 2008: 43). Therefore, if awards gain precedent value, it is reasonable to expect a growing recourse to argumentation by analogy in arbitration awards.

Accordingly, the main research question for this chapter asks whether international awards are characterized by a marked presence of arguments by analogy. A second research question, framed in a genre-based perspective, considers whether arguments by analogy are associated with any specific move within the structure of international awards.

2. Background

Speed and cost-saving are often mentioned, alongside confidentiality, as main reasons to choose arbitration over litigation. However, according to Hunter (2000), this motivation only applies to national disputes, while in an international context preference for arbitration finds its reasons in the enforceability of awards across states and, most importantly, in ICA's international character, i.e. its independence from national courts:

> The main reason why we see arbitration clauses in international commercial contracts is that corporations and governmental entities engaged in international trade are simply not willing to litigate in the other party's 'home' court (Hunter 2000: 382).

If arbitration took place in the country of one of the parties, the other would find itself in a disadvantaged position, if only from a linguistic point of view: all its documents and witness testimony would have to be translated into the language of the court. But the disparity might not finish there: if the two parties come from nations with different legal systems (common law vs. civil law), the 'guest' party would have to adapt to the local legal system, possibly without having direct experience of it.

In tune with this supra-national drive, international arbitration today presents itself as an "autonomous dispute resolution process, governed primarily by non-national rules and accepted international commercial rules and practices" (Lew 2006: 181). The effort towards a harmonization of ICA rules and practice, which started with the New York Convention on the Recognition and Enforcement of Foreign Awards (1958) resulted in the creation of UNCITRAL Arbitration Rules (1976), "a set of procedural rules upon which parties may agree for the conduct of arbitral proceedings" (<www.uncitral.org>), and Model Law (1985), a model for national laws on arbitration, aimed to "assist States in reforming and modernizing their laws on arbitral procedure" (Lew 2006: 181).

Within the framework provided by these international instruments, arbitrators are not bound to follow prior awards when deciding a new case. However, as argued by Nariman (2000), in the last thirty years, a flourishing of arbitration journals, books and newsletters reporting the *ratio decidendi* of hundreds of awards, has given rise to a sort of international jurisprudence, making arbitration increasingly precedent-bound, as well as increasingly similar to litigation. This state of things diverts from the original spirit of arbitration in two ways: in the first place, it disregards the principle that an arbitral tribunal should limit itself to reach a result that "commends itself as *just* in the particular case [since] the private nature of arbitration is inconsistent with any law-making function" (Nariman 2000: 262). Secondarily, if prior awards acquire, *de facto*, the status of precedent, arbitration will end up sharing one of the tenets of common law, thus betraying its distinctive feature of not being embedded in any specific legal system.

2.1. The doctrine of precedent

As Kaufmann-Kohlers (2006: 357) observes,

> it is common knowledge that international arbitration lacks a doctrine of precedent, at least as it is formulated in the common-law system.[1]

According to the same author, the theory is at least partially confirmed by the practice, as a survey of recent awards shows that earlier cases do not have significant precedent value in commercial arbitration, albeit not so in sports and investment arbitration (Kaufmann-Kohlers 2007: 373). Other authors, however, make the point that reference to prior cases is becoming an increasingly common practice for arbitral tribunals (Nariman 2000; Commission 2007; Kaufmann-Kohlers 2006). In most legal systems courts take prior judgments into account to some extent. The difference between common law and civil law legal systems, though, lies in the fact that in the former precedents have "a leading role" as opposed to a supporting role in the latter (Kaufmann-Kohlers 2006: 359). Therefore, the mere presence of reference to earlier cases in international awards, cannot be considered per se symptomatic of a common-law drive in arbitration, but an increase in such practice could – in the long run – determine a change of status for precedent in arbitration.

2.2. Argumentation by analogy

Reference to prior cases in arbitration awards, as well as in court judgments is meant to have a persuasive function, which is pursued by justifying one's reasoning on the basis of a precedent established in an analogous case, i.e. through an argument based on a relation of analogy.

An argument is

> an arranged set of statements or propositions (the premises) advanced by an agent in order to support the truth or acceptability of another statement or proposition (the conclusion) (Juthe 2005).

[1] When referring to precedents a distinction must be drawn between the notion of 'binding precedent', holding under the doctrine of *stare decisis* and that of 'persuasive precedent', i.e. "a decision that is not legally binding but is entitled to respect and careful consideration" (Kaufmann-Kohler 2007: 357), applied by courts without a legal obligation to do so.

Recent categorizations (cf. for example Walton *et al.* 2008) distinguish three main forms of arguments: deductive, inductive and defeasible arguments, the latter of which include argument by analogy. While deductive and inductive arguments enjoy a long-standing tradition in logic, defeasible arguments have only in more recent times been acknowledged a status on the same footing as the other two.

In a deductive argument the premises, arranged on a general-to-particular pattern, preclude that the conclusion is false, therefore if the premises are accepted also the conclusion must be accepted, as is the case in the *modus ponens* (Juthe 2005: 2). In inductive arguments, on the other hand, reasoning proceeds from "a collected set of data" to "statistical conclusion drawn from the data" (Walton *et al.* 2008: 10), thus following a particular-to-general flow, and the conclusion is only probable, since it does not derive from a logically binding form of reasoning.

In a defeasible argument the conclusion can be accepted tentatively in relation to the evidence known so far in a case, but may need to be retracted as new evidence comes in (Walton et al. 2008: 2). Its validity does not depend on logic, rather it should be evaluated as strong or weak in specific respects by subjecting it to critical questioning (Walton *et al.* 2008:61-62). In the case of argument by analogy, for example, where the "inference goes via an analogical relation, in contrast to an inductive or deductive relation" (Juthe 2005: 4) the strength of the argument rests on the similarity of the objects of the comparison.

If we consider the following example, taken from van Eemeren *et al.* (2002: 99):

> It's not necessary to give 10$ allowance to Jimmy, because his brother always got just 5$ a week.

The crucial premise is that Jimmy and his brother are equal and must therefore be treated similarly. The strength of the argument can be checked by testing the validity of the premise, i.e. by asking whether there is any difference between the two objects of comparison, such as for example a change in the cost of life.

From a pragmatic point of view, defeasible arguments are typically used in contexts of epistemic uncertainty, i.e. when reasoning is conducted against a context of only partial knowledge (Cummings 2004; Walton *et al.* 2008: 45). This is probably the reason why analogy is at the basis of case law, where courts' decisions are not derived from a systematized body of rules, as is the case in legal systems based on deductive reasoning.

3. Method and materials

The analysis is carried out on a corpus of the International Chamber of Commerce of Paris (ICC) awards extracts contained in the Kluwer Bank database, from which only final awards were selected. The corpus, amounting to 445,000 words, includes files spanning over two decades (1984 to 2003), as shown in Table 1):[2]

1984	1	1991	5	1998	2
1985	1	1992	8	1999	6
1986	-	1993	3	2000	2
1987	4	1994	7	2001	2
1988	3	1995	6	2002	1
1989	8	1996	4	2003	2
1990	7	1997	1		

Table 1. Award distribution through the years.

In order to answer the main research question, a corpus based approach was adopted. Relying on a list of indicators of argument by analogy drafted by van Eemeren *et al.* (2007), the corpus was analysed to verify whether there was an increase of arguments by analogy over the time lapse examined. Here is the list I used, selecting from the original one that included also other indicators not likely to feature in a corpus of legal language, being too colloquial:

> compar*,[3] simil*, equivalent*, parallel*, as, like, too, also, as well, either, no less than, likewise, both, the same, then, now, analog*

As a first step concordances were extracted and analysed manually to eliminate occurrences of the indicators which actually at close reading did not classify as arguments by analogy. At the end of this operation the over 6,000 original lines were streamlined to 57.[4]

As for the second research question, I followed a corpus-driven approach, analysing through close reading the occurrences of arguments

---

[2] For corpus statistics, see Garzone, this volume. The uneven text distribution across the years simply reflects the availability of awards on the database.

[3] Wildcards are used to retrieve also inflected forms.

[4] Of course the overall number of arguments based on analogy may be higher than that. this datum refers only to schemes in which the relation of analogy was explicitly codified by one of the indicators included in the above list.

by analogy in their broadest context, i.e. the award in which they were employed, limiting the scope to one award per year. I intended, once recurring moves across the awards were identified, to verify whether regular arguments by analogy tended to occur in specific moves.

4. Results

As mentioned in the previous section, all the relevant occurrences of arguments by analogy in the corpus have been retrieved, by means of a Wordsmith Tools' concordancer (Scott 2004). Below I report the initial part of the streamlined concordance output, related to the indicators *also* (collocating with the verb "see") and *as*:

N	Concordance
15	its falseness, (8) to his injury'. Id. See also New York University v. Continental
16	Arbitration § 11.03 (2d ed. 1990). See also Prima Paint Corp. v. Flood &
17	WL 65717, *5 (S.D.N.Y. 1997); see also Reed, Roberts Assoc., Inc. v.
18	BGE 47 II 86, 95 II 39, 96 II 233; see also the non-published decision of the
19	pp. 667 et seq., espec. section 4; see also the Swiss Supreme Court's decision
20	profit picture' (601 F. 2d at 614). See also Van Valkenburgh, Nooger and
21	136 (2d Cir. 1990) (per curiam). See also Walther v. Bank of New York, 772
22	(translation) [10] "In other awards it was also decided that by resorting to a
23	13-01-42, it upheld the validity of other analogous clauses, each case being
24	but not limited to the initial debtor. [8] 'As stated by the French Cour de
25	aim of serving the interest of Algeria - as is the case in the two
26	consequence. In effect, and as the Supreme Court has held, one
27	of the parties' contractual autonomy. As it was said in ICCaward no. 1512,(1)
28	activities', there are different views, both as expressed by commentators and as
29	case of doubt, he does not. Conversely, as underlined in the 1907 leading case, if
30	he must be able to draw on the credit. As stated by Lord Denning in Pavia &
31	agreement of the parties is established. As stated by the Indian Supreme Court
32	claims and counter-claims. However, as the Tribunal concludes that the
33	X' wine sold by respondent would lead, as in the Falstaff case, to the conclusion
34	per se a violation of fair trading, at least as interpreted by the Supreme Court." 2.
35	of the arbitrator is not any more (as the decision of arbitrator Lagergren in

Concordance 1. 'Also'/ 'as'.

By enlarging the context for each line it was possible to visualize a meaningful unit of text which allowed to reconstruct the argument. The following extract will provide an example of reconstruction of argumentation resting on a relation of analogy:

> (1) In the case at issue before us, the defendant does not, at any time, claim direct application of Art.57LEC in this arbitration, but rather its analogous application, which is also inadmissible since it overlooks (i) that in this case there exists no legal vacuum which must be filled by analogy to Art.57LEC, […](ii) *that there do not exist common characteristics between the case regulated by Art.57LEC and the case presented to us, given the substantive differences existing between internal judicial process and international arbitration* […]. (1987)

Reconstructing the argumentative sequence, one can summarize the defendant's claim, resting on an argument by analogy, in the following terms: Art.57LEC is admissible in this arbitration case, because Art.57LEC was admissible in a previous case, and this case and the previous case are comparable. The arbitral tribunal rejects such a claim, basically by asking the critical question for arguments by analogy, i.e. 'Are there any significant differences between the two cases?', the answer to which is 'Yes: substantive differences exist between an internal judicial process and international arbitration'.

4.1. Research question 1

Moving on to consider quantitative data, the incidence of argument by analogy over the time span taken into consideration has been calculated in order to answer the first research question, i.e. whether the recourse to argument by analogy, the foundation of common law systems, has increased over time. Dividing the corpus in three time spans, the following data emerge:

1984-1990	*1991-1997*	*1997-2003*
21%	43%	39%

Table 2. Incidence of arguments by analogy in the corpus.

The percentages in the Table represent the ratio between the number of awards in which there are one or more examples of argument by analogy and the total number of awards for one year. For example, in 1987 arguments by analogy are present in 1 award out of 4, that is in the 25% of the cases. The same ratio was calculated for all the years investigated, and the average for each time span was then calculated on the single years' ratios. Data for the first time span are reported in the Table below for the sake of exemplification:

Year	*Total files*	*Files with arg. by analogy*	*Ratio*
84	1	0	0
85	1	0	0
87	4	1	25%
88	3	1	33%
89	8	1	13%
90	7	4	57%
			21%

Table 3. Exemplification of the procedure followed to obtain the data reported in Table 2.

Returning to the synthetic data for each time span reported in Table 2, it can be observed that in the first span (1984-'90) arguments by analogy are present in 21% of the awards, against 43% and 39% percent in later years. These data testify that there has been an increase in the recourse to arguments by analogy, a datum that can be interpreted as symptomatic of a growing influence of common law systems on arbitration practices.

If for the purposes of this study argument by analogy has been taken as the representative feature of common law systems, the words *law* and *code* can be considered as indicators of deductive reasoning, and by extension of civil-law systems, where cases are principally judged on the basis of statute law. While recourse to arguments by analogy has increased throughout the years, as demonstrated above, interestingly enough data about the frequency of the words *law* and *code* show the opposite trend:

law	1984-1990	1991-1997	1998-2003
per 1,000w	6,48	4,51	3,8
code	1984-1990	1991-1997	1998-2003
per 1,000w	2,11	1,27	0,8

Table 4. Frequency of reference to statutory sources of law in the corpus.

The figures in Table 4 represent the incidence of the node word in the awards, with reference to each time span. For example, considering the word 'code' in the time span 1984-90, the value 2.11 is the average of its frequency in each single award (cf. the figures reported in the column 'per 1000' below):

N	File	Words	Hits	per 1,000
1	1985_1.txt	1.963	12	6,11
2	1987_1.txt	7.292	15	2,06
3	1987_3.txt	4.717	1	0,21
4	1988_3.txt	7.890	11	1,39
5	1989_1.txt	2.409	1	0,42
6	1989_2.txt	1.444	3	2,08
7	1989_5.txt	9.314	17	1,83
8	1989_6.txt	4.124	9	2,18
9	1990_1.txt	2.833	2	0,71
10	1990_2.txt	4.296	27	6,28
11	1990_3.txt	5.620	2	0,36
12	1990_4.txt	2.928	11	3,76
13	1990_6.txt	8.540	6	0,70
14	1990_7.txt	6.811	10	1,47

Table 5. Breakdown of frequency of the word 'code'

The frequency trends related to both indicators of arguments by analogy and to the words *law* and *case* suggest that the case-based model has gained ground in international awards, to the detriment of deductive reasoning.

4.2. Research question 2

Coming to the second research question, i.e. whether arguments by analogy tend to occur in particular moves, I have considered in what part of the award the arguments by analogy identified through the concordancer occur. Due to the necessity of extensive reading, in this second part of the study the scope was limited to one file per year. The following scheme illustrates the distribution of arguments by analogy within each award considered:

1987	*A. Jurisdiction*
1988_3	*II. Main questions*
1989_7	III. Meaning of Art. 12 of the agreement
1990	*II. Jurisdiction*
1991_3	*II. Merits of the dispute*
1992_1	III. Damages and compensation
1993	I. Lack of conformity
1994	*I. Jurisdiction*
1995	II. Termination of the licence
1996	II. The legal effect of mandatory rules of a foreign country
1999	*I. Background*
2000_2	*I. Preliminary issues* *III. Partial arbitral award on the preliminary issue*
2001_1	*I. Claimant's title to claim*
2002_1	*I. Claim for final relief* *II. Determination of the issue*

The first observation to be made is that it was not possible to recognize a homogeneous structure across the awards, as not all of them are organized into the same number of sections and the sections are given different titles. However, despite such apparent diversification, a sort of pattern can be identified, in that whatever the structure of the awards and the title given to the sections, arguments by analogy tend to occur in the initial moves. These are the parts where mainly jurisdictional and substantive reasoning unfolds, the former being concerned with matters of jurisdiction and procedure, and the latter with the "evaluation of factual and legal position of the parties" (Webster 2006: 431), i.e. with the merits. The following example will illustrate how an argument based on analogy is used to substantiate jurisdictional reasoning:

> (2) 1990_1 II Jurisdiction
>
> [7] "The principal issue in this proceeding is whether the contract on which [seller] relies binds [buyer] .... Because that contract contains the arbitration clause by which this Tribunal has been constituted, the issue is in the first instance jurisdictional. In accord with the familiar principle of Kompetenz-Kompetenz, Art. 8(3) of the ICC Rules gives this tribunal authority to determine its own jurisdiction.(1) See Craig, Park & Paulsson, International Chamber of Commerce Arbitration § 11.03 (2d ed. 1990). See also Prima Paint Corp. v. Flood & Conklin Mfg. Co., 388 U.S. 395 (1967).

Under the section 'jurisdiction' the extract reports the tribunal's statement that it has the authority to determine its own jurisdiction on the basis of ICC rules, of specialized literature and of a previous case (*Prima Paint*

Corp. v. Flood & Conklin Mfg. Co), which is mentioned with the function of persuasive precedent. Focusing on the latter, the scheme of the argument based on analogy can be reconstructed as follows: in this case the tribunal has the authority to determine its own jurisdiction because the tribunal had the authority to determine its own jurisdiction in the Prima Paint Corp. v. Flood & Conklin Mfg. Co. case and the two cases are comparable

From a pragmatic perspective the concentration of arguments by analogy in these preliminary stages of arbitration, can be explained as an attempt to make the award less likely to be challenged in the future. That arbitral awards ensure "one-stop adjudication" is a concern for both arbitral institutions and national courts, which do not wish to see the effectiveness of arbitration hampered by subsequent court litigation (Webster 2006). In this respect, the effort to make the award 'unchallengeable' concentrates particularly on jurisdictional reasoning, since it is practice for national courts not to annul awards on the ground of merits, but only for matters of procedural and jurisdictional reasoning.

5. Conclusions

Framed in the ongoing debate on the precedent value of awards, this chapter aimed at discovering whether there has been an increase of reference to prior cases used with precedent value in international arbitration awards. In order to do so, indicators of arguments by analogy, the scheme on which case-law is based, were used to retrieve the occurrences in which earlier cases are quoted in awards, applying *de facto* the doctrine of precedent.

The quantitative analysis thus conducted has highlighted an increase in the recourse to arguments based on analogy in arbitration awards from 1984 to 2003 and a concomitant reduction in references to statutory sources. Considered jointly, these two data have been interpreted as an indicator of a growing influence of common law on arbitration, both in conceptual and procedural terms, in parallel with a progressive decrease in the use of deductive reasoning, which is to civil law what argument by analogy is to common law.

A second research question addressed the distribution of references to prior cases within the textual structure of awards. Despite structural heterogeneity, it has been observed that arguments by analogy are particularly frequent in the moves dedicated to substantive and jurisdictional reasoning. Such a concentration of reference to earlier cases with precedent value was explained as responding to the wish of making the award as sound as possible, with special regard for jurisdictional meaning, so to ensure 'one-stop adjudication', as far as possible.

That the increasing recourse to prior awards with precedent value can be attributed to the influence of common law remains in part an open question, since links of direct causality are difficult to ascertain. Further research in this direction, possibly entailing interviews to practitioners, might add insights into the perception of the phenomena described in this chapter from within the arbitration community of practice.

References

Bhatia, Vijay K., Christopher N. Candlin and Jan Engberg. 2008. "Concepts, Contexts and Procedures in Arbitration Discourse". In *Legal Discourse Across Cultures and System,* edited by Vijay K. Bhatia, Christopher N. Candlin and Jan Engberg, 3-31. Hong Kong: Hong Kong University Press.

Commission, Jeffery P. 2007. "Precedent in Investment Treaty Arbitration: The Empirical Backing". *Transnational Dispute Management* (draft version available at <http://www.linklaters.com/pdfs/Publications/us/tdm2007_article22_1.pdf).

Cummings, Louise. 2004. "Analogical Reasoning as a Tool of Epidemiological Investigation". *Argumentation* 18: 427-444.

Gotti, Maurizio. 2005. "English in Intercultural Settings: Globalising Trends and Local Resistance". In *Identity, Community, Discourse; English in Intercultural Settings*, edited by Giuseppina Cortese and Anna Duszak, 139-165. Bern: Peter Lang.

—. 2008. "Cultural Constraints on Arbitration Discourse". In *Legal Discourse Across Cultures and Systems*, edited by Vijay K. Bhatia, Christopher N. Candlin and Jan Engberg. Hong Kong: Hong Kong University Press.

Hunter, Martin. 2000. "International Commercial Dispute Resolution: The Challenge of the Twenty-First Century". *Arbitration International* 16, no. 4: 379-392.

Jolivet, Emmanuel. 2006. "Access to Information and Awards". *Arbitration International* 22, no. 2: 265-274.

Juthe, André. "Argument by Analogy". *Argumentation.* 19, 2005, 1-27.

Kaufmann-Kohler, Gabrielle. 2007. "Arbitral Precedent: Dream, Necessity or Excuse?" *Arbitration International* 23, no. 3: 357-378.

Lew, Julian D.M. 2006. "Achieving the Dream: Autonomous Arbitration". *Arbitration International* 22, no. 2: 179-204.

Nariman, Fali S. 2000. "The Spirit of Arbitration: The Tenth Annual Goff Lecture". *Arbitration International* 16, no.3: 261-278.

Scott, Mike. 2004. *WordSmith Tools 4.0*. Oxford: Oxford University Press.

van Eemeren, Frans H., Rob Grotendorst and Francisca Snoeck Henkemans. 2002. *Argumentation. Analysis, Evaluation, Presentation*. Mahwah, NJ: Lawrence Erlbaum.

van Eemeren, Frans H., Peter Houtlosser and Francisca Snoeck Henkemans. 2007. *Argumentative Indicators in Discourse: A Pragma-Dialectical Study*. Dordrecht: Springer.

Walton, Douglas, Christian Reed and Fabrizio Macagno. 2008. *Argumentation schemes*. Cambridge: Cambridge University Press.

Webster, Thomas H. 2006. "Review of Substantive Reasoning of International Arbitral Awards by National Courts: Ensuring One-Stop Adjudication". *Arbitration International* 22, no. 3: 431-462.

CHAPTER NINE

LINGUISTIC AND TEXTUAL FEATURES OF ITALIAN COMMERCIAL ARBITRATION AWARDS*

MICHELE SALA

1. Introduction

Arbitration is an alternative dispute resolution method aimed at the drafting of an arbitral award which is meant as a definitive measure for the settling of disputes, thus representing an economical and time-saving alternative to traditional litigation (Nariman 2000; Belotti 2003; Bocchini 2006). Such a procedure is based on the free will of the parties to agree and resolve their disputes without recourse to ordinary jurisdiction, but through the appointment of experts as arbitrators who are ultimately required to write an arbitral award meant as a definitive resolution. Nonetheless, in the Italian context "the parties do not hesitate to opt for litigation when the outcome does not favour them" (Gotti and Anesa 2011: 190). As a matter of fact, in Italy, especially before 1994, arbitration laws lacked specific provisions to make awards unchallengeable thus allowing for various forms of appellate review (cf. Ceccon 2000; Belotti 2003). In Italy, in recent years new laws have been enacted to promote arbitration in civil and commercial issues and reinforce the definitiveness of the arbitral decision by limiting the possibilities of challenge (*Legislative Decree 5/2003, Legislative Decree 40/2006, Legislative Decree 113/2008*, cf.

* The research on which this chapter is based is part of the International research project "International Commercial Arbitration Practices: A Discourse Analytical Study", headed by Prof. Vijay Bhatia. It also contributes to the National Research Programme "Tension and Change in English Domain-specific Genres" directed by Prof. Maurizio Gotti (prot. 2007JCY9Y9).

Gotti and Anesa 2011; Maci 2011).[2] In addition to this, for the sake of judicial definitiveness, the appointment of lawyers as arbitrators has become the preferred practice, strongly recommended by Chambers of Commerce, in the process of establishing the Board of Arbitrators, while professional experts are usually selected as consultants. In fact, lawyers are expected to have both the juridical competence to conceptualize and represent states, events, actors, roles and relations in ways that are juridically clear, and the domain-specific linguistic competence to discuss such concepts in ways that are appropriate to a legal context and to formulate decisions which have the impact and deontic force of a normative act. Nevertheless, arbitration proceedings (in the case of standard arbitration, i.e. *arbitrato rituale*) can still be appealed in the local courts for nullity, revocation or third party opposition. This makes the validity of the award somehow problematic, at least when it is perceived as being non-coherent or non-convincing.

The main assumption at the basis of this analysis is that arbitration is significantly influenced by litigation in terms of practices and language. This might not only be a necessary consequence of the presence of lawyers on the Board of Arbitrators (Nariman 2000), but could be purposefully intended to confer a specific deontic connotation on the award, so as to make it recognizable and acceptable as a normative text rather than a text simply expressing the specialist's opinion concerning the case in point. In consideration of this, the purpose of this chapter is to investigate the ways arbitrators use to reinforce the juridical validity of awards. The main focus will be on the rhetorical strategies used by the drafters to express evidentiality, epistemic and interactive meanings to confer authority and definitiveness on their judgment.

2. Material and methodology

The corpus analysed consists of 20 commercial arbitration awards mostly dealing with disputes in business and private contexts, pronounced between the year 2000 and 2006 and written in Italian (totalling over 900,000 words), available in the archives of the Chambers of Arbitration of Bergamo, Milan and Reggio Emilia. The quantitative searches were based on both automatic and manual investigations. Wordsmith Tools 4.0 (Scott 2004) and Portable Document Format (PdF program) search options

[2] On Italian arbitration awards, cf. also in this volume Antelmi and Santulli, Chaper Six.

were used for word counts. The results were then filtered through a stage of manual correction to rule out non-relevant occurrences.

For an in-depth discussion of the discourse strategies used in arbitration awards it is helpful to stress the particular nature of the arbitral procedure, which has to take into account two specific and crucial aspects, namely:

1) *The ideological distance between the parties*. Usually, the opening lines of the award clearly state that the arbitral procedure is the consequence of a failed attempt at conciliation, through formulations like the following:

(1) [N]on risultava possibile esperire il tentativo di conciliazione. [it was not possible to carry out an attempt at conciliation.]

(2) Esperito il tentativo di conciliazione, che dava esito negativo […]. [After carrying out an attempt at conciliation, which was unsuccessful (…).]

Such expressions signal from the very onset that, on the one hand, a conciliatory, non-adversary and cooperative procedure to reach a settlement agreement through the assistance of a third neutral body is no longer possible, and, on the other, that drastically different positions (interests, needs, expectations) are held by the parties as to the matter of the dispute, which are explicitly represented within the text as hard to reconcile and harmonize.

2) *The challengeability of the award.* As already mentioned, although the arbitration procedure is meant as a definitive resolution, its outcome does not have (nor is perceived as having) the same juridical value as a courtroom judgment, especially in consideration of the fact that there are cases where appeals are possible (Ceccon 2000), among which the action for nullity is the most common. An award can be appealed as null for several reasons, some of which concern purely formal or procedural factors (i.e. the arbitrators were not appointed in the form and manner laid down by law; the award failed to meet mandatory formal requirements or was delivered outside the prescribed time limit), whereas others pertain to aspects closely related to the matter of the dispute (i.e. the award exceeds the scope of the arbitration agreement, it contains contradictory provisions, or there is justifiable doubt as to the arbitrators' impartiality (cf. Consolo 2006; Lino 2006; Cutolo and Esposito 2007). Although the challengeability

is not perceived as a concern by the arbitrators themselves[3] it is indeed a problem for the juridical validity of the text of the award.

These two factors have a considerable impact on the definitiveness of the award. To bypass the obstacle represented by the different ideologies of the parties and the possibility of challenge, the award needs to be presented and perceived as an authoritative, coherent and convincing whole, in other words, it has to be persuasive in terms of meaning: the argumentation of the considerations leading to the final decision should be, or sound, compelling and, consequently, the final decision should be accepted as necessary, expected and unquestionable.

To account for these aspects the scope of the present analysis is two-fold. The first part investigates the use of formulaic and standardized expressions in the whole text of the awards to convey specific meanings. The second part deals solely with the argumentative section of the award, that is the *Motivazioni* (Reasons for the Decision) macro-move, given its function as a preparatory step for the final decision, with a specific focus on the rhetorical strategies exploited by the arbitrators in order to organize the final pronouncement and make it clear, coherent, convincing, and accepted as binding. More specifically, the focus of this second part will be both on markers of evidentiality and epistemic modality (cf. Chafe and Nichols 1986; Palmer 1990), to see how drafters present interpretations and evidence, and on interactive strategies (cf. Thompson 2001; Hyland 2005), to see how arbitrators account for the parties' expectations and competence in the construction and articulation of meaning.

3. Results

3.1. Standardized and formulaic expressions in the award

This section analyses conventional and marked expressions where the terms *Arbitro* and *Collegio* (Arbitrator and Board/Panel/Arbitral tribunal) are used as grammatical subjects, and especially on word-order in such subject-verb collocations so as to ascertain their function and value in the textualization of arbitral awards.

Scanning the text of the awards it is possible to note that the simple form subject (S) + verb (V) + object + adjunct form (or zero subject + verb + object + adjunct) is not always respected. More specifically, cases where

[3] For this information I am much indebted to Paola Catenaccio (University and Milan) and Ulisse Belotti (University of Bergamo), who interviewed arbitrators at the Chambers of Arbitration of Milan and Bergamo. Some of this material can also be found in Belotti (forth.).

the verb is placed before the relevant subject are rather frequent. The use of V+S collocations, if not ungrammatical in Italian and quite frequent in everyday language (cf. Benincà/Salvi 1988, Frison 1988, Sornicola 1994), is quite marked in legal contexts in that it places communicative emphasis on the juridical roles of the grammatical subjects (cf. Rovere 2000: 30; Mortara Garavelli 2001: 86-93, 163).

A search through the Web and especially in corpora of written Italian texts available online (CODIS and CORIS, compiled at the University of Bologna, cf. Rossini Favretti 2000, 2008) revealed that such VS forms are found especially in sentence-final position in literary prose (i.e. *disse lui/lei* [said he/she], which are also common in Anglophone literary prose) or in media discourse reports to tag reported speech (i.e. *sostengono i testimoni,* [as the witnesses claim], *afferma il Ministro* [the Minister claims]). A crucial piece of evidence is that in written and everyday language VS collocations in sentence-initial or sentence-medial position are remarkably rare, while they are relatively more frequent in texts dealing with legal matters (either authored by or addressed to experts belonging to the legal profession). More precisely, such constructions are frequently used in normative texts like contracts, statutes, regulations, etc. (i.e. *stabilisce la legge/normativa che* … [the Law/regulations establish/-es that…]), as well as in informative texts, mainly judicial news reports (i.e., *sostiene l'accusa/difesa* [the defence/prosecution claims]), and even in very informal contexts like entries on web forums or blogs where lawyers or law students comment on legal matters. This is symptomatic of the fact that in legal contexts, also in contexts even remotely dealing with the law, standardized formulations and conventionally established collocations are used as formulae, that is as codified and effective ways of conveying meanings, both for their transparency regarding the content and intelligibility for the addressee.

In the corpus analyzed the terms *Collegio* and *Arbitro* occur 805 times. 284 of these cases have the function of subject, while the remaining instances are dependent on verbs or prepositions and will not be examined here. These collocations are found both in the narrative sections of the award, which is the synthesis of the content of the *Memorie* [Pleadings] presented to the Board by the parties, and in the most typically normative part of the text, which is the *Motivazioni* [Reasons for the Decision] section and the concluding part usually introduced by the formula PQM (standing for *Per Questi Motivi* [for these reasons]) marking the boundary between the introductory and the core parts of the award.

As to the position of the verb combined with the subject *Collegio/Arbitro*, it is possible to further distinguish two main groups: the first consists of 183 cases where the subject precedes the verb (SV); the second includes 101 cases where the subject follows the verb (VS). Concerning the function of the verbs in the two groups, other distinctions are possible. As regards the SV collocations, most of the verbs (128 out of 183) have a narrative function, are frequently in the past tense and synthesize the various stages of the juridical procedure or the discussion of the evidence (in the *Memorie* section) (i.e. *il Collegio/l'Arbitro assegnava, disponeva, prorogava, richiedeva, fissava,* etc. [The Board/Arbitrator assigned, decided, deferred, requested, established, etc.]), as in example (3) below. A smaller number of clusters (51 out of 183) has an evaluative function (i.e. *il Collegio/l'Arbitro ritiene, osserva, stima*, etc. [the Board/Arbitrator believes, observes, estimates, etc.]); these formulations may also have the purpose of mitigating the possible threat represented by the norms or the procedural decisions established by the Arbitrators, as in examples (4) and (5). Finally, very few occurrences (4 out of 183) are combined with a declarative verbal form (i.e. *il Collegio/l'Arbitro dichiara* [The Board/Arbitrator declares]), as in example (6). Instances of the various verbal functions are found in the following examples:

> (3) Preso atto di ciò, *il Collegio fissava* una riunione al 18.1.05. [In consideration of this the Board arranged a meeting on 18.1.05.]

> (4) *Il Collegio ritiene* di dover prender norma principalmente da ciò che è stato possibile accertare attraverso la consulenza tecnica. [The Board finds it necessary to mainly consider valid what was established through advice from specialists.]

> (5) *Questo Arbitro prospetta* la possibilità che il Collegio eserciti ex officio il potere espressamente riconosciutogli dall'art. 1384 C.C. [This Arbitrator advances the possibility for the Board to exert ex officio the authority expressly conferred upon it by Art. 1384.]

> (6) *Il Collegio dichiara*: tenuta [X] a corrispondere alla [Y] l'importo di € 4.619,75. [The Board establishes that [X] shall pay to [Y] the amount of € 4,619.75.]

As regards VS collocations, most of the verbs (93 out of 101) have a markedly evaluative function and are used to introduce and reinforce the Arbitrator's judgment about aspects of the dispute or of the judicial procedure so as to strengthen the validity of the final decision (i.e., *il Collegio/l'Arbitro ritiene, osserva, stima*, etc. [the Board/Arbitrator finds, thinks, believes, observes, estimates, etc.]), as in examples (7) and (8). A very small number of occurrences (8 out of 101) has an imperative function (i.e. *accerti il Collegio* [the Board should ascertain]), as in (9) below. Examples of these functions can be found in the following texts:

(7) A tale conclusione *ritiene il Collegio* di dovere addivenire. [The Board thinks it necessary to reach this conclusion.]

(8) *Osserva il Collegio* che l'art. 34 del contratto 13.11.2002 – che reca la rubrica "ritenute di garanzia-pagamenti" – prevede che l'anticipazione da parte del committente del 10% dell'importo dovuto a forfait all'appaltatore doveva essere a cura di quest'ultimo garantito da fideiussione bancaria. [The Board observes that Article 34 of the contract 13.11.2002 – which contains the expression "withholding payments" – states that the advanced payment of 10% of the amount due to the contractor by the client should have been made by the latter and accompanied by a letter of guarantee issued by the bank]

(9) *Accerti il Collegio Arbitrale*, e per l'effetto condanni al relativo pagamento la [X] i seguenti crediti della [Y] ai sensi e per gli effetti degli artt. 1671 c.c. e 73 del contratto. [The Board should ensure and consequently condemn [X] to the relevant payment of the following credits of [Y] in compliance with Articles 1671 and 73 of the contract.]

The occurrences of SV and VS forms are outlined in the following table:

	Narrative	Evaluative	other
Subject + Verb (183)	128	51	4
Verb + Subject (101)	-	93	8

Table 1. Frequency and distribution of *Arbitro/Collegio* + verb formulations.

The data in the table are quite significant in that they are indicative of the tendency to use formulaic VS collocations for evaluative purposes or to posit norms and formulate binding decisions (cf. Rovere 2000). The same piece of evidence acquires even more significance when considering the type of evaluation expressed by the various verbs. Examining the 144 evaluative verbs that occur in combination with the term *Collegio/Arbitro* (51 in the SV group + 93 in the VS group), it is possible to distinguish 3 main groups. The first is made up of verbs expressing positive evaluation, through which arbitrators endorse claims made by one of the parties through formulations of the type *The Board/Arbitrator finds it right, good, admissible to…*, as in the following examples:

(10) Il Collegio ritiene tale orientamento *fondato*. [The Board finds such an interpretation well founded.]

(11) Ritiene il Collegio di *potere affermare* che a quegli spetti la invocata 'maggiorazione'. [The Board finds it possible to affirm that the requested 'increase' is owed to them.]

The second group consists of verbs expressing negative evaluation, by which arbitrators reject previous claims or requests through formulations of the type *The Board/Arbitrator finds it wrong, bad, inadmissible to…*, as in the following cases:

(12) L'arbitro ritiene che il Tribunale Arbitrale sia *incompetente* a decidere la presente controversia. [The Arbitrator finds the Board of Arbitrators unqualified to deliberate on the present dispute.]

(13) Quanto agli eventuali futuri esborsi […] ritiene il Collegio che […] non resti che dichiarare allo stato e in questa sede *inammissibile* la domanda. [As to the possible forthcoming disbursements, the Board believes the only measure is to declare at this moment and in this hearing the request inadmissible.]

The third group comprises those verbs expressing neutral evaluation, by which arbitrators express judgment about (the necessity or correctness of) aspects of the judicial procedure through structures of the type *The Board/Arbitrator finds it necessary/appropriate to proceed in a given way,* rather than evaluating the admissibility of the requests made by the parties, as can be seen in the following examples.

(14) Per determinare, dunque, il corrispettivo spettante a [X], il Collegio ritiene *doversi riferire* agli importi di cui ai contratti 27.5.03 (E 115.000) e 5.11.03 (E 40.000). [In order to determine the compensation due to [X], the Board thinks it necessary to make reference to the amounts in the contracts 27.5.03 (E 115.000) and 5.11.03 (E 40.000).]

(15) Rileva l'Arbitro procedente *l'opportunità* […] di una verifica in merito al rispetto del procedimento disciplinare come previsto dagli artt. 90 e 91. [The Arbitrator in charge of the procedure points out the opportunity for a verification regarding compliance with the disciplinary measures as provided for by articles 90 and 91.]

The frequency and distribution of such formulations are outlined in the following table.

Type of evaluation	SV (51)	VS (93)
Positive	23	13
Negative	5	45
Neutral	23	35
Total	51	93

Table 2. Frequency and distribution of evaluative verbs.

As we can see in the table, in the SV group (consisting of 51 evaluative verbs) 23 verbs are positive, 5 are negative, and 23 are neutral. In the VS group (93 evaluative verbs) 13 verbs are positive, 45 are negative, and 35 are neutral. The data reveal that VS are not only more frequent in combination with evaluative verbs, but, most significantly, they are generally found in negative evaluative contexts, as if particularly effective in conveying critical meanings.

After considering the use of subject + verb structures to confer authoritativeness and impact to specific parts of the text of the award, the next sections focus on the strategies used in the *Motivazioni* move to introduce and motivate the final decision.

3.2. Evidentiality and epistemic markers in the *Motivazioni* move

The linguistic concept of evidentiality refers to any linguistic expression of attitude towards the truth of a state of affairs, or indicating the nature of evidence or the source of knowledge (Chafe and Nichols 1986; Wierzbicka 1994; Nuyts 2000; Taavitsainen 2001). In this section, the different expressions used to represent knowledge claims, observations and interpretations have been divided into two main categories:

- mediated resources: those expressions where the evaluating agent is lexicalized and the knowledge claim is explicitly framed within a subjective perspective;
- non-mediated resources: those formulations representing an interpretation or a state of affairs without any reference to the semantic agent.

More specifically, mediated forms are those expressions of attitude associated with the terms *Collegio* or *Arbitro* with the grammatical function of subject or object (both direct and indirect) through which arbitrators express their viewpoint and which are indicative of a subjective interpretation, such as formulations like *il Collegio ritiene, viene ritenuto da questo Collegio, a parere del Collegio, X ha portato il collegio a...* (The Board thinks, it is thought by the Board, according to the Board, X has led the Board to…), as those in the examples below:

(16) Ritiene in proposito il Collegio di non potere condividere il criterio X. [In this respect, the Board feels it cannot share criterion X.]

(17) [Tali] motivazioni […] *hanno portato il Collegio Arbitrale* a respingere l'eccezione. [Such reasons have led the Board to reject the exception.]

(18) *Sembra a questo Collegio* che l'utente sarebbe indotto a X. [It seems to this Board that the user would be led to X.]

Non-mediated resources are those expressions where any reference to the evaluating-agent is missing as in the case of:

- constructions with the verb *essere* [to be] + adjective, such as *è evidente, è noto, è chiaro, è possibile* (it is evident, it is well-known, it is clear, it is possible) where the reference to the agent is omitted or implicit;
- impersonal constructions with the pronoun *si*, such as *si ritiene, si rileva, si presume* (it is believed, it is observed, it is assumed);
- formulations with verbs like *sembra, pare, appare, risulta* (it seems, it appears, it results), especially when used with a predicative function (as variants of the verb 'to be').

Instances of these resources can be found in the following example:

(19) *È infine paradossale* ritenere […] che la nomina del terzo arbitro debba essere rimessa al Presidente del Tribunale competente. [Finally it is paradoxical that the appointment of the third arbitrator should be conferred on the Head of the relative Court.]

(20) *Appare dunque fondata* la richiesta della […]. [The request for […] appears well-founded.]

(21) *Non si può trascurare*, inoltre, il fatto riferito dal Sindaco di […]. [Moreover, the fact reported by the Mayor of […] cannot be ignored.]

The table contains the frequencies of such expressions both in absolute and normalized figures (per 10,000 words).

MEDIATED FORMS	**Abs.**	**Norm.**	**NON-MEDIATED FORMS**	**Abs.**	**Norm.**
Collegio/arbitro			*È* + adj	72	15.8
+ subject/agent	65	14.3	*risulta*	47	10.34
+ object/patient	9	1.98	*sembra*	1	0.22
+ preposition	25	5.5	*appare*	30	6.6
			pare	12	2.64
			Si + verb	73	16.1
TOTAL	**99**	**21.7**		**235**	**51.7**

Table 3. Occurrence of mediated and non-mediated resources in the *Motivazioni.*

The data in the table significantly show the high frequency of non-mediated evidentiality markers, irrespective of their epistemic values or pragmatic function as boosters (i.e. *è chiaro, è ovvio,* etc.) or hedges (i.e. *sembra, è possibile,* etc.).

3.3. Interactive strategies: logical markers in the *Motivazioni* move

Since the *Motivazioni* macro-move in judicial documents has a markedly argumentative function (Santulli 2006; Degano 2010), the way causality is represented is fundamental for the articulation and interpretation of meaning.

For this reason, this section analyses those connectors (conjunctions, adverbs and adverbial expressions) used to express textual and semantic coherence by lexically representing the cognitive relationship between different conceptual units or meanings. The focus is on both poles of the causality range, that is on consecutive logical markers (markers of causality) and contrastive logical markers (those connectors presupposing a causality link between claims by expressing it in negative terms, that is as contrast, opposition, concession).

Consecutive logical markers: Several studies on Italian legal language (Ferrari 1999; Mortara Garavelli 2001) distinguish two main modes in the expression of causality, namely:

a) a *regressive mode*, represented by those formulations rhetorically expressing the link between a final state and its original condition, such as *perchè, poichè, giacchè, siccome, dato che, per il fatto che* (because, since, given that, etc.). Through the use of such connectors the subordinate clause, irrespective of its position within the text, always lexicalizes the cause or the justification of a specific state of affairs which is represented as a given, as can be seen in the following examples:

(22) X è d'altra parte escludibile, *poiché* il rilascio dei titoli costituiva obbligazione prevista nell'ambito del contratto. [X is, however, to be excluded, since the issue of the securities was provided for as part of the contract.]

(23) Ha precisato, inoltre, che il diverso comportamento processuale assunto dai due Comuni non smentisce la conclusione suesposta, *dato che* tale valutazione "non può che essere riferita alla situazione sostanziale". [X has also specified that the conduct of the two city councils during the trial does not disprove the above mentioned conclusion, given that such an evaluation "cannot but refer to the actual situation".]

b) a *progressive mode*, represented by those forms pointing to the (possible) effect of a given cause, emphasizing the link between an original condition and its consequence, like *perciò, quindi, dunque, di conseguenza, conseguentemente* (so, thus, therefore, as a consequence, consequently, etc.), as can be seen in the following examples:

(24) *Conclusivamente*, *dunque*, per le prestazioni contrattuali effettivamente svolte l'attore ha diritto ad un compenso pari al 15% del finanziamento. [Thus, conclusively, for the contractual services actually provided, the party is entitled to a compensation amounting to 15% of the financing.]

(25) Quanto alle domande [...] per danni da eventi atmosferici o da terzi, il C.T.D. ne ha escluso l'esistenza e *quindi* nulla compete a X. [As to the request for damages due to weather conditions or a third party, C.T.D. excluded such a possibility, thus nothing is due to X.]

This distinction between regressive and progressive markers (Mortara Garavelli 2001: 129) will prove particularly fruitful for the present analysis.

Contrastive markers: This group includes those formulations representing opposition, contrast, concession between two ideas or conceptual units. More specifically these markers are used to voice alternative meanings and represent different or even contrasting views, while at the same time inferring a semantic and cognitive hierarchy between them, thus favouring a given interpretation. Such markers are connectors like *malgrado, sebbene, nonostante*, etc. (even though, although, nonetheless, etc.), as used in the following examples:

(26) L'appaltatore può avvalersi della facoltà di scegliere [...] la prosecuzione del rapporto *nonostante* il ritardo. [The contractor may resort to the faculty of opting for the prosecution of the contract despite the delay.]

(27) *Benché* il contenuto dell'incarico conferito a X abbia natura schiettamente professionale, va *nondimeno* rilevato che Y ha deliberato di affidare detto incarico ad un proprio socio. [Although the type of task assigned to X is of a clearly professional nature, it must nonetheless be noted that Y decided to entrust one of his associates with such a task.]

(28) La posizione assunta dalle parti in proposito ha valore unicamente di argomentazione difensiva, che non vincola in alcun modo la decisione del giudice, il quale può ritenere conforme a legge una tesi, *anche se* non sostenuta dalla parte che vi avrebbe teoricamente avuto interesse. [The position held by the parties on this issue has the mere validity of a defensive argument, which does not bind in any way the decision of the judge who may consider a thesis conforming to the law even though not supported by the party who may have an interest in doing so.]

The tables below reproduce the frequencies of logical markers in our corpus.

REGRESSIVE MODE	**Abs.**	**Norm.**
perchè	23	5.06
poichè	10	2.2
giacchè	11	2.42
siccome	4	0.88
dal momento che	0	
dato che	1	0.22
in quanto	39	8.58
per il fatto che/di	0	
TOTAL	**88**	**19.36**

Table 4. Frequency of regressive markers in the *Motivazioni*.

PROGRESSIVE MODE	Abs.	Norm.
perciò	5	1.1
quindi	53	11.6
dunque	40	8.8
di conseguenza	1	0.22
conseguentemente	10	2.2
infatti	44	9.68
pertanto	36	7.9
	189	**41.58**

Table 5. Frequency of progressive markers in the *Motivazioni*.

CONTRASTIVE MARKERS	Abs.	Norm.
anche se	6	1.32
benché	2	0.44
Malgrado	2	0.44
nonostante	12	2.64
per quanto	22	4.84
pur/ pure	32	7.04
(pur) tuttavia	9	1.98
sebbene	1	0.22
seppur/-e	5	1.1
	91	**20.0**

Table 6. Frequency of contrastive markers in the *Motivazioni*.

An interesting aspect which can be observed from the data in the tables is the high number of consecutive markers (both progressive and regressive). A closer look also reveals that progressive markers are used twice as frequently as either regressive or contrastive markers (respectively 41.58 vs. 19.36 and 20.0). This tendency seems to indicate that an orderly exposition moving from the cause to the effect, from the condition to the consequence, is the preferred mode of argumentation in Italian arbitral discourse, possibly because this facilitates the processing of the information on the part of the parties and is likely to make the content of the final decision more convincing.

4. Discussion

Although a corpus of 20 awards can hardly be exhaustively representative of arbitration discourse, it is nonetheless symptomatic of the way language is used and argumentation is organized in this domain. On this basis, it is now possible to interpret the results in the tables above in the light of a need for coherence and impartiality which, as observed above, are among the main requirements for an award to be considered valid.

The data presented in section 3.1 suggest that Italian Arbitrators tend to use formulaic and marked VS collocations "to better consolidate the legal importance and validity of arbitral awards" (Gotti and Anesa 2011) and mark the most crucial parts of the texts of the award. As a matter of fact, we can find VS forms in those sections which are meant to express disagreement with one of the parties and rejection of their requests, or which are intended to change a state of affairs in a damaging way for one of the parties. Such decisions, in fact, need to sound authoritative and binding, and VS forms and formulaic constructions seem to adequately perform this function by conferring on the judgment a marked deontic connotation and impact. Arbitrators use VS clusters also to comment on elements relevant to the judicial procedure leading to the final decision, stressing through these formulae its correctness, exhaustiveness and completeness. In this way the final judgment is represented as a necessary, unchallengeable and incontestable conclusion, with the purpose of reinforcing the sense of definitiveness which is at the core of arbitration as a valid alternative dispute resolution.

Some remarks are needed at this point to give some perspective to these results, which can be meaningfully interpreted in the light of the Italian legal context. The Civil Law system which characterizes Italian jurisdiction hinges on the primacy of the code and the written norm (Apple and Deyling 1995; Gibbons 2003): for this reason in this context standardized codifications or conventionally established ways of conveying meanings are favoured in order to effectively shape legal meanings (cf. Santulli 2006; Mortara Garavelli 2001). Strictly related to this is the absence in the Italian juridical culture of an impactful movement like The Plain English Movement (PEM, cf. Mellinkoff 1963; Tiersma 1999) has been for Anglophone legal cultures. PEM, primarily aimed at simplifying legal language, introduced the crucial distinction between the linguistic form and its function, more precisely, between the codification and its cognitive impact, on the one hand, and the validity or pragmatic value of its normative meaning, on the other. Such a distinction is significantly less marked (if not completely missing) in Civil Law contexts, where the 'form' is, instead, taken to directly point to, reflect, and reinforce the 'function'. This results in the traditional conservativism typical of Italian legal language (cf. Mortara Garavelli 2001), distinctively featured by the remarkable presence of frozen expressions, Latinisms, archaisms or unusual linguistic constructions, of which VS collocations can be seen as an example.

As to the use of markers of evidentiality in the *Motivazioni* move (cf. 3.2.), the quite marked predominance of non-mediated forms for the presentation of the content seems to respond to the need for impartiality, which is a crucial requirement for the arbitral procedure. Arbitrators tend to construct evidentiality and present meaning in a depersonalized, detached, and almost axiomatic manner (through expressions like *è evidente che, il Collegio ritiene che,* etc. corresponding to the English 'it is evident that', 'the Board believes that', etc.), as though the truth of such meanings were self-evident and unquestionable, as necessarily resulting from observation or general knowledge, common sense, or legal competence. The discrepancy between mediated and non-mediated resources seems also to suggest that arbitrators offer interpretations (usually through the formulaic expression l*'Arbitro/Collegio ritiene* [the Arbitrator/Board thinks]) only after the truth of a state of affairs has been established through non-mediated strategies. In other words, arbitrators rhetorically represent themselves not as much as actors subjectively evaluating a state of affairs, but rather as commenting and discussing objective truths (previously introduced by expressions such as *è chiaro, è ovvio* [it is clear, it is obvious]).

Another step towards impartiality is represented by the use of contrast markers, which equals the use of regressive markers. This is meant for the sake of completeness, comprehensiveness, and exhaustiveness, so as not to leave out any relevant views that the parties might have, even representing those meanings which appear to be contrary or indeed detrimental to establishing the arbitrator's viewpoint. In reality, contrastive resources, besides this function, are strategic devices used to guide interpretation by inferring a semantic hierarchy between meanings.

As to the coherent and persuasive presentation of the *Motivazioni* move (cf. 3.3.), the use of logical markers in general (both consecutive and contrastive) plays a key role, as they are meant to guide and facilitate the hermeneutic process by emphasizing the logical relationships between meanings, thus making the text more cognitively 'reader-friendly'.

More specifically, the predominance of progressive markers is quite significant. Mortara Garavelli (2001), in studying Italian statutory texts, observes that the regressive mode is the most widely used, since for a deontic text to have a certain impact it is quite expected and appropriate to first introduce a state of affairs and subsequently justify it. This standard is not respected in the *Motivazioni* move of the awards. This is possibly due to the fact that this move is the argumentative section of a performative text and, as such, it does not need to have an impact, but rather must be convincing, clear and coherent: here the interplay between meanings and their logical and sequential ordering is crucial. Placing the causes and conditions in a thematic position creates expectations and, at the same time, offers cognitive guidelines as to how the new information should be interpreted, i.e. the consequence, which in turn completes the overall meaning. In this way, by introducing and preparing each piece of informative material such strategies not only reflect a reader-friendly textualization – requiring a linear and consequential processing that minimizes decoding efforts – but also minimize the possibility of semantic contradictions, obscurities and misinterpretations, thus allowing the parties to understand the meaning, recognize the sense and the purpose of the provisions in the final decision, and eventually accept the award as binding.

References

Apple, James G. and Robert P. Deyling. 1995. *A Primer on the Civil-Law System*. Washington, D.C.: Federal Judicial Center,.

Belotti, Ulisse. 2003. "Generic Integrity in Italian Arbitration Rules". In *Legal Discourse In Multilingual and Multicultural Contexts: Arbitration Texts in Europe,* edited by Vijay Bhatia, Christopher Candlin and Maurizio Gotti, 19-40. Bern: Peter Lang.

—. forh. "'They say (.) what do you want (.) mind your own business': The Voices of 'Others' in Italian Arbitration Narratives". Paper presented at the *Colloqium on Exploring the discourses and practices of International Commercial Arbitration.* XVII European Symposium on Languages for Specific Purposes (Aarhus School of Business, University of Aarhus, 17-21 August 2009).

Benincà, Paola and Giampaolo Salvi. 1988. "L'ordine normale degli elementi nella frase semplice". In *Grande grammatica italiana di consultazione. Vol I. La frase. I sintagmi nominale e preposizionale*, Lorenzo Renzi, 119-129. Bologna: Il Mulino.

Bocchini, Ermanno (ed.). 2006. *L'Arbitrato*. Padova: CEDAM.

Ceccon, Roberto. 2000. "La Corte Arbitrale di Venezia, una nuova istituzione per attrarre l'arbitrato internazionale in Italia". *Le prospettive dell'arbitrato interno ed internazionale: il Regolamento della Corte Arbitrale di Venezia*, 7-12. Torino: Giappichelli.

Chafe, Wallace and Johanna Nichols (eds). 1986. *Evidentiality: The Linguistic Encoding of Epistemology*. Norwood, NJ: Ablex.

Consolo, Claudio. 2006. *Le impugnazioni delle sentenze e dei lodi.* Padova: CEDAM.

Cutolo, Daniele and Antonio Esposito. 2007. "The Reform of the Italian Arbitration Law. The Challenging of Arbitrators and the Setting of Time Limits". *Journal of International Arbitration* 24, no. 1: 49-62.

Degano, Chiara. 2010. "Indicators of Argumentation in Arbitration Awards: A Diachronic Perspective". In *The Discourses of Dispute Resolution*, edited by Vijay Bhatia, Christopher Candlin and Maurizio Gotti, 189-205. Bern: Peter Lang.

Ferrari, Angela. 1999. "Tra rappresentazione ed esecuzione: indicare la 'causalità testuale' con i nomi e con i verbi". *Studi di Grammatica Italiana* 18: 113-144.

Frison, Lorenza. 1988. "La struttura della frase semplice". *Grande grammatica italiana di consultazione. Vol I. La frase. I sintagmi nominale e preposizionale*, edited by Lorenzo Renzi, 7-87. Bologna: Il Mulino.

Gibbons, John. 2003. *Forensic Linguistics.* Oxford: Blackwell.

Gotti, Maurizio and Patrizia Anesa. 2011. "Professional Identities in Italian Arbitral Awards: The Spread of the Lawyers' Language". In *Discourse and Identity in the Professions*, edited by Vijay K. Bhatia and Paola Evangelisti Allori, 189-212. Bern: Peter Lang.

Hyland, Ken. 2005. *Metadiscourse.* London: Continuum.

Lino, Vincenzo. 2006. *Cassazione e Arbitrato.* Cercola: Edizioni Giuridiche Simone.

Maci, Stefania M. 2011. "Arbitration in Italy. Litigation Procedures in Arbitral Practice". In *Discourse and Identity in the Professions*, edited by Vijay K. Bhatia and Paola Evangelisti Allori, 213-237. Bern: Peter Lang.

Mellinkoff, David. 1963. *The Language of the Law.* Boston: Brown & Co.

Mortara Garavelli, Bice. 2001. *Le parole e la giustizia.* Torino: Einaudi.

Nariman, Fali S. 2000. "The Spirit of Arbitration: The Tenth Annual Goff Lecture". *Arbitration International* 16, no. 3: 261-278.

Nuyts, Jan. 2000. *Epistemic Modality, Language, and Conceptualization.* Amsterdam / Philadelphia: John Benjamins.

Palmer, Frank R. 1990. *Modality and the English Modals.* London: Longman.

Rossini Favretti, Rema. 2000. "Progettazione e costruzione di un corpus di italiano scritto: CORIS/CODIS". In *Linguistica e informatica. Multimedialità, corpora e percorsi di apprendimento,* edited by Rema Rossini Favretti, 39-56. Roma: Bulzoni.

—. 2008. “Text, Collocations and Frames”. In *Frames, Corpora and Language Representation*, edited by Rema Rossini Favretti, 79-94. Bologna: BUP.

Rovere, Giovanni. 2000. “L’avverbiale strumentale nel linguaggio giuridico”. In *Traduttori e giuristi a confronto. Interpretazione traducente e comparazione del discorso* giuridico, edited by Leandro Schena and Rita Snel Trampus, 25-35. Bologna: Clueb.

Santulli, Francesca. 2006. “Strutture argomentative e scelte lessicali nel linguaggio della giurisprudenza”. In *Prospettive nello studio del lessico italiano, Atti SILFI 2006*, edited by Emanuela Cresti, 461-469. Firenze: FUP.

Scott, Mike. 2004. *WordSmith Tools - Version 4*. Oxford: Oxford University Press.

Sornicola, Rosanna. 1994. “On Word Order Variability: A Study From A Corpus of Italian.” *Lingua e Stile* 29, no. 1, 25–57.

Taavitsainen, Irma. 2001. “Evidentiality and Scientific Thought-Styles: English Medical Writing in Late Middle English and Early Modern English”. In *Modality in Specialized Texts: Selected Papers of the 1st Cerlis Conference*, edited by Maurizio Gotti and Marina Dossena, 21-51. Bern: Peter Lang.

Thompson, Geoff. 2001. “Interaction in Academic Writing: Learning to Argue with the Reader”. *Applied Linguistics* 22, no. 1: 58-78.

Tiersma, Peter M. 1999. *Legal Language.* Chicago: University of Chicago Press.

Wierzbicka, Anna. 1994. “Semantics and Epistemology: The Meaning of ‘Evidentials’ in a Cross-Linguistic Perspective”. *Language Sciences* 16: 81-137.

CHAPTER TEN

CONTRASTIVE STUDY OF INTERNATIONAL COMMERCIAL ARBITRATION AND COURT JUDGMENTJUDGMENTS: INTERTEXTUALITY THROUGH METADISCOURSE IN ACTION

IGNACIO VÁZQUEZ AND DIANA GINER

1. Introduction

Arbitration is one of the key members of Alternative Dispute Resolution (ADR) mechanisms of solving disputes, together with conciliation and mediation. Companies are increasingly turning to ADR as the means to resolve their disputes, as a faster and less costly alternative to litigation. The parties themselves design their method of dispute resolution and choose the seat of arbitration and also the procedures. In arbitration, the parties agree to be bound by the decision of the arbitration tribunal. They do so by incorporating an arbitration clause in their contract. In principle, arbitration lies somewhere in between mediation and litigation, however, in practice there is an emerging view (Nariman 2000: 261; Bhatia 2008: 169) that international commercial arbitration, which emerged as an alternative to litigation to resolve disputes outside the courts, is being increasingly 'colonized' by litigation, thus threatening the integrity[1] of arbitration practice, which is contrary to the spirit of arbitration as a non-legal practice. One of the ways to investigate this view is to analyse and compare specific aspects of the discourses of arbitration and litigation in

[1] We refer here to the notion of "generic integrity", as was put forward by Bhatia (2004: 152). We understand that generic integrity is not static or pre-established. On the contrary, generic integrity is built as a response to the communicative needs associated with a particular professional culture.

order to see to what extent they have their own individual integrity. This study reports on one such attempt to compare certain aspects of arbitration awards and litigation court judgments.

More specifically, this chapter investigates the extent to which the use of hedges and boosters can shed light on the phenomena of hybridization and colonization of arbitration discourse by litigation practices and explore the motivations for such a process. Drawing on Fairclough's (1992) notion of intertextuality and Hyland's (2005) metadiscourse framework, we examine more specifically how judges and arbitrators use hedges and boosters as interactional resources to adopt a stance on both their propositions and their audience, and to express doubt and certainty in the negotiation of claims made. The central concern of the chapter is how texts (or rather judges and arbitrators as writers) negotiate past decisions, integrate these texts into their own texts and align themselves with such past decisions. Furthermore, we will argue that legal reasoning and interpretation is not primarily and exclusively an exercise of conclusive logic leading to inevitable outcomes, as claimed by traditional legal theory, but rather an exercise in inter-subjective positioning and making choices, though not entirely unrestricted ones.

Section 2 sets out the theoretical framework for the study. We argue for the dialogic nature of judgments and arbitration awards, by focussing on the use and distribution of some features of metadiscourse in different parts of the two genres. We draw on Bhatia's definition of genre as a configuration of text-internal and text-external resources, thus highlighting two kinds of relationship involving texts and contexts: a) within and across texts focusing primarily on text-internal properties (intertextuality); b) within and across genres involving primarily text-external resources (interdiscursivity). The focus of this section is the relationship between language, context and social practice. Here we are concerned with the social construction of dialogue in judgments and arbitral awards, which are the outcome of litigation and arbitration respectively. They both bear traces of various discursive events, some overtly and explicitly, some tacitly and implicitly. Judgments and awards both refer to events in real life, which are reconstructed discursively by the litigants in conference with their lawyers, or by the parties in an arbitration process. They are further re-contextualized in lawyers' submissions to the court or the arbitration tribunal, by the evidence given both in court and before the arbitration panel, and by the arguments made and the precedents cited by lawyers on behalf of their clients. The final step is for judges and arbitrators, after having considered the arguments and the evidence, to make a decision and to justify it in writing, further re-contextualizing what they read and heard in court.

The argument is that all structural elements of judgments and arbitration awards are dialogic, to a certain degree, but different elements draw on different kinds of dialogue. This section also discusses the rhetorical structure of both genres with a special focus on the way hedges and boosters are used as interactional metadiscourse markers.

Section 3 features the contrastive analysis of judgments and arbitration awards presented as instantiations of professional discursive practices. Finally, some concluding remarks are made.

2. Theoretical framework

When judges and arbitrators write judgments and arbitration awards, they make sense of their texts in relation to other similar and related texts. This is what we refer to as *intertextuality*. Intertextuality can operate at two levels. At one level, there can be the presence of specific words of others mixed with the words of the writer in question. This can be marked by a clear, explicit boundary between a writer's own text and another text, such as quotation marks. At another level, there can be a combination of different genres and different discourses. This is referred to as interdiscursivity[2] (Fairclough 1992; Chouliaraki and Fairclough 1999).

2.1. Fairclough and Intertextuality

A specific strength of Critical Discourse Analysis (CDA), according to Fairclough, is the extension of context to include intertextuality. This makes it possible to show and follow the traces of other texts and discourses in a text, and this, it will be shown, is one aspect of great importance in arbitral awards and judgments as instances of legal discourse.

The principle of intertextuality is, in fact, a re-conceptualization of the principle of the dialogic nature of texts, as the meaning of a particular text is seen as arising from relations between texts and social viewpoints, not from the minds of individuals. We make sense of texts in relation to similar and different texts. However, while all texts form intertextual links, different texts and different communities form different intertextual links: which texts are valued, why and how, and which ones are omitted.

---

[2] In Fairclough (1992) there is a distinction between intertextuality and interdiscursivity. The former is also referred to as "manifest intertextuality", the latter as "constitutive intertextuality" (or interdiscursivity).

Intertextual analysis in Fairclough's model of CDA provides the means to go beyond the analysis of texts and to analyse the discursive practices of text production, distribution and consumption. An intertextual perspective of text as a link in a chain of prior and future texts emphasizes the historicity of texts (text production). It explores the paths along which texts move, become transformed and shift from one text type to others (text distribution). And it emphasizes that text interpretation is shaped by prior texts, which a reader brings to bear on the interpretation of a new text (Fairclough 1992: 84f).

Fairclough raises several issues related to intertextuality. One of them is metadiscourse as "a peculiar form of manifest intertextuality where the text producer distinguishes different levels with her own text, and distances herself from some level of the text, treating the distanced level as if it were another, external text" (Fairclough 1992: 122). Metadiscourse can be marked lexico-grammatically through modality markers (hedges and boosters), expressions such as "sort of" or "definitely", or it can be marked as belonging to another domain of discourse by means of expressions like "in legal terms" or "technically speaking". The concept of "metadiscourse" implies that a speaker or writer is positioned outside a discourse or that he wants to distance himself from the represented discourse. Metadiscourse is a clear manifestation of intertextuality and is closely related to the dialogic nature of the documents under scrutiny.

This is the type of strategy used by the judges in a criminal appeal, for example, when they write: "Neither disputed that they dug a grave, although they called it 'a hole'" in the following paragraph extracted from (Osland v The Queen).

> "[3] The prosecution case was that Mrs Osland and David Albion together planned to murder Mr Osland. It was put that, in furtherance of their plan, they dug a grave for their intended victim during the day of 30 July 1991. Later, on the evening of the same day and in furtherance of the plan alleged, Mrs Osland mixed sedatives in with Mr Oslands dinner in sufficient quantity to induce sleep within an hour. According to the prosecution case, David Albion carried the plan to finality after Mr Osland went to bed by fatally hitting him over the head with an iron pipe in the presence of Mrs Osland. And later, he and Mrs Osland buried Mr Osland in the grave they had earlier prepared. Mrs Osland and David Albion both gave evidence at the trial. Neither disputed that they dug a grave, although they called it "a hole".

This strategy allows the judges to represent the defendants' discourse (evidence given at the trial) in their own discourse (the judgment) and at the same time to distance themselves from the defendants' representation and to put forward their own representation of the other text. This is done through constantly reminding the reader that the information displayed comes from the party's contention (Mrs Osland).

Our hypothesis assumes that the same applies to arbitrators when they write awards. Central to these arguments is the idea of dialogue and negotiation. If legal literacy involves negotiating a dialogue between different levels of textuality, at a basic level it requires a capacity simultaneously to use texts effectively in practical circumstances and also to be aware of its contingency, its political and ideological functionality and its generic conventionality. In a judgment, the writer enters into a number of dialogues with previous texts: with the evidence, arguments and submissions made by the litigants in court and with similar decisions in the past (precedent). In an arbitration award, the same applies to previous awards.

Both judges and arbitrators also enter into a dialogue with possible future texts: with a possible appeal against their decisions, and with other judges and lawyers who will be involved in similar cases in the future. And finally, writers may enter into a dialogue with their colleagues on the bench who may have decided a case differently.

2.2. Hedges and boosters as instantiations of Interactional Metadiscourse

For the purpose of studying the use of hedges and boosters we adopted Hyland's taxonomy of interactional metadiscourse (Hyland and Tsé 2004; Hyland 2005). Hyland (2005) proposed an overall typology[3] of the resources employed by writers to express their positions and connect with readers. The model provides a comprehensive and integrated way of examining the means by which interaction is achieved in academic argument and how the discoursal preferences of different cultural contexts construct both writers and readers. Hyland uses metadiscourse as the "cover term for the self-reflective expressions used to negotiate interactional meanings in a text, assisting the writer (or speaker) to express a viewpoint and engage with readers as members of a particular community" (Hyland 2005: 46). Metadiscourse thus offers a way of understanding the interpersonal resources judges and arbitrators use to present propositional

[3] Many other definitions and taxonomies of metadiscourse have been proposed: Vande Kopple (1985), (2002); Crismore and Fansworth (1990); Markkanen *et al.* (1993(; Luuka (1994); Bunton (1999); Hyland (2000); Hyland and Tse (2004); Dafouz (2003).

material, and therefore a means of investigating the way they reason.

According to Hyland (2005), there are five categories of interactional metadiscourse: hedges, boosters, attitude markers, engagement markers and self-mentions. Of these, we decided to study two complementary rhetorical strategies (hedges and boosters), as they generally emerge as the most frequently employed interactional metadiscourse markers. Hedges and boosters are two sides of a same coin. They are communicative strategies used for increasing or reducing the force of statements. Their importance in professional discourse lies in their contribution to establishing an interactive tenor, conveying both epistemic and affective meaning. [4]

As a summary of the theoretical framework, we combine intertextual analysis from Fairclough's model of (Critical) Discourse Analysis (Fairclough 1992), which provides the means to go beyond the analysis of texts and analyse the discursive practices of text production, distribution and consumption, with Bhatia's multiperspective model of discourse (Bhatia 2004: 18-19), which makes it possible to view discourse as text, genre, professional practice or social practice, and Hyland's model of metadiscourse.

2.3. Role of judgments and awards

Both in the common law and in the civil law legal systems, judgments are extremely important texts; they are a source of law. On a practical level a judgment is the final decision in a legal dispute, which is argued and settled in a court of law representing an order of the court determining winners and losers. However, the function of a judgment goes beyond the settlement of specific disputes. It has wider implications with respect to

---

[4] More specifically, hedges are linguistic devices that indicate the writer's decision to recognize alternative voices and viewpoints and so withhold complete commitment to a proposition. Boosters, on the other hand, are linguistic resources that allow writers to close down alternatives and express certainty in what they say. They are most commonly expressed through deontic and epistemic modality markers, modal verbs, and lexical items. According to the broad definition adopted in this study, boosters include: *always, beyond doubt, certain, certainly, clear, clearly, conclusively,, definite, definitely, demonstrate, doubtless, evident, evidently, find, finds, found, incontestable, indisputable, must (possibility), obviously, prove, show, undeniable,* etc. Hedges include: *about, almost, apparently, appear, approximately, broadly, claim, argue, estimate, fairly, feel, frequently, in general, in my opinion, likely, maybe, might, mostly, perhaps, plausible, possibly*, etc. (Cf. Hyland 2005).

the past as well as the future. With respect to the past, a judgment justifies a court's decision and persuades the court's audience of the correctness of this decision – that is, that the decision is based on law. This includes providing a public account of the reasoning process, which leads to a judge's decision. With respect to the future, judgments have a guiding function for other judges, lawyers and the general public. A judgment states what the law is, and by stating the law, a judicial decision becomes binding for similar cases in the future. Thus, a judgment has a *justifying* as well as a *declarative* function (Maley 1985).

In the same way, an arbitral award is a determination on the merits by an arbitration tribunal, and is analogous to a judgment in a court of law. It is referred to as "award", even where all of the claimant's claims fail (and thus no money needs to be paid by either party), or the award is of a non-monetary nature. It also has wider implications with respect to the past and to the future. With respect to the past, an arbitration award justifies an arbitral tribunal's decision and persuades the parties of the appropriateness of this decision. This also includes providing a public account of the arbitrators reasoning process. With respect to the future, arbitration awards also guide other arbitrators and the general public. Therefore, also arbitration awards have a justifying as well as a declarative function.

Judgments are not only reasoning and justifying texts, they are also coercive texts. They can force people to do things. In criminal proceedings they can affect bodies in a physical sense by sending people to prison, or even, in some countries, to death. In civil proceedings they can force people to pay compensation for harm done to others, or to perform actions agreed on in contracts, to give just a few examples. In arbitration procedures arbitral awards also seem to perform a coercive function as they are binding on both parties.

2.4. The language of judgments and arbitral awards: declaring and justifying

At the macro level, a generic structure of arbitration awards and judgments has been identified (Maley 1985; Bhatia 1993) as well as a relationship between the structural elements and the communicative functions of declaring and justifying. Judgments consist of five parts or stages:

1. Facts: account of the events
2. Issue(s): problem(s) to be solved
3. Reasoning: justification of decision
4. Conclusion: principle or rule that applies to case
5. Finding: Solution to problem posed in Issue.

The structure of arbitral awards is not so well established as that of judgments, but there are, nonetheless, certain elements that seem to be essential for the generic structure of each award to be fully developed. The following structure is tentatively proposed on the basis of our analysis only:[5]

1. Introduction / The parties
2. Procedural History/ Summary of procedure
3. Summary of facts and Parties' Contentions/ Factual Background
4. Analysis of issues /Considerations / Applicable law / Legal Considerations
5. Decisions.

Both judgments and arbitral awards have some features in common. They have a justificatory, a declaratory and a coercive function. The justificatory function of a judgment is represented by the structural elements 'issue' and 'reasoning' ("Procedural history" and "Summary of Facts" in awards). The declaratory function is represented by the elements 'conclusion' and 'finding' in judgments and by "considerations" and "decisions" in awards. The coercive function affects all parts of both judgments and awards.

In general terms, we can rely on studies of the communicative purpose and the macro structure of judgments and arbitration awards[6] and we have some insights into the realisation of communicative purpose and structural elements, but the reasoning of judges and arbitrators, the negotiation of previous decisions, the positioning of writer and reader are still a relatively unexplored territory.

---

[5] Alternative descriptions of the structure of arbitration awards are proposed in other studies in this volume; cf. Bhatia and Lung, Chapter Three; Bhatia and Han, Chapter Eleven.

[6] Maley (1985) and Bhatia (1993) are the main references when dealing with the structure of judgments.

2.5. Arbitral awards and judgments as instantiations of professional discursive practices

When comparing awards and judgments, the first impression we have is that in both cases we are dealing with legal genres: special items or words that have a legal flavour or a special meaning in legal documents like judgments - such as *claimant, respondent, construction, privilege* - also appear in arbitral awards. We also come across functional expressions that have the same flavour, for example *hereto* and *notwithstanding*. This may sound too superficial; therefore, we should be looking more in depth into other aspects of the linguistic practices of both professional genres, such as their rhetorical structure, their communicative purpose and their way of reasoning, to assess whether superficial similarities are also a manifestation of deeper similar discursive practices.

The two genres analysed in this study have been selected for being the final expression of two legal professional processes. Judgments and arbitral awards are outcomes of the processes of litigation and arbitration respectively, of which they represent the most crucial documents, where authors have to defend their viewpoints strongly in order to make their decisions appear fair and well grounded and, therefore, credible. The central argument here is that the discourse of arbitration, as it appears in arbitration awards, is constituted by identifiable professional and linguistic practices which make it specific (arbitrators have the authority to impose their decision on the parties, but their intervention is meant to be less authoritative than that of judges, as they have been selected by the parties themselves), but at the same time it shares features with the professional practices of litigation discourse. This is the result of mixing "private intentions" with "socially recognized communicative purposes" and often of genre "bending" (Bhatia 2004: 73), which amounts to appropriation of genres and generic resources, including the textual resources, generic conventions, the professional practices and the disciplinary cultures that motivate these practices. What we find here is an inter-generic hybridization of arbitration awards by judgments.

Drawing on documentary data, the study investigates the extent to which the integrity of arbitration principles is maintained in arbitration practice, pointing out phenomena of hybridization and colonization of arbitration discourse by litigation practices and exploring the motivations for such an inter-discursive process.

3. Analysis of judgments and arbitration awards

In this section we are going to deal with the different instantiations of interactional metadiscourse markers in arbitration and litigation practices. As a pilot study, we have selected a sample of three items per category (three arbitral awards and three judgments). We will take examples where intertextuality through metadiscourse occurs and we will analyse each example to see what the intention of the author appears to be in relation to the context where these elements appear.

3.1. Awards

The awards used for the analysis in this chapter have been randomly selected from the Investment Treaty Arbitration website. The cases are Mondev International. Ltd. V. United States, Desert Line v. Yemen, and BG Group Plc v. Argentina. In the following examples, we will see instantiations of hedging that intend to distance the author from the content expressed in the propositions. In this way, in example (1) below "could possibly constitute" and "might arguably have violated" are pointing to an alternative interpretation of the facts. In addition, we see an instance of an enhanced alternative viewpoint thanks to the combination of a booster and a hedge ("must still be possible"). Once the alternatives have been exposed, the author proceeds to conclude. The reader can notice the concluding character of this statement thanks to the insertion of the booster "cannot". "Cannot assist" conveys a high level of commitment on behalf of the author to the propositional content of this concluding remark.

> (1) 70. Thus events or conduct prior to the entry into force of an obligation for the respondent State may be relevant in determining whether the State has subsequently committed a breach of the obligation. But it *must* still *be possible* to point to conduct of the State after that date which is itself a breach. In the present case the only conduct which *could possibly constitute* a breach of any provision of Chapter 11 is that comprised by the decisions of the SJC and the Supreme Court of the United States, which between them put an end to LPAs claims under Massachusetts law. Unless those decisions were themselves inconsistent with applicable provisions of Chapter 11, the fact that they related to pre–1994 conduct which *might arguably have violated* obligations under NAFTA (had NAFTA been in force at the time) *cannot assist* Mondev.
> (Mondev International Ltd. v. United States, page 11)

Excerpt (2) below is an example of intertextuality in which the legal bindings related to arbitration are exposed. That is, expressions typical of litigation are making appearance in this document in order to provide legal support to the argumentation. Of course, the final decision would be valid even if this was not made explicit in the award. However, the arbitrator prefers to remind both parties of the legal consequences of this decision. Although most of the metadiscursive devices are contained in the legal quotation, in selecting the text the author is aware of the binding connotations these boosters have. Here, "established", "shall decide", "shall be binding" and "established" are functioning as deontic modality markers and they are brought into the award in order to warn or remind the parties that the arbitrator's decision, subjective as it may be, is binding (unless they decide to take the case to litigation).

> (2) 100. Article 1131 of NAFTA provides that:
> "1. A Tribunal *established* under this Section *shall decide* the issues in dispute in accordance with this Agreement and applicable rules of international law.
> 2. An interpretation by the Commission of a provision of this Agreement *shall be binding* on a Tribunal *established* under this Section."
> (Mondev International Ltd. v. United States, page 16)

On the whole, in the reasoning section of the awards we can observe that both boosters and hedges are being used in favour of the author with self-distancing or engaging purposes towards the propositional content of other texts or of the author's own words. Consequently, we could say that these interactional elements also fulfil a justifying or declaring function within the reasoning section of the awards analysed in this chapter. In the conclusions section, the author also appears to be using intertextuality through metadiscourse in order to make the tone more declarative when presenting the arguments that are going to support the final decision. Example (3) illustrates this point with "should never have been brought". The combination of the hedge "should" and the booster "never" create a statement with a clear declarative function. Thanks to the combination of these two elements ("should" and "never"), the effect produced is that of closing down alternatives. A similar effect is achieved through the use of the modal "should" in example (4), in which the author shows a fairly high degree of commitment to the statement containing it. Therefore, it can be affirmed that this element entails a declarative function and signals the approximation to the final decision.

(3) 58. As to the question of costs and expenses, the United States sought orders that Mondev pay the Tribunal's costs and the legal expenses of the United States on the basis that its claim was unmeritorious and *should* never have been brought.
(Desert Line Projects LLC v. Yemen, page 26

(4) 247. The content of the minimum standard *should* not be rigidly interpreted and it should reflect evolving international customary law.
(BG Group Plc v. Argentina , page 41)

In example (5), taken from the conclusions section, we see that the author uses the booster "cannot be", expressing high epistemic modality, with the effect of ruling out alternative views to the one here expressed.

(5) 152. But the distinction between conduct compliant with or in breach of NAFTA Article 1105(1) *cannot be* co–extensive with the distinction between tortuous conduct and breach of contract. For example, the Massachusetts legislation immunizes public authorities from liability for assault and battery. An investor whose local staff had been assaulted by the police while at work *could well claim* that its investment was not accorded "treatment in accordance with international law, including... full protection and security" if the government were immune from suit for the assaults. In such a case, the availability of an action in tort against individual (*possibly unidentifiable*) officers *might not be* a sufficient basis to avoid the situation being characterised as a breach of Article 1105(1).
(Mondev International Ltd. v. United States, page 25)

This opening statement is developed further in the same paragraph with information that intends to justify such affirmation. In the process of justification the author employs legislation relevant to the case, selects information and presents it in a way that will best support the initial statement. This exposition of information contained in the legislation is not made "raw" though, but there is ample recourse to more metadiscursive elements. In this way, "could well claim", "possibly unidentifiable" and "might not be" are resulting from this initial premise. The author ends this argumentation by concluding that "the availability of an action in tort against individual officers might not be sufficient" for the situation to be considered a breach. These words already give the audience a pretty evident clue to the final outcome in this award, as if the author wanted to orient the audience towards receiving his decision as the most suitable or commonsensical one.

In example (6), the author prefers to keep an impersonal tone when stating his/her personal opinion, by using third person self-reference ("the

Arbitral Tribunal"). However, the reference to the Arbitral Tribunal entails a declarative function given the powerful character of arbitral figures in contemporary society. In consequence, although "consider" and "necessary" might be suggesting a personal opinion lacking authority in other circumstances, in this context the result is a declaration. In addition, this argument anticipates the final decision while at the same time supporting it. Thus, in this case, intertextuality is realised through an expression that has the same function as a booster since it is used to express commitment to the propositional content of the statement in question.

> (6) 215. There is therefore no reason to scrutinize the other violations of the BIT alleged by the Claimant and contested by the Respondent. The Arbitral Tribunal *considers* it *unnecessary* to determine whether the factual record ultimately also supports a finding of liability under other provisions of the BIT.
> (Desert Line Projects LLC v. Yemen, page 34)

Then, in example (7), the author concedes the possibility ("may") that the supporting argumentation is brief and not too specific ("may be exceptionally succinct"), but is still stating that he agrees with it, although this agreement could include the exception of minor details ("the present Arbitral Tribunal broadly comes to the same conclusion").

> (7) 272. The Arbitral Tribunal observes that the Yemeni Arbitral Tribunal held with this regard that "[t]his claim is not based on legal or contractual grounds" (Exh. CM–88, p. 36). This reasoning *may be exceptionally* succinct, but the present Arbitral Tribunal *broadly* comes to the same conclusion, as explained herein below.
> (Desert Line Projects LLC v. Yemen, page 40)

Equally, in the final part of the award, the decision (example 8 below), we can find metadiscursive elements that are meant to be playing in favour of the main author's intentions.

> (8) C. Award
> In view of the above, the Arbitral Tribunal hereby *orders* that:
> 1. The Arbitral Tribunal has jurisdiction over the present dispute;
> 2. The Settlement Agreement contravened the Respondent's obligations under Art. 3 of the BIT and, therefore, it is not entitled to international effect;
> 3. The Yemeni Arbitral Award *shall be implemented* in its entirety, and be fully respected as definitively binding on both Parties;

4. The Respondent's counterclaims *shall be dismissed…*
(Desert Line Projects LLC v. Yemen, pages 44-45)

The ultimate purpose of the award is to reach a decision that suits both parties and, in order to do so, the arbitrator needs to resort to certain strategies that will allow him or her to put a slant on the document. To start with, the author shows full commitment to the propositional content by making use of a booster that gives these final words a fastening or compelling tone. As can be seen, this is where the metadiscursive elements "orders", "shall" and "will" come into play. Even though the document has legal power of its own, the author seems to prefer to use this kind of term not only to signal that the final decision is coming, but also to endow this decision with an extra dose of legal authority. Possibly, the author hopes in this way to avoid any questioning of this decision too. Example (8) displays various instantiations of the booster "shall" ("shall be implemented", "shall be dismissed") and the performative verb "order" conveying a clear declarative function to the text.

In example (9), drawn from the decision of another award, the same strategy is deployed. The author makes use of boosters as part of the declarative discourse that states the decision taken. We even notice in this award that the booster has been typed in capital letters ("DECIDES"). Again this seems to have a double purpose. On the one hand, the author is facilitating the visualisation of the decision and, on the other hand, he is enhancing the subsequent propositional content.

(9) For the foregoing reasons, the Tribunal unanimously DECIDES:
[…]
(e) That each party shall bear its own costs, and shall bear equally the expenses of the Tribunal and the Secretariat.
(Mondev International Ltd. v. United States, page 26)

The same applies to example (10), from another award, where the booster "decision" appears separated from the actual decision.

(10) XII. Decision
467. For the foregoing reasons, the Arbitral Tribunal unanimously renders the following award:
[…]
(3) The Republic of Argentina breached Article 2.2 of the Argentina–U.K. BIT.
(4) The Republic of Argentina shall pay BG Group Plc. the sum of US$185,285,485.85 (one hundred and eighty five million two hundred and eighty five thousand four hundred and eighty five US dollars and 85/100)

for damages to BG Group Plc.'s investment claimed in this arbitration.
(5) The Republic of Argentina shall pay BG Group Plc. interest on the sum set out in decision (4) above from 6 January 2002 until the date of payment, at the average interest rate applicable to US six–month certificates of deposit, compounded semi–annually.
(BG Group Plc v. Argentina, page 60)

3.2. Judgments

In this section, we will carry out a similar analysis of metadiscourse in judgments in order to obtain contrastive results to be compared with those related to arbitral awards. The judgments in this section have been randomly selected, as was the case for the awards. They were rendered in three different cases: Indeni Petroleum v. V.G. Limited (from the Southern African Legal Information Institute), Federal Deposit Insurance v. Cromwell Crossroads Ltd. (United States District Court of Connecticut), and Yorli v. Sheanan (United States Court of Appeals, Seventh Circuit). The analysis will first address the reasoning sections and subsequently the conclusions and finding sections of the judgments.

In example (11), from the reasoning section of Indeni Petroleum v. V.G. Limited, the booster "must" is repeated twice ("must have been tried" "there must be a judgment"), thus enhancing the propositional content, namely the conditions that "must" be fulfilled for the Law Reform Miscellaneous provisions to be applicable.

(11) The main thrust of Mr. Kabukas argument is that for the court to exercise its discretion under Section 4 of the Law Reform Miscellaneous Provisions) Act, Cap 74 the proceedings *must* have been tried by a court of record and there *must* be a judgment.
(Indeni Petroleum v V.G. Limited, page 12)

A similar effect is produced in examples (12) and (13). In example (12), referred to the case of Yorli v. Sheanan, the author stresses the necessity that certain conditions be fulfilled for the relevant legislation to apply, through the booster "must". In example (13), from the same case, the author presents the contention of one of the parties with a high degree of commitment, while attaching a tone of subjectivity to the exposition of such contention.

(12) In order to establish a violation of § 1983, a plaintiff *must* show "he was deprived of a right secured by the Constitution or laws of the United States and that the deprivation was caused by a person acting under color of state law." Kelley v. Myler, 149 F. 3d 641, 648 (7th Cir. 1998) (emphasis

added). In order to establish the causation element of a § 1983 violation, a plaintiff *must* show that the defendant "was personally involved or acquiesced in the alleged constitutional violation." Kelly v. Municipal Courts of Marion County, Indiana, 97 F.3d 902, 909 (7th Cir. 1996).
(Yorli v. Sheanan, page 8)

(13) *It is undisputed that* Lewis *felt* as far back as 1994 that he was the victim of discrimination. Under Hardin, the continuing violation cannot save Lewis' claims.
(Yorli v. Sheanan, page 25)

In example (14) the author uses the hedge "presumably" with the main intention of reducing his commitment to the statement referring to a typographical error.

(14) As there was, *presumably*, a typographical error in the Plaintiff's motion to enforce, the court denied the Plaintiff's motion without prejudice and allowed the motion on or before January 31, 2006.
(Federal Deposit Insurance v Cromwell Crossroads, page 14)

Moving on to the conclusions sections, also here we have encountered cases where strategies of commitment modulation are used to orient the reception of the judgment. To emphasise the reasons that led the defendants to ask that some parts of the plaintiff's statements be struck, in example (15), the author quotes their words attributing them explicitly to the parties by means of the projecting clause "they argue". In addition, the use of the verb "argue" has a hedging effect, as it signals a certain distance of the drafter from the defendants' personal opinion.

(15) Defendants Fred and Frank Guerra and Andrew Douvris have filed motions to strike plaintiffs' local rule 56.1 statements. They *argue* that the court *should* strike certain paragraphs of plaintiffs' responses to defendants' fact statements because these paragraphs "do not squarely and concisely respond to [defendant's] Statement of Facts, but instead, assert additional matters, or that admit the statement of fact but then assert various other matters."
(Yorli v. Sheanan page 30)

In example (16), the judge describes a past action. However, in doing so, the author makes use of a hedging expression in order to distance himself from that action. Therefore, the description is "re-constructed" adding up the personal perspective of the author through metadiscourse.

(16) The court granted this motion on January 4, 1994, but *it appears that* the change in this action's title caption was not effected.
(Federal Deposit Insurance v Cromwell Crossroads, page 28)

As it seems to be typical of the finding sections of both the awards and the judgments analysed in this chapter, the authors prefer to make use of boosters that are meant to provide their discourse with a tone of commitment and enforceability. Even though in both cases authors are granted the legal power to make their decisions enforceable, they seem to make recourse to discursive strategies that highlight the presence of the author. Example (17) and (18) below clearly illustrate this point:

(17) (1) the Clerk of the Court *shall* change the title caption in the docket for this case so that "Federal Deposit Insurance Corporation as Receiver of Central Bank" is removed and substituted with "C.C. Cromwell Limited Partnership" as the plaintiff; (2) all further submissions by the parties *shall* contain the following caption: Limited Partnership, Plaintiff, v. Cromwell
(Federal Deposit Insurance v Cromwell Crossroads page 28)

(18) For the reasons we have given, we *find* no merit in the appeal which we dismiss with costs. The costs *are to be taxed* in default of agreement.
(Indeni Petroneum v V.G. Limited, page 15)

In particular, in example (17), the expressions "shall change" and "shall contain", are reminiscent of the constructions found in the conclusions sections in the awards. In example (18) "are to be taxed" expresses a sense of obligation, while "we find", which Hyland includes in his boosters taxonomy (2005: 221), conveys a sense of strong commitment to the propositional content of the statement containing it. Furthermore, through the use of this verb, the reader can easily identify this statement as the judge's final decision.

4. Final Considerations

Litigation and arbitration are two different conflict resolution methods. However, as explained in the introduction section of this chapter, they perform very similar functions in our society: they both declare winners and losers in a dispute, and in both judgments and arbitration awards the author unfolds information extracted from the parties' contentions and legal documents with the aim of reaching a ruling. In addition, the two genres share a similar structure, with sections in which the arguments of the parties and the related legal background are exposed to the public, followed by sections in which, on the ground of such reasoning process, conclusions are drawn and the final ruling is declared.

Drawing on Fairclough's conception of metadiscourse as a form of intertextuality whereby the author distances herself from some levels of the text (Fairclough 1992: 122), we have focussed in particular on the categories of boosters and hedges as interactional metadiscourse markers. Their distancing or committing effects have been investigated in comparable samples of awards and judgments, and the results obtained clearly confirm that intertextuality through metadiscourse is common in both genres.

Intertextuality prototypically appears in the shape of quotations embedded in a text, and this is also the case in our samples. After all, both judgments and awards must include the parties' contentions, legal references and other relevant information that supports the argumentation of the author. As it would be impossible to quote these discourses entirely in the final documents, the author picks the information that he or she considers most important or relevant to support the final decision, an operation which is not neutral in itself. However, intertextuality takes also a more indirect form: the information selected is not reported "raw", as the author constructs his or her own argumentation using strategies that help him or her show a higher or lower level of commitment towards the propositional content of their statements, among which boosters and hedges play a fundamental role

In the analysis here carried out, on the one hand, we have been able to see how hedges can open alternative paths to develop the author's argumentation, or lessen the author's commitment to the propositional content of a particular statement with the aim of leading the reader to an agreement with the final decision or ruling. Hedges perform, then, a justifying function. On the other hand, boosters perform an enhancing effect on the propositional content, by focussing the attention of the reader on certain arguments that result crucial for the development of the reasoning leading to the final decision. In consequence, hedges and boosters are strongly related to the justifying function of language inasmuch as they appear within the reasoning sections of both awards and judgments. In the conclusions and decision sections of both the awards and judgments analysed in this chapter, authors use a more authoritative tone and make use of boosters with that objective in mind. Thus, it could be affirmed that boosters perform a clear declarative function in these sections, and even more so in the decision sections.

The two distinct language functions can be identified then in both judgments and awards, with the justifying function located mainly in the reasoning section, while the conclusions and findings display a prevalence of the declarative function. Incidentally, this shows that the two functions that Maley found in the language of judgments (1985) are also present, in the language of arbitral awards, realized by means of intertextuality in the shape of interactional discourse markers.

We could have expected differences in the realization of the declarative and justifying functions in judgments and awards since these two processes differ greatly in the way they are meant to solve conflicts. Arbitrators have to be accountable to their customers in a way judges do not need to. On the one hand, judges stand in front of the two parties with the mere obligation of deciding on a verdict based upon the facts they are given and the whole process is based on litigation. On the other hand, arbitrators have to decide, mainly on the basis of common sense, and convince the parties that their decision is the most logical and coherent according to the facts given. Therefore, it might be expected that awards differ from judgments for a greater effort of arbitrators to actively convince their audience – the audience they have been hired by – of the validity of their decision. Besides, arbitrators may use modality and persuasion to promote themselves for future clients too.

However, after the comparative study carried out, we can conclude that no differences were found in the writers' use of hedges and boosters to present information that will support their final decisions in judgments and arbitral awards. In particular, similarities in hedging and boosting strategies and functions between judgments and arbitral awards presumably depend on the discourse community's expectations, and the addresser's specific intentions. Given that in awards and in judgments alike the expectations of the community and the communicative purpose are to declare a winning and a losing party, both genres require the decisions to be thoroughly justified. These justifications often imply resorting to intertextual examples of relevant legislation or the parties' argumentation. As stated above, the authors of both the awards and the judgments examined in this chapter make use of intertextuality through metadiscourse. They do so in order to support their ideas without sounding too assertive, and also to make declarations in the conclusions and decision sections. These results suggest that there might be other devices or rhetorical strategies arbitral awards and judgments share. Our intention in the future is to carry out, then, an analysis of further common elements within a larger corpus of judgments and arbitral awards with the objective of, perhaps, finding common patterns of argumentation.

References

Bhatia, Vijay K. 1993. *Analysing Genre. Language Use in Professional Settings*. London: Longman.
—. 2004. *Worlds of Written Discourse. A Genre-based view.* London: Continuum.
—. 2008. "Genre Analysis, ESP and Professional Practice". *English for Specific Purposes* 27: 161-174.
Bunton, David. 1999. "The Use of Higher Level Metatext in PhD Theses". *English for Specific Purposes* 18: S41-S46.
Chouliaraki, Lilie and Norman Fairclough. 1999. *Discourse in Late Modernity. Rethinking Critical Discourse Analysis.* Edinburgh: Edinburgh University Press,.
Crismore, Avon and Robert Fansworth. 1990. "Metadiscourse in Popular and Professional Science Discourse". In *The Writing Scholar. Studies in Academic discourse,* edited by Walter Nash, 118-136. Newbury Park: Sage Publications.
Dafouz, Milne E. 2003. "Metadiscourse Revisited: A Contrastive Study of Persuasive Writing in Professional Discourse". *Estudios Ingleses de la Universidad Complutense* 11: 29-52.
Fairclough, Norman. 1992. *Discourse and Social Change.* Cambridge: Polity Press.
Hyland, Ken. 2000. "Hedges, Boosters and Lexical Invisibility: Noticing Modifiers in Academic Texts". *Language Awareness* 9, no. 4: 179-197.
Hyland, Ken. 2005. *Metadiscourse*. London: Continuum.
Hyland, Ken and Polly Tse. 2004. "Metadiscourse in Academic Writing: A Reappraisal. *Applied Linguistics* 25. no. 2: 156-177.
Luuka, Minna R. 1994. "Metadiscourse in Academic Texts". In *Text and Talk in Professional Contexts,* edited by Britte-Louise Gunnarson, Per Linell and Bengt Nordberg, 77-88. Uppsala: ASLA (The Swedish Association of Applied Linguistics).
Maley, Yon. 1985. "Judicial discourse: the case of legal judgment". In *The Cultivated Australian,* edited by John E. Clark, 159-175. Hamburg: Buske.
Markkanen, Raija, Margaret S. Steffensen and Avon Crismore. 1993. "Quantitative Contrastive Study of Metadiscourse. Problems in Design and Analysis of Data". *Papers and Studies in Contrastive Linguistics* 23: 137-151.
Nariman, Fali S. 2000. "The Spirit of Arbitration: The Tenth Annual Goff Lecture". *Arbitration International* 16, no.3: 261-278.

Vande Kopple, William. J. 1985. "Some exploratory discourse on metadiscourse". *College Composition and Communication* 36: 63-94.

—. 2002. "Metadiscourse, discourse and issues in composition and rhetoric". In *Discourse Studies in Composition*, edited by Ellen Barton and Gail Stygall, 91-113. New Jersey: Hampton Press.

Awards and judgments[7]

BG Group Plc v. Argentina, UNCITRAL (UK/Argentina BIT) retrieved from <http://ita.law.uvic.ca/documents/BG-Award.pdf>.

Desert Line Projects LLC v. Yemen ICSID case No ARB/05/17 retrieved from <http://ita.law.uvic.ca/documents/DesertLine.pdf>

Federal Deposit Insurance Corp. as receiver of Centralbank v. Cromwell Crossroads Associates, Ltd. Partnership et al. Case No. No. 3:93CV00691(DJS) retrieved from <http://www.ctd.uscourts.gov/>

Indeni Petroleum Refinery Company Ltd v V.G. Ltd (84/2004) [2007] ZMSC 22; SCZ No. 22 of 2007 (4 September 2007) retrieved from <http://www.saflii.org/zm/cases/ZMSC/2007/22.html>

Mondev International Limited v. United States of America, case No. ARB(AF)/99/2 retrieved from <http://ita.law.uvic.ca/documents/Mondev-Final.pdf>

Osland v The Queen (1998) 197 CLR 316. Gaudron, McHugh, Gummow, Kirby and Callinan JJ, On appeal from the Supreme Court of Victoria, Australia.

Yorli P. Huff v. Michael F. Sheahan, in his official capacity as Sheriff of Cook County, case No. 05-1310, retrieved from <http://www.ca7.uscourts.gov/tmp/4W0GKCRF.pd

---

[7] Unless differently indicated, all websites were last visited on 15/03/2012.

CHAPTER ELEVEN

COMPARATIVE GENRE ANALYSIS OF CHINESE ARBITRATION AWARDS AND LITIGATION JUDGMENTS*

VIJAY BHATIA AND HAN ZHENGRUI

1. Introduction

Professional discourses have been a major research focus in the fields of genre studies and applied linguistics for some time now. Through the analysis of highly standardized genres like legislative provisions (Bhatia 1989, 1993, 1997), scientific journal papers (Hyland 2000), and tax forms (Devitt 1991), researchers have found various ways to identify and analyze the linguistic and generic features used in professional genres. The main purpose of these studies has been not simply to learn the discursive characteristics of specific genres, but also to provide instructional materials for related professional training/teaching (Bazerman and Paradis 1991). Researchers have also analyzed professional genres from a much broader social constructionist viewpoint (Berkenkotter and Huckin 1995; Bhatia 2004; Swales 1998) attempting to uncover and reconstruct the professional practices associated with and usually hidden behind these visible genres. This chapter is meant to contribute to this line of research by analyzing arbitration awards and litigation judgments produced in the People's Republic of China, by examining their generic features and their production, consumption, and exploitation in specific arbitral and legal contexts. This research uses the multi-perspective and multidimensional genre analytical framework proposed by Bhatia (2004). Particular attention

* This study draws on the international RGC (HKSAR) CERG funded research project [No. 9041191 (CityU 1501/06H)] --- *International Commercial Arbitration Practices: A Discourse Analytical Study* (led by Vijay Bhatia).

is paid to the issue of interdiscursivity as discussed in Bhatia (2008: 174) and Candlin and Maley (1997: 203).

2. Method

The data set used in this research consists of five Chinese litigation judgments and five Chinese arbitration awards. The disputes handled in these five judgments include intellectual property, personal injury, and international trading, and the disputes handled in the five awards are all related to international trade contracts. In order to examine the extent to which arbitration awards are interdiscursively influenced by litigation judgments, it is necessary to look for the specific textual and generic evidence for the similarities and differences between these two genres. To achieve this, the chosen genre exemplars are analyzed from a generic perspective. The rhetorical moves (Swales 1990: 140; Bhatia 1993: 24-41) of each set of genre exemplars are examined and compared, analyzing specific moves, the sequential order of these moves, the standardization and variation in the realization of these moves, and the typical lexico-grammatical resources employed. In addition, transparency, one conceptual issue related to both genres, is discussed.

Transparency is a concept borrowed from the socio-legal studies which relates to the requirement of accessibility of legal rules and regulations to readers. Broadly speaking, both legal specialists and laymen are the intended readers of litigation judgments and arbitration awards because it is not uncommon for these two professional practices to involve laymen as parties and specialists as agents (Bhatia *et al.* 2009: 2-13; Rogers 2006: 1301; Bhatia *et al.* 2005: 11). Transparency and confidentiality have been identified as two related issues in international commercial arbitration and have attracted increasing attention from both legal scholars (Buys 2003 and Rogers 2006) and linguists (Bhatia *et al.* 2009). However, these notions are not totally uncontroversial in international commercial arbitration, where there seems to be a tension between striving for transparency and warranting confidentiality. In light of this, one of the purposes of this research is to see how the concept of transparency functions in arbitration awards and litigation judgments.

This chapter also draws on narratives of experienced legal specialists and practitioners, i.e. one lawyer and two judges. The lawyer is an established legal practitioner, specializing in corporate law and commercial arbitration. Recently, he sat on behalf of his claimant in Beijing in an arbitration case where the value of disputed goods was over fifty million RMB. One of the two judges is from an intermediate court of a central province in Mainland China, and has been hearing cases for over twenty years. The other judge is relatively young with about five years of juridical experience. Interviews are conducted with our informants, with a twofold aim (Hyland 2000: 138): firstly, to discuss with them general issues including the nature and function of arbitration and litigation, their personal perspectives on the two professional practices, their personal understanding of litigation judgments and arbitration awards; secondly, to solicit their views on specific issues arising from the analysis of the two sets of textual data. They were also encouraged to supply their views and perceptions about issues like the purpose of specific extracts of sample awards and judgments, the way they are produced, and the rhetorical strategies used in them.

3. The move patterns of awards and judgments

The analysis of our data demonstrates that there seem to be some striking similarities between these two genres. Both are highly specialized and standardized in terms of the use of specific lexis and syntactic resources; both largely include their respective conventional components, and both seem to arrange such conventionalized components in a relatively fixed order. The arbitration award has a number of textual indicators of rhetorical structuring, which include titles/subtitles, numbers in text layouts, paragraph boundaries, and purposefully designed text spaces. At the same time, one may also notice discourse markers, such as *however*, *in conclusion*, and *anyway*, and attributive markers, such as *the claimant stated, the respondent replied as follows*, *this tribunal holds*, and *the arbitration is given as follows*, which are helpful to segment texts into meaningful parts. Litigation judgments, on the other hand, include fewer textual indicators because there are no titles or sub-titles, no numbers indicating the beginning of sections and no textual space purposively left between sections. However, attributive markers such as *the plaintiff claimed*, *the defendant defended*, and *this court holds* are put more prominently at the very beginning of paragraphs and sections. With the help of these indicators and other similar textual-mapping devices (Bhatia 1987: 1-10), the analysis of each genre exemplar has been done manually, highlighting the following move patterns:

Arbitration Awards	Litigation Judgments
Heading	Heading
Move 1: Introduction **Step 1**: Summary of the arbitration process **Step 2**: The parties (including lawyers, and tribunal) **Step 3**: Introduction of subject matter	**Move 1**: Introduction **Step 1**: Introduction of the subject matter **Step 2**: Summary of the trial process
Move 2: Facts **Step 1**: Facts mutually agreed by both parties **Step 2**: disputed facts	**Move 2**: Facts **Step 1**: Claims and Defences **Step 2**: Facts identified by the judges
Move 3: Opinions **Step 1**: Clarification of disputed issues **Step 2**: Giving arbitral opinions	**Move 3**: Opinions **Step 1**: Interpretation of law **Step 2**: Application of law **Step 3**: Giving legal opinions
Move 4: Arbitration decisions **Step 1**: Conclusion of case **Step 2**: Notice of the final power **Step 3**: Signature	**Move 4**: Court decisions **Step 1**: Conclusion of case **Step 2**: Notice of the right to appeal **Step 3**: Signature

Table 1. The move pattern of arbitration awards and litigation judgments

As can be seen in this table, the two genres both include four moves which appear in the same sequential order. However, it must be noted that some of the moves of litigation judgments are more complex than the corresponding ones of arbitration awards. For example, compared to arbitration awards, litigation judgments have a more detailed and complex heading (see Appendix A for details). The court, parties, lawyers and attorneys are all listed, and this separate and standardized introduction of litigation participants has no counterpart in arbitration awards, where they are merged with *Introduction*. Award *Introduction* quite informally introduces all participants along with arbitrators' summarization of the arbitration proceeding. The result is that arbitration awards appear to be relatively more informal, more readable and more accessible to non-specialist readers, whereas litigation judgments are formal and very much standardized. The arbitration discourse as shown in awards looks more like an informal version of the litigation discourse in judgments. Let us now look at individual moves in more detail.

4. Move 1: Introduction

In award *Introduction*, arbitrators usually state that the tribunal has followed the related law and parties' arbitration agreement and has ensured both parties to have a fair chance to present their points of view, thus legitimizing the whole process of arbitration. To emphasize this legitimization, arbitrators attempt to disclose as much information about the arbitration process as necessary to specialist and non-specialist readers. As demonstrated in Appendix B, the award *Introduction* is written as story-telling narratives and presents no significant reading challenge to specialists and non-specialist readers alike.

In order to summarize the complete arbitration process, this move often makes use of sentences which indicate actions:

Arbitration Commission took cognizance of dispute
the Arbitration Commission formed the arbitral tribunal
the arbitral tribunal reviewed
On 12 June 1992, an oral hearing was held
both parties presented
the arbitration award is hereby made

The overwhelming use of such sentences reduces the effort on the part of readers in accessing the conveyed meanings, particularly when the described actions are arranged in a chronological order. An early report of the subject matter facilitates readers' understanding of the complete award, as one may need to know what triggers the arbitration in the first place before deciding whether he should take time and effort to read the award. Arbitrators introduce the subject matter in the first sentence of this move, as exemplified below:

(1) [CIETAC] took cognizance of the dispute arising from the delivery of polypropylene under the contract … entered by and between …

There is no separate listing of parties and lawyers participating in the arbitration. They are all introduced through and as part of the arbitrators' summarization of the arbitration process. Major participants in commercial arbitrations are included in this move (taken from the sample award in Appendix B): arbitration commission ("CIETAC"), tribunal members ("Mr. A, B and C"), claimant ("XX Ltd"), and respondent ("YY Ltd"). However, lawyers are not mentioned in this move, thus giving the impression that the parties had handled the specialized and complicated arbitration process all by themselves. Such an observation is not supported by specialist informants who believe lawyers are only textually absent in the final awards, but are mostly present in arbitration practices. The arbitrators make lawyers textually absent to save possible unintended complications or misrepresentations, as explained by the following statement:

> (2) …in tribunal hearings, parties and their agents usually talk interchangeably and collaboratively. Mostly, they talk the same thing, but inconsistency does happen because of the contingency nature of natural talk. To save the efforts and troubles to identify those inconsistencies, the arbitrators intentionally make parties and their agents one whole entity…

The *Introduction* of litigation judgments shows much similarity. Like in awards, it introduces the subject matter and the litigation process, but in a more formulaic and hence standardized manner. For example, subject matters reported in judgments are introduced by means of the following conventional pattern:

> (3) The plaintiff X sued the defendant Y for exchanging cargo on marine transpiration contract.

Very much like in arbitration awards, the judges attempt to summarize the litigation process in this move. However, their purpose in doing so, as it seems, is not to legitimize the litigation by disclosing sufficient information to the readers, but to meet the requirement of the Supreme Court of PRC[1] and to claim the authority of litigation judgments as a legal genre. The summarization they supply can be highly standardized:

> (4) This court accepted the case on September, 26th, 2001. On November 30th, the judge, Huang Qingnan, heard the case in public trial as required by law. Yan Tieying, the agent ad litem of XXX, and Zhao Shuzhou and Sun Jingliang, the agents ad litem of YYY, participated in the trial. This case has now been concluded.

In this excerpt, narrative elements which are typical of arbitration awards, are somehow missing. In arbitration awards, readers are told,

---

[1] The summarization of the entire litigation process is a necessary component in civil judgment, which is required by the Supreme People's Court of PRC. Although the Supreme People's Court issued the official examples of various litigation documents, it does not stipulate specific information to be included in the required summarization of the litigation process; rather, it permits the judges to make appropriate decisions according to specific cases.

though vaguely, how the tribunal is formed, what documents the tribunal has read, what conciliation has been initiated by the tribunal, and even the number of hearings held by the tribunal. Such information mostly is not included in litigation judgments, where they are replaced by general and standardized expressions, like "this court accepted the case", "the judge(s) heard the case", and "this case has now been concluded". In fact, all PRC legal judgments have strictly followed the official sample (Appendix C) issued by the PRC Supreme Court without significant situation-specific particularization. This sample was provided by the Supreme Court in 1993 for lower courts to follow when writing their civil judgments, with a view to pushing Chinese judges to generate a fuller report of the dispute (subject matter) and the trial process. In actual fact, judges have interpreted the guidelines of the Court literally, taking the wording of this official sample as a template for a handy use. Accordingly, all judgment *Introductions* read alike and are featured by highly convergent use of lexis and phrasing and a formulaic list of litigation participants. This move reveals less useful information in terms of litigation process than in terms of arbitration process.

5. Move 2: Facts

The Move *Facts* in awards includes two steps: the facts mutually agreed by the parties and the disputed facts. Arbitrators report the parties' agreed facts (Appendix D) in a chronological order and their writing exactly reflects what happened in the process of implementing the disputed sales contract. This gives readers a better chance to understand what the dispute is about, and how it has developed. Temporal expressions are used frequently in this move in order to attribute exact dates to reported actions:

(5) After signing the contracts
After the first ten days of June
After that
On September 20, 1990
On October 2, 1990

These temporal expressions enable a lively reconstruction of the development of the dispute and the narrative account reflects the negotiable nature of arbitration practices. However, some of these expressions are quite too formal and rigid. For example, the whole dispute occurred in the year 1990; once the first exact reference to the date has been made ("September 20, 1990"), the year ("1990") could have been omitted in the subsequent references, which is actually not the case. The practical consideration for the arbitrators is that the stakes of international arbitrations usually are very high, so they could not afford to leave any possible room for misinterpretation of their writings. The arbitrators do not want the parties or other interested readers to infer that these months and dates in Appendix D refer to the year 1990. In every single instance they write the full date, thus leaving no room for inferences or interpretations, which is clearly a feature of litigation discourse.

After reporting the agreed facts, the arbitrators provide a lengthy discussion of the claimants' claims and the respondents' defences. The arbitrators' writing here includes not much of their analyses and arguments, but many direct quotations from the original documents submitted by the parties to the tribunal. As shown in Appendix E, the arbitrators' discussion of the claimants' claims and the respondents' defences are all numbered points organized by a few attributing sentences:

> (6) In its application for arbitration, the claimant stated: […]
> The respondent stated in its defence: […]
> The claimant made the following statements in solution to the claimant's claims: […]

Although quoting the parties' words is an efficient way to report the important points of their claims and defences, and it can tell a complete arbitration story and produce a convincing arbitration award, it becomes problematic when quotations, direct or indirect, occupy a half or even two thirds of the textual space of this genre. An arbitration award filled with quotation marks becomes a document which reports conclusions rather than negotiating them. Insufficient effort on negotiation reduces the persuasiveness of arbitration awards, minimizes the procedural satisfaction parties could get, and also harms the credibility of arbitration decisions.

Facts in Judgments includes the same two steps, but in a reverse order. Judges conventionally present a summary of parties' claims and defences first and then report the facts they identified in courtroom trials. Judgment *Facts* make use of explicit textual markers ("the plaintiff claimed", "the defendant argued" and "this court holds") to construct a scenario where plaintiffs, defendants and judges utter their respective voices and then negotiate them. Further investigations, nonetheless, suggest that a selective, rather than faithful report of plaintiff's and defendants' voices is more common in the corpus.

Appendix F is extracted from a full indictment submitted to the court by a plaintiff who accused the defendant of improperly using the plaintiff's published work. Appendix G is the judges' report of Appendix

F in the judgment. It can be noticed that Appendix F includes explicit components of argumentation: claims, facts and reasons, and opinions ("the plaintiff argues"), all summed up in one simple sentence in Appendix G ("I sued against Sohu (Ltd.) for its violation of my copyright"). The narrative elements used in Appendix F include time ("August 9 of 2005"), place ("plaintiff's blog and defendant's website"), the subject matter ("the defendant reposted the plaintiff's copyrighted materials"), and the ways of action ("several times", "without prior negotiation and authorization", "without paying the plaintiff"). All these are re-contextualized in Appendix G as "Sohu (Ltd.), without my permission, copied my articles from my blog in 2006". In appendix F, the plaintiff also provides multiple arguments supporting his claims, such as that the defendant should respect the author's copyright, that he reposted the plaintiff's article illegally several times, and acquired a huge amount of unlawful profits, while in Appendix G such information is completely omitted.

In summary, it might be concluded that both arbitrators and judges carefully pick and choose information from arguments submitted by the parties in order to construct the corresponding sections of awards and judgments. Arbitrators tend to let parties' arguments stand on their own by making use of direct quotations and judges reformulate parties' arguments to retain only issues which are relevant for the adjudication of the case. Both avail themselves of their prerogative to analyze and evaluate parties' arguments and retain only those reported in the final awards and judgments. Their deep concern is to highlight the relevant arbitration and legal issues and use them to prepare the final arbitration and litigation decisions.

6. Move 3: Opinions

In the Move *Opinions* of awards, arbitrators discuss parties' disputed issues, interpret arbitration rules used, and disclose their reasoning process. This move is expected to be the most important move because it reflects arbitrators' analytical efforts to strive for arbitration decisions, but it is normally two times shorter than the move *Facts*. This gives the impression that arbitrators are more concerned with reporting *Facts* rather than negotiating *Opinions*, though a sufficiently accessible negotiation of *Opinions* generates more procedural satisfaction for parties and other interested readers (Zhao and Sharma 2003: 56).

Arbitrators' propensity to report, as opposed to negotiating, is evidenced in *Opinions* as well. The analysis of the corpus reveals that award *Opinions* are mostly highly structured and standardized, as shown in the following example:

> (7) PART II OPINION OF THE ARBITRATION TRIBUNAL
> 1. The contracting agreement was legally effective because […] [issue][2] Any party which breached it *should* be liable therefore […] [opinion].
> 2. The respondent failed to provide HK$2 million to renew and improve […][issue]... the respondent should be liable therefore […] [opinion].

This example of *Opinions* consists of a title ("Part II Opinion of the arbitration tribunal") and five numbered issues. Instead of a normal paragraphed text, *Opinions* here includes only itemized issues, each following a fixed pattern: issue + opinion. The arbitrators' opinions are provided at the end of the discussion of each specific issue.

This way of constructing issues and opinions demonstrates the arbitrators' intention to report issues unambiguously and to supply their opinions explicitly. Their rhetorical efforts can be considered successful in that little room has been left for a reinterpretation or misinterpretation. In fact, the same effort could be seen elsewhere in this genre. For example, the majority of award contents are tightly structured in the form of numbered points. The heavy use of numbered or itemized points makes Chinese arbitration awards more like a genre which reports and delivers orders rather than a genre which negotiates facts and persuades parties. The amicability of the Mainland China Arbitration practices found in Zhao and Sharma (2003: 25) finds no evidence here. Although such textual features make arbitrators' writing quite readable for specialist and non-specialist readers, they do not seem to meet transparency requirements because readers cannot easily access arbitrators' reasoning process.

An insufficient disclosure of information is not uncommon in this move. In identifying issues, arbitrators condense particular factual details into general descriptions. In citing arbitration rules, they reduce specialized explanations of arbitration rules to less precise discussions, which increases the accessibility of discourse, but at the same time tends to reduce the specification of information and thus makes their writing less transparent by keeping detailed information undisclosed. After identifying specific issues, arbitrators are expected to weigh up the strength and weakness of the parties' respective arguments and further produce fully-fledged analyses and arguments. In practice, there are no signs indicating

---

[2] The labels [Issue] and [opinion] are added by the present authors for the sake of analysis.

such an intention on the part of the arbitrators. Their opinions are presented as given, without any further analysis or explanation:

> (8) It was verified that the respondent had returned goods valued at US$27,391.55.

> (9) It cannot be disputed that this fund was never invested and [...].

The passive voice in these two examples presents arbitrators' opinions as if they were self-evident and hence require no presentation of supportive evidence and argument. This rhetorical arrangement makes awards less persuasive and accountable, because the arbitrator' opinions to specific issues should be based on actual analysis and evidence, instead of on unspecified presuppositions. Such rhetorical choices put at risk the credibility and authority of awards as a specialized and professional enforceable genre.

Insufficient disclosure of information affects also arbitrators' citations of arbitration rules from time to time. The following examples use imprecise linguistic expressions:

> (10) In accordance with provisions of Articles 18, 19 and 20 of the Foreign Economic Contract Law of PRC, the claimant should indemnify the following economic loss [...]

> (11) Because the respondent's counter-claim concerning insufficient delivery of goods exceeded the time limit for counter-claim as stipulated by the Arbitration Rule [...]

> (12) According to the Regulations on Industrial and Commercial Administration and opinions of Shanghai Administration for Industry and Commerce, no examination or ratification was required [...]

There is an increasing degree of imprecision in these example texts and none of them produces actual discussion or explanation of specific arbitration rules. The first text reports the source of authority ("the Foreign Economic Contract Law of PRC") but quotes no contents of regulations related to the case under question. The second one cites the authority vaguely, in such a way as not to allow its retrievability ("the time limit stipulated in Arbitration Rules"). Specialist and non-specialist readers have no way of knowing what "Arbitration Rules" and what specific stipulations of these "Arbitration Rules" are being referred to. The third text becomes even more imprecise because it refers to one particular organization ("Shanghai Administration for industry and Commerce") rather than any particular documents rendered by this organization used as authority. The arbitrators' opinions are thus presented without much support from any retrievable source of authority, and little effort is seen in the negotiation of award decisions.

Similarly, in litigation judgments *Opinions* is theoretically the most important move, where judges need to identify issues, interpret the law, and apply it to the issues. It is true that judgment *Opinions* usually extends from two to three pages and is considerably longer than award *Opinions*, but the status of *Opinions* is still not prominent in litigation judgments. It seldom occupies more than three pages out of a ten-page long judgment. In writing litigation judgments, judges pay more attention to reporting parties' arguments and courts' factual findings, while their writing of *Opinions* is usually less carefully structured. Judges do not explicitly list the issues to be handled in *Opinions*. After summarizing parties' arguments and reporting the identified facts, judges immediately turn to their legal reasoning, leaving it for readers to figure out what specific issues are actually being addressed. To make things worse, judges use few textual markers such as numbers, spaces, or sub-titles to indicate the structure of their arguments. To figure out the specific issues under discussion requires considerable efforts in understanding and analyzing legalized content, which is possible for specialists only. The less reader-friendly textual arrangements might hinder a sufficient disclosure of the judges' reasoning process to non-specialist readers, thus decreasing the procedural satisfaction litigation judgments are intended to produce. For non-specialist readers, the move *Opinions* in judgments is neither readable nor transparent.

7. Move 4: Decisions

The Move *Decisions* in awards is the final and enforceable section, in the sense that parties do not have the right to challenge it except on the rare basis of procedural flaws. Since it is in this move that arbitrators decide the parties' respective rights and duties, it is necessary for arbitrators to make it as readable as possible for the parties, their lawyers/attorneys, and other interested non-specialist readers. Two ways of presenting decisions are found in the corpus (see Appendix I for details). Award *Decisions* sometimes are a separate section entitled "award" or "award of the arbitration tribunal", and sometimes are included in the move *Opinions*, where there is no explicit attributing markers indicating its existence. This variation in presenting decisions demonstrates that arbitrators enjoy a certain degree of flexibility in writing awards which is not available for judges as discovered in this research.

The step "notice of the final power" is somehow problematic. These notices tend to be realized by simple and short sentences, be it "This award is final" or "This award shall be final". The superficial interpretation of these notices is that arbitrators' decisions are endowed with an ultimate authority and no challenge against them could be raised by any parties. This is true in the sense that parties cannot apply for the same dispute to be heard again by the same or other arbitration tribunals, but it covers the fact that arbitration awards can be challenged on the basis of procedural flaws. Awards can be challenged if any party could provide sufficient evidence proving that there were procedural flaws (Article 58 of Arbitration Law of the People's Republic of China) in the proceedings. The procedural flaws under which arbitration awards can be challenged are common knowledge for legal specialists, who are lawyers, attorneys, judges, or law professors, but not for non-specialist claimants and respondents. *Decisions* says "This award is final", in fact it means 'the award should be final unless there are procedural flaws stipulated in Article 58 of Arbitration Law of the People's Republic of China'. This is never made sufficiently explicit so that it does not undermine the finality of arbitration awards.

Arbitration awards present decisions mostly through Easification tools as discussed in Bhatia (1983: 42), such as numbering and listing individual decisions, arranging information in easily identifiable chunks, etc. The same textual features are also found in litigation judgments (see Appendix J). Compared to award *Decisions*, judgment *Decisions* are more standardized. They are not incorporated within other moves, and clear attributing markers usually declare their existence:

> (13) According to the "Civil Procedure Law of the PRC" article 64 section 1; the Supreme People's Court "Provisions Concerning the Civil Economic Model of Trial Reform" article 3 section 2; "Maritime Law" of the PRC article 42 section 1 item 1 and article 46, the court makes the following judgment: ...

As can be seen in this excerpt, the insufficient disclosure of information is apparent in judgment *Decisions*. Law is textualised by the complex-prepositional structures, such as "in accordance with", "according to", and "in terms of", etc. Such textual references are clear signs of quotations, and readers expect the referred laws to be fully quoted and explained. However, judges conventionally omit a full quotation of the law and take the meaning of the law as unproblematic and shared knowledge. They do not produce detailed interpretations to support the *Decisions*. Judges, like arbitrators, seem unwilling to disclose adequate information about how their decisions have been reached, and they both prefer to make a simple delivery of conclusions rather than negotiate and rhetorically construct them.

8. Conclusions

This chapter examines and compares the move structures of arbitration awards and litigation judgments in the context of PRC, focusing on the extent to which the practice of arbitration is interdiscursively influenced by the practice of litigation. As revealed in this research, these two genres largely present the same moves and arrange these same moves in the same sequential order. Moves of the two genres demonstrate arbitrators and judges' intention to report conclusions rather than their intention to negotiate decisions. The differences lie in the standardization of writing. Litigation judgments are more structured and standardized than arbitration awards. For example, award *Introductions* includes arbitrators' narratives about arbitration proceedings, while judgment *Introductions* includes judges' formulaic repetition of the example judgment prepared by the Supreme People's Court. *Facts* of the two genres are mostly a re-contextualization of parties' arguments submitted to arbitrators and judges. Arbitrators' re-contextualization includes carefully chosen direct quotations, while judges' encompasses only their understanding and selection of parties' arguments. *Opinions* are, theoretically, the most important move in both genres, but neither arbitrators nor judges show sufficient efforts in its construction. *Opinions* on specific issues are written as given rather than as negotiated and argued. Although *Decisions* of both genres are written in a reader-friendly way, much of the important information is vaguely disclosed.

To sum up, although awards sit in arbitration practices where considerable freedom is left for parties to negotiate and judgments sit in litigation practices where the pubic and state power plays a dominant role, not much material differences could be identified between arbitration awards and legal judgments. It is not inaccurate to claim that, in spite of the two different professional contexts, arbitration awards are interdiscursively influenced by legal judgments. The interdiscursivity between arbitration and litigation is not entirely surprising considering that the majority of arbitrators listed by various Chinese arbitration commissions are mostly established law professors and renowned lawyers. This interdiscursivity shows that arbitration, which is a dispute settlement device meant for negotiation and conciliation, has taken on a strong flavour of or has been heavily colonized by litigation, a public or state-oriented legal activity.

References

Bazerman, Charles and James Paradis 1991. *Textual Dynamics of the Professions: Historical and Contemporary Studies of Writing in Professional Communities*. Madison, Wis.: University of Wisconsin Press.

Berkenkotter, Carol, and Thomas N. Huckin. 1995. *Genre Knowledge in Disciplinary Communication: Cognition/Culture/Power*. Hillsdale, NJ.: Lawrence Erlbaum Associates.

Bhatia, Vijay K. 1983. "Simplification v. Easification: The Case of Legal Texts". *Applied Linguistics* 4 (1): 42-54.

—. 1987. "Textual-Mapping in British Legislative Writing". *World Englishes* 6 (1): 1-10.

—. 1989. "Legislative Writing: A Case of Neglect in EA/OLP Courses". *English for Specific Purposes* 8 (3): 223-238.

—. 1993. *Analysing Genre: Language Use in Professional Settings*. London: Longman.

—. 1997. "Genre-Mixing in Academic Introductions". *English for Specific Purposes* 16 (3): 181-196.

—. 2004. *Worlds of Written Discourse: A Genre-Based View*. London: Continuum.

—. 2008. "Towards Critical Genre Analysis". In *Advances in discourse studies*, edited by Vijay K. Bhatia, John Flowerdew and Rodney H. Jones, 166-178. London and New York: Routledge.

Bhatia, Vijay K., Christopher N. Candlin and Rajesh Sharma 2009. "Confidentiality and Integrity of International Commercial Arbitration Practice". *Arbitration* 75: 2-13.

Bhatia, Vijay K., Jan Engberg, Maurizio Gotti and Dorothee Heller. 2005 "Introduction". In *Vagueness in Normative Texts,* edited by Vijay K Bhatia, Jan Engberg, Maurizio Gotti and Dorothee Heller, 10-13. Bern: Peter Lang.

Buys, Cindy G. 2003. "The Tension between Confidentiality and Transparency in International Arbitration". *The American Review of International Arbitration* 14: 121-138.

Candlin, Christopher N., and Yon Maley. 1997. "Intertextuality and Interdiscursivity in the Discourse of Alternative Dispute Resolution". In *The Construction of Professional Discourse*, edited by Britt-Louise

Gunnarsson, Per Linell and Bengt Nordberg, 201-222. London and New York: Longman.
Devitt, Amy J. 1991. "Intertextuality in Tax Accounting: Generic, Referential, and Functional". In *Textual Dynamics of the Professions: Historical and Contemporary Studies of Writing in Professional Communities*, edited by Charles Bazerman and James Paradis, 336-357. Madison: University of Wisconsin Press.
Hyland, Ken. 2000. *Disciplinary Discourse: Social Interactions in Academic Writing*. Harlow: Pearson Education Ltd.
Rogers, Catherine A. 2006. "Transparency in International Commercial Arbitration". *Kansas Law Review* 54: 1301-1337.
Swales, John M. 1990. *Genre Analysis: English in Academic and Research Settings*. Cambridge: Cambridge University Press,.
—. 1998. *Other Floors, Other Voices: A Textography of a Small University Building*. Mahway, N.J.: Lawrence Erlbaum Associates.
Zhao, Yuhong and Rajesh Sharma 2003. "Introduction to the Legal System of the People's Republic of China". In *Multilingual and Multicultural contexts of legislation*, edited by Vijay K. Bhatia, Christopher N. Candlin, Jan Engberg and Anna Trosborg, 25-57. Berlin: Peter Lang.

Appendix A
(Judgment Heading)

Guangzhou Maritime Court of the PRC
Civil Judgment
(2001) GHFCZ No.212
Plaintiff: Shenzhen Bao An Gaoke Electronic Co., Ltd.
Address: High-tech Industrial Park, No.8 Tang Hang Rd.,
Shiyan County, Shenzhen
Legal Representative: Zhao Jinhai, General Manager
Agent ad litem: Yan Tieying, lawyer of Guangdong Wanshang Law Firm
Defendant: Beijing Hui Hang International Forwarding Ltd.
Shenzhen Branch
Address: Room AB, 26/F, Shenzhen Development Bank Tower,
No.5047, Shen Nan Dong Rd., Luo Hu District, Shenzhen
Representative: Li Ming, Manager
Agents a d litem: Zhao Shuzhou, Sun Jingliang,
lawyers of Wang Jing & Co. Law Firm
Defendant: Wan Hai Lines Ltd.
Address: 10/F, No. 136, Song Jiang Rd., Taipei, Taiwan, China]
Legal Representative: Chen Chaoheng, Chairman of the Board of Directors
Agents a d litem: Zhao Shuzhou, Sun Jingliang,
lawyers of Wang Jing & Co. Law Firm

Appendix B
(Award Introduction)

China International Economic and Trade Arbitration Commission took cognizance of the dispute arising from the delivery of polypropylene under the contract mentioned herein, in accordance with the arbitration clause set out in the contract 91RV-HPMT7011 (P) entered by and between the claimant, XX Ltd and the respondent, YY Ltd, and upon the written application for arbitration submitted by the claimant.

In accordance with the arbitration rules the Arbitration Commission formed the arbitration tribunal having Mr. A as the chief arbitrator, Mr. B and Mr. C as arbitrators to hear the case.

The arbitration tribunal reviewed the application for the arbitration submitted by the claimant and the statement of reply by the respondent as well as materials of evidence provided by both parties respectively.

On June 1992, an oral hearing was heard in Beijing. However, the respondent failed to appear at the hearing.

The claimant participated in the hearing, made oral presentation and answered questions on facts from the tribunal.

After the first hearing the respondent requested a second hearing. The second hearing was held in Beijing on 9 September 1992 by the tribunal.

Both parties presented their case and carried out a debated at the hearing.

Based on the facts ascertained by the tribunal and through discussion among the arbitrators, the arbitration award is hereby made.

Appendix C
(Official Sample of Civil Judgment by the PRC Supreme Court)

Sample of Civil Trial Judgment
×××× People' Court
Civil Judgment
(××××) ×Case No.
Plaintiff [...]
Defendant [...]
The plaintiff ... sued the defendant ... for ... This court accepted the case, constituted collegiate panel (... as the sole judge), and held (public) hearings... (Names of trial participants) appeared in court and participated in the suit. Now the case has been concluded.

Appendix D
(Report of "Agreed Facts" in Award Facts)

After signing the contracts, the respondent sent its representative to Tongjiang, China to supervise the processing of the caviar. After the first ten days of June (which was the end of the flood season) 3.5 tons of sturgeon fish was caught and 404kg sturgeon caviar were collected… After that, the respondent examined and confirmed ….	Smooth implementation of contract
On September 20, 1990, the respondent opened a letter of credit ... On October 2, 1990, the respondent opened another letter of credit for 4.5 tons of sturgeon fish. Due to a discrepancy with the actual quantity of 3.5 tons the claimant demanded that the letter of credit be amended.	The occurrence of a problem
On November 2 and 5 of 1990, the band issuing the letter of credit pointed out those discrepancies… Consequently, the issuing bank refused to negotiate the payment and stated that the applicant for the letter of credit had denied payment.	Unpleasant results
On November 8, 1990, the respondent told the claimant that it would not effect payment... On December 6, the respondent requested ... The claimant refused this offer. In its application for arbitration, the claimant stated [...]	Fruitless efforts to negotiate

Appendix E
(Re-contextualization of arbitration parties' arguments)

(*The claimant's claims*)
In its application for arbitration, the claimant stated:
1[...]
2[...]
3. Since the respondent had already taken away and sold the 517 kg of caviar, it should effect payment through collection if the issuing bank refused to make payment. However, the claimant received no meaningful reply from the respondent after repeated negotiation...

(*The respondent's defences*)
The respondent stated in its defence:
1[...]
2. The claimant's material breach of contract caused the respondent to suffer los. Immediately after signing the contracts, the respondent sent its technical personnel to the boat factory in Tongjiang to supervise the processing of the sturgeon caviar and fish. In order to obtain higher profits, the claimant offered low prices to purchase the sturgeon from fisherman but was unsuccessful in attracting sales. After the flood season only 404kg of caviar and 3.5 tons of fish had been bought and processed in the boat factory of Toingjiang. That amount was way below what was agreed in contracts no.006 and 007, (i.e. 2-3.5 tones of caviar and 35 tons of fish). As early as, or even before, the beginning of the 1990 flood season, the respondent had already signed or reached sales agreements with several clients -- selling three tongs of caviar to FF Co. of Sweden at the unit price of US$295/kg, FOB Beijing; and selling 35 tons of sturgeon fish to Denmark DD Co. at the price of US$7/kg, FOB Dalian. Due to the claimant's failure to deliver the full amount of the goods, the respondent incurred loss of profits in the sum of US$239,400 for the sturgeon caviar and it had to pay US$180,000 for liquidated damages to FF Co. The claimant's act constituted a fundamental breach of the contracts. Therefore, the claimant should reimburse the respondent for the above-mentioned losses, totaling US$545,400 and bear the arbitration fee for the present proceedings.

Appendix F
(Indictment)

Claims: 1, To order the defendant to stop the violation immediately [...]
2, To order the defendant to pay the plaintiff the due mount of XXX for compensation
3, To order the defendant to reimburse the plaintiff [...]

Facts and reasons: The plaintiff has made it clear "prior negotiation and authorization are required for citation or quotation of the copyrighted materials". On August 9 of 2005, the plaintiff posted in blog "Six thoughts about Baidu goes crazy, Matsa comes, and Alibaba is sold". The defendant reposted this article on its own website on August 9 of 2005 while it did not negotiate with the plaintiff or acquire prior authorization, did not mark the article source, and did not pay the author... The plaintiff argues she, as the lawful copyrighter, should enjoy legal protection of her writings ...the defendant should respect the author's copyright, but it, without prior negotiation and authorization, reposted the plaintiff's article illegally several times and thus acquired huge amount of unlawful profits. So the defendant should be held responsible for its violation of plaintiff's copyright. The plaintiff hereby files this case with the Court for your adjudication.

Appendix G
(Judges' Re-contextualization of Indictment)

The plaintiff, Qin Tao, claimed: Sohu (Ltd.), without my permission, copied my articles of my personal blog in 2006, and I sued against Sohu (Ltd.) for its violation of my copyright. During the litigation, Sohu (Ltd.) and I signed a reconciliation agreement under which Sohu (Ltd.) should pay me RMB 50,000 for compensation. Until now, Sohu (Ltd.) had not fulfilled its obligation of payment, so I sued and required the court to order Sohu (Ltd.) to pay me RMB 50,000 as agreed in our reconciliation agreement.

Appendix H
(Judgment Opinions)

This court holds: According to the stipulations of the General Principles of Civil Law of PRC, citizens enjoy legal protection of their rights to reputation and it is not permitted to violate other people's rights to reputation by insults or calumnies. The law of the place where an infringing act is committed shall apply in handling compensation claims for any damage caused by the act. So, General Principles of the Civil Law of PRC should be applied to the present case of violation of Zhang Tielin's (with a foreign citizenship) rights to reputation. Zhang Tielin claimed Zhou Meiying's sayings in Chengdu Business Times (June 29, 2003 and July 4, 2003) violated his rights to reputation while Zhou Mieying defended that she never said things like "treat with sex" or "The emperor' proposed strange requests". According to reports from various media on and after that day … (Zhou Meiying's sayings) in those newspaper articles are real … Zhou Meiying's actions have violated Zhang Tielin's rights to reputation, and she should be held responsible … her defences could not be accepted by this court. Chengdu Business Times reported the "sex scandal"… on basis of Zhou Meiying's statement … the contents are basically authentic, and does not exaggerate or distort facts. So Chengdu Business Times can not be held responsible for the violation of Zhang Tielin's rights to reputation.

Appendix I
(Award Decisions)

A: Award of the arbitration tribunal:
The Applicant's claim against the respondent for damages in the amount of US$ xxx is untenable and shall be rejected.
Sales confirmation No XX was formed.
The applicant shall be responsible for payment of the arbitration costs in this case, amounting to US$ XXX [...]
This arbitration award shall be final.

B: Opinion of the arbitration tribunal and award:
It was held by this arbitration tribunal that:
The respondent shall return to the applicant […]
The respondent shall reimburse the applicant for its losses arising from the freight and custody expenses incurred [...]
The costs of the arbitration shall be borne by [...]
This award shall be final.

CHAPTER TWELVE

"APPELLANTS" IN SPORTS ARBITRATION MAKE STRONGER CLAIMS THAN "APPLICANTS" IN COURT: THE REPORTING STYLES OF JUDGES AND ARBITRATORS*

PAOLA EVANGELISTI ALLORI

1. Introduction

This chapter explores the use of reporting verbs made by judges and sport arbitrators respectively in their exposition of the procedural action leading to the final pronouncement. The pronouncements issued by the two categories of legal professionals, as judging bodies in international court sentences and arbitral awards, have been analysed in terms of lexical selection and internal organisation; in both cases they were found to exhibit notable differences (Evangelisti Allori 2011). Of particular interest was the perceived difference in the selection of reporting verbs in the two kinds of documents.

Reporting verbs signal the presence of, very often strongly evaluative, authorial comment on the propositional content reported. In legal pronouncements, where they are used to report the actions undertaken by the parties in the procedure, they implicitly express the judging body's view of the parties' attitude towards the case.

* This chapter is part of the research carried out under the national MIUR-funded, PRIN project "Tension and Change in English Specialized Discourse", protocol N. 2007109911_005: "Tension and Change in English Juridical Discourse".

1.1. Arbitration vs litigation styles

The present study is linked to a wider research project[1] aimed at investigating whether, and eventually the extent to which, the discourse and practice of arbitration is losing its generic integrity in favour of litigation practice and discourse as a colonising genre. The phenomenon appears to be evident in commercial arbitration where there seems to be a growing tendency for the parties to prefer the assistance of legal professionals in arbitration so as to make sure that their financial interests are better protected. Such a tendency dictated by "practical" issues is bound to affect, in a kind of domino effect, the discursive practices of arbitration, thus making the discourse and practice of arbitration more and more similar to the legal discourse and practice of litigation. As pointed out by Bhatia (2007: 1), the recourse to legal experts as arbitrators

> often encourages the importation of typical litigation processes and procedures into arbitration practices. This in turn *leads to an increasing mixture of discourses* as arbitration becomes, as it were, 'colonized' by litigation practices, threatening the integrity of arbitration practice to resolve disputes outside of the courts, and thus going contrary to the spirit of arbitration as a non legal practice.

The mixture of discourses mentioned by Bhatia would thus result in a hybrid type of legal discourse where the language and concepts of arbitration are, as it were, colonized by forms and concepts typical of the legal language used in litigation procedures.

Trying to investigate whether and to what extent such hybridization is taking place, i.e. whether and to what extent the discourse of litigation procedures is colonizing the discourse of arbitration, and eventually to identify the discursive practices at work in the world of arbitration, is a challenging task for the linguist analysing legal discourse. Such a task implies careful analysis and comparison of the contexts typical of the two kinds of social practice and of the procedures carried out in each, besides the analysis of discourse proper. This is what the international group of researchers coordinated by Bhatia in the CERG Project proposes to do

[1] The project referred to here (led by prof. Vijay K. Bhatia of the City University of Hong Kong) is an international RGC (HKSAR) CERG funded research project entitled *International Commercial Arbitration Practices: A Discourse Analytical Study* For a description of this project cf. in this volume Bhatia, Garzone and Degano, Chapter One.

through the analysis of both written texts and of narratives of practice by arbitrators interviewed.[2]

1.2. Arbitration in Sport

Within the context of arbitration, it seems interesting to investigate whether the same sort of colonization, and consequent discourse hybridization, is taking place in other fields where arbitration is applied as a possible substitute for litigation. In sports, for instance, where recourse to arbitration is quite frequent both at national and at international level, in day to day activities and during worldwide events such as the Olympic Games.

Sports arbitration offers the further advantage of being probably the only case of arbitration carried out *exclusively* by legal professionals, whom the parties can chose only from a closed list of lawyers and judges proposed by the sole international arbitration authority worldwide, the Court of Arbitration for Sport (CAS). It can be hypothesised that, in this case, given the exclusively legal background of the arbitrators, many features of legal reasoning and of legal discourse could be detected in the arbitration documents produced. To this end, the final pronouncements, i.e. sports arbitration awards and court judgments, were selected as the most complete documents of legal reasoning in the two fields since, in giving the judgment, both kinds of judging bodies summarize the facts and report on the whole procedure, including the reasoning which led to the final decision.

2. The documents analysed

The analysis was carried out on two specialized corpora of final pronouncements on international cases: judgments given by the European Court of Justice (ECJ) and awards by the International Court for Arbitration in Sport (CAS).

The two kinds of final pronouncements are comparable on a number of grounds: (a) they are given by unique international judging bodies (both ECJ and CAS are the only court in their field), (b) they are international in composition (both individual European court's Chambers and CAS's

---

[2] See for instance the Symposium on *Interdiscursive colonization of arbitration practices in the changing world*, organized by V.K.Bhatia and M. Gotti, at the '15th AILA World Congress of Applied Linguistics', Essen, Germany, 24-29 August 2008.

Panels are made up of judges or arbitrators from different countries); (c) they are both "appeal" bodies, i.e. bodies judging over cases already judged by other, lower level, tribunals whose pronouncement is appealed against by one of the parties because unsatisfactory; and (d) in both cases the decision is made on written evidence provided by the parties or in the form of reports from hearings.

For our present purposes, the ECJ and the CAS corpora were analysed in terms of the actions attributed by the two different judging bodies to the Appellant or Applicant, according to the case, as the party who set the procedure in motion through his/her application for judgment. These were identified through an analysis of the reporting verbs used in each corpus in relation to that party.

2.1. Conceptual structure of the pronouncements

As a first step in the comparison, the macro-structure of the two kinds of final pronouncements was analysed. Although often exhibiting different terminology, particularly concerning the three fundamental aspects of the judgment giving process – Participants, Procedure and Matter of dispute (Evangelisti Allori 2010) –, the awards and court judgments analysed present similar internal structures and organisation of content.

The conceptual layout of the pronouncements can be thought of as a four move structure (see also Maci 2011) in which the judging body proceeds to:

1. identifying the case;
2. establishing facts of the case;
3. arguing the case;
    a giving a history of the case;
    b presenting arguments;
    c deriving *ratio decidendi*;
4. pronouncing judgment.

Both genres present identical hierarchically structured moves realised in the documents by the following conceptual organization:

the OPENING: the Court/Panel and the case to be judged;
the FACTS: identification of the parties and description of the events which led to the present request for arbitration or judgment.
the PROCEDURAL FACTS (or Legal Analysis): lengthy description in which

(a) the Facts described in 1. above are taken up individually,
(b) the general Laws/Regulations applicable to the case are identified,
(c) the Participants' Actions (Claims, counter-claims, arguments, etc.) are reviewed individually and "weighed" against the specific relevant norms (articles, rules, etc.),
(d) the conclusion of the Court or Panel at each individual step is provided.
the CONCLUSIVE PRONOUNCEMENT:
(f) the closing formula ("On those/these grounds…") introduces the essence of the court/panel decision,
(g) costs are adjudicated.

In other words, the pronouncement opens with formal bureaucratic information meant to identify the case: mention of the Court, the composition of the tribunal/panel, case number, mention of the parties and the reasons they brought before the judging body. There follows a detailed description of the facts which led to the present request for arbitration or for judgment. The following section examines the (legal) grounds on which each fact is to be judged, presents the considerations/ interpretation by the tribunal/panel according to the relevant provisions and the conclusion arrived at. This is followed by the decision on costs and their distribution between the parties, while the final pronouncement (consisting of a closing formula plus the essence of the judgment/award) acts as closure just before the judges', or arbitrators', signatures.

3. The judging body as narrator / evaluator

In the description of the procedural facts in the legal analysis section, the judging body assumes the simultaneous double function of narrator and of evaluator. On the one hand, it narrates the way the final decision is reached by describing each individual fact/event and the procedural action taken at each step in view of reaching the final decision but, in so doing, it also provides indirectly an evaluation of the parties' actions in the procedure. The latter function is indicated by the overwhelming presence, in section 3, of reporting verbs that convey the author's stance. Here, the Appellant/Applicant's action and position towards his/her opponent(s) and the case are represented, i.e. filtered, through the eyes of the narrator who, from a position of detached, external reporter of facts in section 2, becomes an evaluator while also being a co-participant in the action being narrated.[3]

Section 3, appropriately labelled "Legal Analysis" in some of the CAS awards, "Grounds" in ECJ sentences, is also conceptually and linguistically more complex than the previous one in which the Court or Panel simply describe the participants and the events; it exhibits all the logico-cognitive and discursive features of argumentation.

3.1. Arguments in pronouncements

The analysis of each issue brought in for judgment – introduced by the positions of the parties which, in turn, are examined and evaluated against the relevant norms, calls for argumentative reasoning. It is here that the Appellant/Applicant's claims are set "in explicit or implicit opposition to deviant or alternative propositions" (Werlich 1983: 40) such as those attributable to an antagonistic position, represented in this case by the Respondent's counter-claim. The reasoning on each claim follows an established conceptual path, or *frame,* which is realised by a complex network of logical relations initiating with an expectation raising statement followed by a denial of the truth validity of that statement and culminating in the cause/effect relation – as the heart of the syllogism (Evangelisti Allori 1989, 1990). It is interesting to note, though, that in this case the whole argumentative sequence is triggered off by the initial reported clause, where the quality of the reporting verb is relevant in the interpretation of the argument that follows, as in example (1):

> (1) 7. The applicant complains that the Commission infringed the rights of the defence in failing to inform the applicant of the fresh conclusions which it had reached after the enquiries carried out in 1968 into the price increase in dyestuff and [...]
>
> 8. [Expectation raising] During the course of the administrative procedure the undertakings concerned must be informed of the essential elements of fact on which the Commission bases its objections against them.
> [Denial of truth validity] However, it is not necessary for the contents of the file to be made available in their entirety. [...]

[3] Here, following the legal tradition of use of impersonal style (see Gotti and Anesa 2011) the panel refers to itself in the third person: 'the Court' or 'the Panel', e.g. "The Court finds/considers/observes….that", "The Panel holds/acknowledges/is of the opinion…that".

[Justification/Cause] The Commission's Notice of Objections, sent to the applicant by letter on 11 December 1967, sets out all the facts necessary for determining the objections taken into consideration.
9. [Conclusion/Effect] This submission is therefore unfounded. (ECJ - 49/69)

In the documents analysed, such sequence is usually embedded in larger sequences in which the pattern is repeated a number of times according to the complexity of the case so that we may find recursive structures as illustrated below:

a. Court as Narrator (1):	Appellant *claims* that
b. Court as Evaluator (1):	(i) Concession
	(ii) Denial of Truth validity of (i)
	(iii) Justification
	(iv) Conclusion
c. Court as Narrator (2):	Appellant further *claims* that
d. Court as Evaluator (2):	i) Concession
	(ii) Denial of Truth validity of (i)
	(iii) Justification
	(iv) Conclusion
e. Court as Narrator (3):	Furthermore, Appellant *complains/ argues* that
f. Court as Evaluator (3):	(i) Concession
	(ii) Denial of Truth validity of (i.)
	(iii) Justification
	(iv) Conclusion

The set of evaluative sequences thus schematized culminates in the final and definitive evaluation "It follows from all the foregoing considerations that the applicants' application must be declared (un)founded."

In such a process, the Court as narrator does also step in as actor in the narrator-evaluator sequence; it does so referring to itself in the third person, particularly in the step immediately after the introduction of the claim and before the concession, e.g.

(2) 40. The applicants claim in substance to be entitled to [...] and that the Council must refund to them the differences [...]
41. *The Court considers that the applicants' claim of set-off against the Council must be analysed as a claim for indemnity* [...]
In order for the applicants to be able to claim compensation for the damage allegedly suffered, they must demonstrate a service-related fault [...]

42. In the present case, however, it has not been established that the Council committed a fault [...] (ECJ, T-24/91)

4. Reporting verbs as signals of evaluation

Evaluation is concerned with authorial stance in the construction of discourse. Among the range of linguistic devices available[4] to signal evaluation, reported speech is probably the most explicit. Originally studied in narrative analysis as a linguistic strategy available to the narrator for the presentation of a character's speech or thought (Leech and Short 1981), reported speech has also been implicitly behind critical discourse analysts' treatment of the "representation" of facts, particularly in the news (Fowler 1991, Fairclough 1995).

Reporting verbs themselves have been considered as "one of the clearest signals of the presence of evaluation" (Thompson and Ye 1991: 369). They are the means available to the writer to express his/her view on the propositional content expressed in the reported clause. As expression of the writer's position in relation to that information, they have been looked at through the lens of lexical semantics in the analysis of reported speech in newspaper articles (Bergler 1991, 1993). The impact of reporting verbs as carriers of author's evaluation has also been shown to be strong in academic discourse. In looking at the verbs used in citations, for example, Thompson and Ye (1991) classify such verbs in terms of their denotation, i.e. in terms of the processes they refer to, and of their evaluative potential, i.e. in terms of whether they refer to the writer's stance, the reported author's stance, or the writer's interpretation of the reported information. Indeed, one relevant feature of reporting verbs, also pointed out by Hyland (2000/2004: 38-9), is that they function to indicate at the same time the status of the information reported while being indicative of the writer's position in relation to that information. Hyland also points out that, while

[4] Studies carried out in the past few years (Huston and Thompson 2000; Hyland 2000/2004) have highlighted the variety of linguistic elements contributing to the indication of evaluation/author's stance in discourse. Such studies have indicated that evaluative meaning does not only reside in overtly evaluative lexical items. Grammatical structures have also been shown to be indicators of evaluation (Labov and Waletsky 1967; Labov 1972) as well as lexico-grammatical sequences (Huston and Sinclair 2000).

Appendix J
(Judgment Decisions)

[···] in accordance with the stipulations of Article 42 (1) 1-3, Article 55, Article 71 and Article 72 of the Maritime Code of the PRC, the judgment is hereby given as follows:

I The Defendant YYY shall compensate to the Plaintiff XXX the loss of cargo in amount of … and loss of interest thereof based on the loan interest of the People's Bank of China applied in the corresponding period (calculating from April 24, 2001 to the date of payment as specified by this judgment);

II Other litigation requests of the Plaintiff XXX shall be dismissed.

Of the acceptance fee of this case in amount of … the Plaintiff XXX shall pay … and the remaining … shall be borne by the Defendant YYY. This court shall not refund to … The defendant YYY shall pay …

The payment of the above sums shall be completed within 10days upon coming into effects of this judgment.

Should there be any objection to this judgment, a statement of appeal with copy/copies in the number of the opponent party/parties may be submitted to this court within 15 days upon the service of this judgment, for appealing before the appeal court Guangdong Higher People's Court.

> generally writers in all fields tended to indicate their position about cited material more indirectly [...] writers in the soft disciplines [...] were far more likely to depict authors as adopting a particular stance towards their work either presenting their view as true, false or tentatively correct. (Hyland 2000/2004: 39).

He adds that such "explicitly evaluative strategies are better suited to the more disputational style of argument favoured by the humanities". Where an oppositional argumentative style is called for, as, for instance, in our specific kind of humanistic discourse, it is common to find more explicit evaluative strategies using "strong" reporting verbs such as *argue, reject, assert*, and so on.

4.1. Reporting verbs in legal pronouncements

In line with the argumentative style of the documents analysed, the kind of reporting verbs found in the pronouncements belong mostly to the "strong" category.

4.1.1. Reporting verbs in judgments and in sport awards

Statistically, court judgments present a lower number of reporting verbs, exactly a half if compared with awards:

ECJ JUDGMENTS		**CAS AWARDS**	
Reporting verbs	0.02%	Reporting verbs	0.04%

Table 1. Statistical amount of reporting verbs in the two corpora.

At the same time, they present fewer verb types (5 vs. 27). Table 2 shows the statistically relevant types of verbs used to report on the Applicant or the Appellant's actions in the two kinds of pronouncement, in the order in which they appear in the top frequency lists from the two corpora:

ECJ	CAS	
1. CLAIM 2. MAINTAIN 3. ARGUE 4. ASSERT 5. COMPLAIN ============	1. CONTEND 2. SUBMIT 3. CLAIM 4. REQUEST 5. RAISE issues/ questions ======================	
	6. OBJECT 7. POINT out 8. INVOKE 9. STRESS 10. CHALLENGE 11. COMPLAIN 12. ARGUE 13. MAINTAIN 14. ASSERT 15. HOLD 16. ALLEGE	17. BRING criticism 18. UNDERLINE 19. PUT FORTH 20. COMMENT 21. ESTABLISH 22. CONCEDE 23. CONCLUDE 24. TAKE position 25. MAKE admissions 26. TRY to impose 27. CONFIRM

Table 2. Reporting verbs related to the Appellant/Applicant.

A few things are worth noting in this table. Firstly, the difference in verb types appearing in the top five positions: ECJ judgments show a prevalent preference for the five main types, which alone account for 99.97% of the reporting verbs, and these are exclusively "strongly" evaluative verbs. In the CAS awards, the verbs in the top five positions account for 60.82% of the total, the remaining being distributed among the other types found, thus confirming numerically the greater variety of use. Here, in top position, there also appear such reporting verbs as *request, point out, underline, put forth* which are apparently more "neutral" as to the writer's stance.[5] Further, it is also interesting to note that, although the verbs used to refer to the Applicant in ECJ do also appear in the CAS list, they do not hold the same prominent position. *Claim*, for instance, which is the topmost reporting verb in ECJ (37.24%), appears only in third

[5] In fact, such verbs, usually not appearing in the classifications of 'strong' evaluative verbs, acquire evaluative force when followed by a *that*-clause in the context of the legal documents analysed.

position in CAS (11.44%), after *contend*, the statistically most frequent reporting/evaluative verb (20.48%), and *submit. Claim* is also the only verb from the ECJ list appearing in the top five position in CAS, while *maintain, argue, assert* and *complain* appear lower down, as statistically less relevant (all at 3.1%). Table 3 shows the statistical import of the main verbs used in the two corpora to represent the procedural actions performed by Applicant and Appellant:

ECJ - Applicant		**CAS - Appellant**	
1.CLAIM that	37.24 %	1. CONTEND that	20.48 %
2. MAINTAIN that	30.53 %	2. SUBMIT that	13.85 %
3. ARGUE that	21.47 %	3. CLAIM that	11.44 %
4. ASSERT that	6.71 %	4. REQUEST that	7.83 %
5.COMPLAIN that	4.02 %	5. RAISE issues/ questions	7.22 %
Total	99.97 %	Subtotal	60.82%
Other	0.03 %		
		OBJECT to	4.81 %
		POINT out that	4.81 %
		INVOKE	4.21 %
		STRESS that	4.21 %
		CHALLENGE	3.61 %
		MAINTAIN that	3.01 %
		ARGUE that	3.01 %
		ASSERT that	3.01 %
		COMPLAIN that	3.01 %
		HOLD that	.20 %
		Total	95.71 %
		Other	4.29 %

Table 3. Statistical import of the procedural actions attributed to the Applicant / Appellant in judgments and in awards.

According to the selection and percentage of reporting verbs, it would seem that judges and arbitrators hold different views of the participants in the litigation and arbitration procedures. For instance, the Appellant in CAS "claims" less than the "Applicant" in ECJ but he/she "contends" more; by the same token, he/she "argues" less but "raises" more issues, and makes more "requests"; he/she "complains" less but, at the same time "objects", "challenges", "holds". In addition, the selection of such verbs as "bring criticism against", "take position", "try to impose", "blame", "concede" (see Table 2) not included in the above CAS list because statistically not highly substantial, contributes to project an image of the Appellant in sport arbitration as a dynamic and assertive individual who fights to have his/her point of view recognized. An image clearly more dynamic and assertive than that of the Applicant to the European Court projected by the selection of reporting verbs made by the ECJ judges.

5. Conclusion

The analysis of reporting verbs carried out on two specialised corpora of legal discourse, i.e. final pronouncements given by court judges and by sport arbitrators on international appeal cases, has highlighted notable differences in the selection and use of the verbs chosen to report on the action undertaken by the Applicant/Appellant as the party who sets the legal appeal procedure in motion.

In reporting on the case in their final pronouncement, the two judging bodies follow much the same conceptual schema, where the core of the legal reasoning appears after the formal identification of the case and the exposition of the facts which led to the request of appeal. This section, often called "legal analysis", presents a complex schema of reasoning where the judging bodies, in analysing and discussing each issue, alternatively take up the roles of narrator, evaluator and participant. In such a complex network, reporting verbs play a relevant role in the creation of the image of the Applicant in court litigation or of the Appellant in arbitration and of his/her attitude towards the case.

As for their narrative styles, the linguistic analysis depicts judges as more rigidly tied to a conventional schema of reporting on their legal reasoning than arbitrators. In particular, they tend to use a restricted number of verbs which, as a consequence, appear more frequently in the corpus, thus acquiring heavier statistical weight on the whole. At the same time, also the quality of the reporting verbs used more frequently is found to vary, e.g. *claim* vs *contend*.

Such differences in style concur in projecting a diverse image of the Applicant or Appellant as the party who set the appeal procedure in motion. Through the selection of the reporting verbs analysed, the sport arbitrators project an image of the Appellant as a dynamic and alert participant in the procedure who fights eagerly to have his/her point of view accepted by the judging body. The court judges, on the other hand, project an image of the Applicant as a more static, almost detached participant in the background.

Since it can be presumed that Court Applicants are as eager as the appellants in Arbitration to have a positive pronouncement, it must be assumed that the differences observed are due to different legal conventions in drafting the pronouncement. In other words, judges and sport arbitrators, although belonging to the same 'legal professional' category seem to behave differently according to the legal contexts they are operating in. Thus, the linguistic analysis of judges and arbitrators' evaluative style and patterns confirms the independence of sports arbitration from court litigation already pointed out in previous analyses (Evangelisti Allori 2010, 2011) and adds further evidence to the adherence to different legal discourses and professional styles which, in turn, show that the process of colonization by traditional legal proceedings is not evident in the field of sport arbitration, in spite of the sport arbitrators acting themselves, at different times, also as lawyers and judges in legal fields different from arbitration.

References

Bergler, Sabine 1991. "The Semantics of Collocational Patterns for Reporting Verbs". In *Proceedings of the Fifth Conference of the European Chapter of the Association for Computational Linguistics,* April 1991 – Berlin, 216-221.

—. 1993. "Semantic Dimensions in the Field of Reporting Verbs". In *Proceedings of the Ninth Conference of the University of Waterloo Centre for the New Oxford English Dictionary and Text Research.* Oxford, England, 1-8.

Bhatia Vijay K. 2007. "Interdiscursivity in critical genre analysis". In *ANAIS Proceedings of the 4th International Symposium on Genre Studies*, edited by Adair Bonini, Débora de Carvalho Figueiredo and Fábio José Rauen. Tubarão – Santa Catarina: CD-Rom Publication ISSN 1808-7655, University of Southern Santa Catarina, Tubarão, Santa Catarina, Brazil - August 15th-18th.

Evangelisti Allori, Paola. 1989. "What's in an Argument: A Case for the Analysis of Clause Relations". In *Il Muro del Linguaggio. Conflitto e Tragedia*, edited by Lidia Curti, Laura Di Michele, Thomas Frank and Marina Vitale, 427-438. Napoli: Istituto Universitario Orientale.

—. 1990. "An Analysis of Arguments as Frames". In *English Past and Present*, edited by Jean Aitchinson, Thomas Frank and Nicola Pantaleo, 251-267. Bari: Schena.

—. 2010. "Content as Indicator of Genre Identity. Key Concepts in Sports-related Arbitral Awards". In *Discourse, Identity and Roles in*

Specialized Communication, edited by Giuliana Garzone and James Archibald, 39-162. Bern: Peter Lang.

—. 2011. "The Legal Identities of Sport Arbitrators and Judges in International Pronouncements: A Case for Genre Variation?" In *Discourse and Identity in the Professions: Corporate, Legal and Institutional Citizenships*, edited by Paola Evangelisti Allori and Vijay K. Bhatia, 147-170. Bern: Peter Lang.

Fairclough, Norman. 1995. *Media Discourse.* London: Edward Arnold.

Fowler, Roger. 1991. *Language in the News. Discourse and Ideology in the Press.* London: Routledge.

Gotti, Maurizio and Patrizia Anesa. 2011. "Professional Identities in Italian Arbitral Awards". In *Discourse and Identity in the Professions: Corporate, Legal and Institutional Citizenships*, edited by Paola Evangelisti Allori and Vijay K. Bhatia,189-212. Bern: Peter Lang.

Huston, Susan and John Sinclair. 2000. "A Local Grammar of Evaluation". In *Evaluation in Text: Authorial Stance and the Construction of Discourse*, edited by Susan Hunston and Geoff Thompson, 75-101. Oxford: Oxford University Press.

Hunston, Susan and Geoff Thompson. 2000. *Evaluation in Text: Authorial Stance and the Construction of Discourse*. Oxford: Oxford University Press.

Hyland, Ken. 2000/2004. *Disciplinary Discourses. Social Interactions in Academic Writing*. Ann Arbor: The University of Michigan Press.

Labov, William. 1972. *Language in the Inner City.* Philadelphia: University of Pennsylvania Press.

Labov, William and Joshua Waletsky. 1967. "Narrative analysis". In *Essays on the Verbal and Visual Arts*, edited by Helm June, 12-44. Seattle: University of Washington Press.

Leech, Geoffrey N. and Michael H Short. 1981. *Style in Fiction. A Linguistic Introduction to English Fictional Prose.* London: Longman.

Maci, Stefania. 2011. "Arbitration in Italy. Litigation Procedures in Arbitral Practice". In *Discourse and Identity in the Professions: Corporate, Legal and Institutional Citizenships*, edited by Paola Evangelisti Allori and Vijay K. Bhatia, 213-237. Bern: Peter Lang.

Thompson, Geoff and Yiyun Ye. 1991. "Evaluation in the Reporting Verbs Used in Academic Papers". *Applied Linguistics* 12, no. 4: 365-382.

Werlich, Egon. 1983. *A Text-Grammar of English.* Heidelberg: Quelle & Meyer.

CHAPTER THIRTEEN

INTERTEXTUAL MARKERS IN SPORTS-RELATED ARBITRATION: PAST AND PRESENT*

MICHELA MENGHINI

1. Introduction

This study carries out a diachronic analysis and comparison of the use of intertextual devices and their functions in a corpus of sports-related awards issued by the Court of Arbitration for Sport between 1991 and 2010, in the attempt to establish whether significant differences can be found between old and recent awards, and whether such differences can be ascribed to the process of hybridisation with litigation that has recently been hypothesised for commercial arbitration (Hunter 2000; Nariman 2000; Bhatia 2008).

The study consists of two steps. First, the occurrences and distribution of intertextual features are analysed comparing recent awards and older awards, organised in two sub-corpora (the Recent Awards sub-corpus, and the Archive sub-corpus, cf. Section 4 below), mostly using WordSmith Tools 5 (Scott 2009). This initial step aims at giving a general view of the use of intertextuality in the sport arbitration corpus, following Bhatia's (1998) analysis of intertextuality in legal discourse, and at detecting possible differences in a diachronic perspective. As a second step, one specific award from each subcorpus is selected and analysed for a more detailed investigation and comparison of textual realisations, of the use and functions of intertextual devices in specific examples, which will illustrate the intertextual play at work.

---

* The research on which this chapter is based is part of the National Research Programme *Tension and Change in Domain-specific Genres* funded by the Italian Ministry of University (PRIN Grant No. 2007JCY9Y9).

2. Background: Sport Arbitration

The Court of Arbitration for Sport (CAS) is an independent tribunal, which aims to facilitate the settlement of sports-related disputes "through arbitration or mediation by means of procedural rules adapted to the specific needs of the sports world", in the words of its website.[1] Its statutes were officially ratified by the International Olympic Committee (IOC) in 1983, and came into force in 1984. The CAS was subsequently restructured and made more independent of the IOC in 1994, when the "Agreement concerning the constitution of the International Council of Arbitration for Sport" (also known as the "Paris Agreement") was signed by the major sports-related authorities and the "Code of Sports-related Arbitration" (subsequently revised in 2004 and 2010 and amended on 01/01/2012) came into force. Article R27 of the 2010 Code reads as follows:

> These Procedural Rules apply whenever the parties have agreed to refer a sports-related dispute to the CAS. Such disputes may arise out of an arbitration clause inserted in a contract or regulations or of a later arbitration agreement (ordinary arbitration proceedings) or involve an appeal against a decision rendered by a federation, association or sports-related body where the statutes or regulations of such bodies, or a specific agreement provides for an appeal to the CAS (appeal arbitration proceedings).[2]

Arbitration clauses were included in sports federations' and associations' rules since 1991, but after the Paris Agreement an arbitration clause referring disputes to the CAS was included in the statutes of all Olympic International Federations and several National Olympic Committees.[3]

---

[1] See <http://www.tas-cas.org/20question>. Unless otherwise indicated, all websites were last accessed on 15/03/2012.

[2] See < http://www.tas-cas.org/rules >.

[3] The CAS website provides for the Arbitration Clause to be used in the statutes of sports bodies: "Any decision made by ... (insert the name of the disciplinary tribunal or similar court of the sports federation, association or sports body which constitutes the highest internal tribunal) may be submitted exclusively by way of appeal to the Court of Arbitration for Sport in Lausanne, Switzerland, which will resolve the dispute definitively in accordance with the Code of sports-related arbitration. The time limit for appeal is twenty-one days after the reception of the decision concerning the appeal." It also provides for the Arbitration Clause to be included in contracts: "Any dispute arising from or related to the present contract will be submitted exclusively to the Court of Arbitration for Sport in Lausanne,

CAS is also the officially recognised appeals body for all international doping-related disputes, according to Article 13 of the World Anti-Doping Code, promulgated by all Olympic Committees as well as by many governments since 2003, thus setting doping-related disputes apart from all other kinds of disputes at international levels.

The jurisdiction and independence of the CAS were challenged a few times by athletes, who appealed to the Swiss Federal Tribunal against CAS awards, even after the 1994 reform. The Federal Tribunal dismissed such appeals, concluding in a 2003 decision that the CAS was sufficiently independent of the IOC, and recognised its relevance and fundamental role within the international sport community (as reported and cited in the "History of the CAS – The 1994 Reform" section of the CAS website).[4]

Such challenges to arbitration decisions are deemed to be among the possible causes of the colonisation of commercial arbitration by litigative genres and practices, as companies now prefer to have legal experts (rather than, for instance, technical or accounting experts, as arbitration would allow them to have), both as their advisors and representatives and as arbitrators, in order to avoid formal errors that would increase the risk of a challenge (Nariman 2000; Hunter 2000). Lawyers and judges are thus more and more often involved in arbitration procedures. It is part of the aims of the present chapter to ascertain whether also sport-related arbitration is affected by this type of colonisation.

In previous studies (Fazio and Menghini 2010; Evangelisti Allori 2004, 2010; Menghini 2011), CAS awards showed some significant lexical and terminological differences from both judgments and commercial arbitrators' awards, which seemed to indicate a significantly less pervasive colonisation of sports-related awards by litigative genres, although the athletes' representatives and the arbitrators are usually legal experts. This chapter aims at further investigating the hypothesis of a colonising influence from litigation, through the study and comparison of the use of intertextuality in old and recent CAS awards, to establish whether any possible diachronic changes may be attributed to such a colonisation.

3. Intertextuality in legal discourse

The term "intertextuality" was first introduced in studies on polyphony and dialogism, based on Bakhtin's work and theory on Russian literature

Switzerland, and resolved definitively in accordance with the Code of sports-related arbitration." (<http://www.tas-cas.org/clause-templates>).

[4] See <http://www.tas-cas.org/history>.

(1981, 1984). Rephrasing Bakhtin, Kristeva defined intertextuality saying that "any text is constructed as a mosaic of quotations; any text is the absorption and transformation of another" (Kristeva 1980: 66). Allen (2000), in his study on the history and usage of the term from its origins in Bakhtin's works to its recent developments in postmodern theory, observed that "intertextuality seems such a useful term because it foregrounds notions of relationality, interconnectedness and interdependence in modern cultural life" (Allen 2000: 5). More recently, Bauman (2004) studied intertextuality in oral genres and offered the following definition: "By *intertextuality* I mean the relational orientation of a text to other texts, [...] the ways in which each act of textual production presupposes antecedent texts and anticipates prospective ones" (Bauman 2004: 4). With a polyphonic perspective and an intertextually-oriented interest in "structures expressing interactional meaning", Fløttum *et al.* (2006: 29), analysed academic discourse and the several voices within academic texts. For the purposes of this chapter, their analysis of integral references and reported speech as "the explicit presence of the other(s)" (Fløttum *et al.* 2006: 230) seems particularly interesting:

> If we understand polyphony as the presence of several voices in one and the same text, or even in one utterance, reported speech is the polyphonic phenomenon par excellence [...]. The locutor (corresponding to the author) gives the floor to another person, the represented locutor, whether directly by transferring complete responsibility for the reported sequence to the represented locutor, [...] or indirectly by transferring responsibility of content only (and not form) of the reported sequence to the other [...] (2006: 230)

This kind of polyphonic interplay particularly characterizes legal genres (Bhatia 1998 and 2007; Flowerdew 2002; Gibbons 2003; Gotti 2003), contributing to the precision required in legal texts, which make constant reference to, and are often connected with other, usually preceding, legal texts. Indeed, according to Bhatia (1998), in legal discourse intertextuality "is used to serve the general function of textual coherence", as legal texts must usually "be interpreted in the context of something expressed elsewhere"; and intertextual devices are used to point readers to that "elsewhere". Intertextuality is also used to serve "generic and disciplinary functions of making laws clear, precise, unambiguous and all-inclusive". This might be all the more relevant in sport arbitration discourse, in view of the risk of challenges, as CAS jurisdiction has often been challenged and sport arbitration cases have sometimes been taken to national civil courts, thus distorting their nature of sports disputes.

4. Corpus and methodology

The corpus for this study consists of awards issued by the Court of Arbitration for Sport and is divided into two subcorpora: the Recent awards subcorpus is comprised of 116 awards issued between 2005 and 2010, while the Archive awards subcorpus is comprised of 33 awards issued between 1991 and 1999.[5] "Archive" is in fact the name of a section in the CAS website in which older awards files are collected and made available. "Recent Decisions" is the section of the same website where recent awards are published and made available for a limited period of time. Table 1 shows statistics about tokens and types for each subcorpus, as computed using WordSmith Tools 5 (Scott 2009). The average number of words differs: in the Recent subcorpus it adds up to 10,129 words, while in the Archive subcorpus it adds up to 5,280. As can be seen in Table 1, Archive awards feature a higher type/token ratio, which implies a higher lexical density, i.e. a higher number of different types of words is used. While the Recent awards, though generally longer, apparently use a more standardized, less varied lexicon.

Court of Arbitration for Sport <http://www.tas-cas.org>	
Years 2005-2010 ("Recent awards subcorpus") 116 awards Tokens 1,167,534; Types: 19,133 Type/token ratio (TTR): 1.75 Standardised TTR: 32.69	Years 1991-1999 ("Archive awards subcorpus") 33 awards Tokens: 183,084; Types: 7,731 Type/token ratio (TTR): 4.44 Standardised TTR: 34.54

Table 1. Corpus composition.

In order to identify all intertextual markers, the subcorpora were tagged through a partially manual 'search and substitute' procedure, so that the WordSmith Tools concordancer could locate and count all their occurrences as a first step of analysis; then, the frequency and distribution of intertextual markers across the two sub-corpora were explored quantitatively, by means of wordlists and concordances. As a second step, two sample awards, a recent one and an old one, were selected, for a

[5] For the purposes of this study, awards in languages other than English were discarded.

similar quantitative analysis and comparison of occurrences of intertextual features as well as for in-depth qualitative analysis of the same features.

5. Markers of intertextuality in the Sport Arbitration Corpus

The most significant intertextual markers, i.e. the expressions introducing intertextuality, which were found in the corpus mostly correspond to those that Bhatia (1998) mentioned for legal discourse: *in accordance with, pursuant to, within the meaning of, referred to in, for the purposes of, subject to, notwithstanding, without prejudice to*, etc. Most of them are complex prepositional phrases, of widespread, almost formulaic usage in legal language.

In addition to these, this investigation also includes parts of texts in quotation marks, both single words and longer "integral citations" (Swales 1990), in order to analyse how other texts are explicitly given voice in sport arbitration texts. According to Swales' definition, in an integral citation the actual words of a different text are explicitly cited along with details about the source of the citation, corresponding to a "fully integral reference" in Fløttum, Dahl and Kinn's (2006: 226-227) terminology. In the sport arbitration texts, articles of rules or codes, or tribunals' previous decisions are mostly cited, though there are other cases too, which will be illustrated later on. Such integral citations are usually two or more lines long in the sports-related awards. Short expressions of just one or very few words in quotation marks were analysed separately and are referred to in this chapter as "quotations", to distinguish them from integral citations.

As we will see in the analysis of the two sample awards, there are other intertextual devices and expressions, but these above-mentioned markers are the most significant ones in the corpus as a whole.

5.1. Functions of intertextual markers

The functions of the selected intertextual devices were investigated in the CAS corpus according to Bhatia (1998)'s classification of them for legal discourse, so that for each function one or more intertextual markers were identified:

- the function of signalling textual authority, i.e. referring to the source of authority that supports a statement or attributes rights, is mostly performed through the use of integral citations and devices such as *in accordance with* and *pursuant to*;

- the function of providing terminological explanation, i.e. explaining a legal term/concept through reference to articles of law, is usually performed by short quotations, sometimes preceded by *within the meaning of*;
- the function of facilitating textual mapping, i.e. pointing to the legal text or part of text where a concept is defined or circumstances are set out, etc., is mainly performed by the complex prepositional phrase *referred to in*:
- the function of defining legal scope, i.e. specifying the scope of a legal provision, *for the purposes of* is used. As for sub-categories of 'defining legal scope', *subject to* is used as a conflict-avoiding textual link, i.e. a link used to restrict the scope and explain conditions of applicable rules, as in the following example: "subject to the primacy of applicable FIFA's regulations, Swiss Law shall apply complementarily" [award #1448]; *notwithstanding* and *without prejudice to* are used as conflict-resolving textual links, i.e. devices used to acknowledge priority of rules or articles of law for the case, as in the following example: "the Appellant submits that he had been denied the possibility to attend a hearing [...], notwithstanding the provisions of Article 98 FDC [...]" [award #1155].

5.2. Quantitative analysis and comparison of intertextual markers

The frequency values of intertextual markers for each subcorpus were computed for statistical analysis. Graph 1 shows a comparison of the percentage values of occurrences for each intertextual device in the sub-corpora.[6]

As can be seen, percentage values are very similar between the subcorpora, with the exceptions of *within the meaning of*, which is four times more frequent in the Archive Awards sub-corpus, and *notwithstanding*, which is almost twice more frequent in the Recent Awards sub-corpus.

Although percentage values of occurrences are similar, the dispersion, i.e. the distribution of the markers *across* all the texts is definitely more uniform in the Recent Awards subcorpus, ranging from a minimum of 15% to a maximum of 99% of texts featuring intertextual devices, while in

[6] Percentage values were calculated on total number of words.

the Archive subcorpus we find a minimum of only 6% up to a maximum of 94% of texts featuring intertextual devices (see Table 2 and Graph 2).

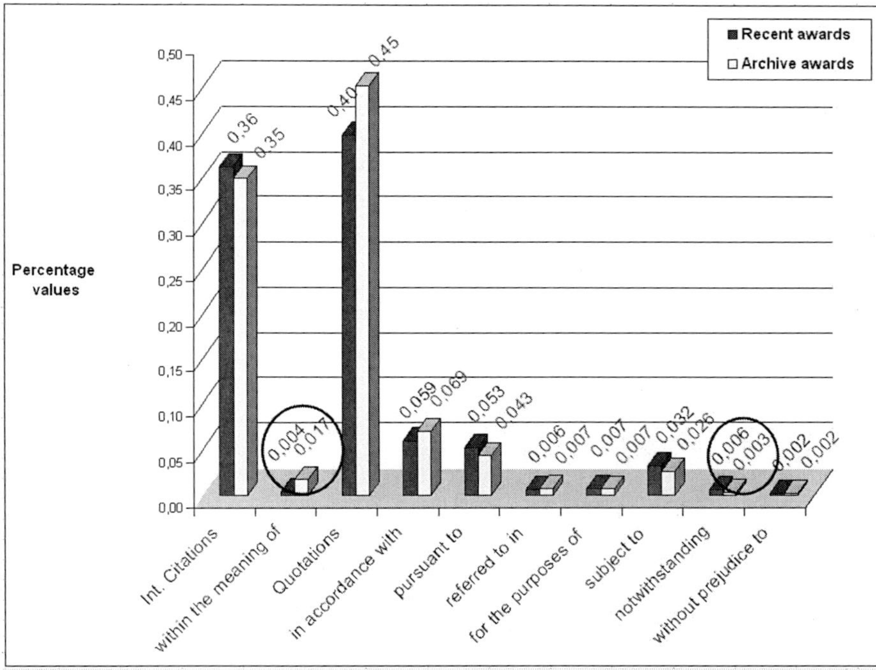

Graph 1. Comparison of percentage values of intertextual markers in the subcorpora.

Moreover, in the Recent awards dispersion values *within* each text are also generally higher than they are in the Archive awards. For example, in the Recent subcorpus 61% of texts show a dispersion value for integral citations higher than 0.70, indicating a generally uniform distribution of integral citations within each text, while in the Archive subcorpus only 42.4% of the texts show a dispersion value higher than 0.70, indicating a generally sparser distribution of integral citations within each text. This implies that in Archive awards integral citations tend to cluster in some sections of each text and are not found at all in other sections. This might be related to the legal analysis sections, which in the Archive awards seem to be shorter, less detailed and which do not explicitly report parts from the Appellants' submissions, as we will see.

	Percentages		Distribution across texts	
	%	%	Tot.: 116	Tot.: 33
Intertextual markers	Recent	Archive	Recent Texts (%)	Archive Texts (%)
int. citations	0.36	0.35	113 (97.41)	31 (93.94)
in accordance with	0.059	0.069	107 (92.24)	29 (87.88)
pursuant to	0.053	0.043	108 (93.10)	24 (72.73)
within the meaning of	0.004	0.017	27 (23.28)	6 (18.18)
quotations	0.40	0.45	115 (99.14)	30 (90.91)
referred to in	0.006	0.007	37 (31.9)	8 (24.24)
for the purposes of	0.007	0.007	41 (35.34)	6 (18.18)
subject to	0.032	0.026	94 (81.03)	21 (63.64)
notwithstanding	0.006	0.003	42 (36.21)	5 (15.15)
without prejudice to	0.002	0.002	17 (14.66)	2 (6.06)

Table 2. Percentages and dispersion values in the subcorpora.

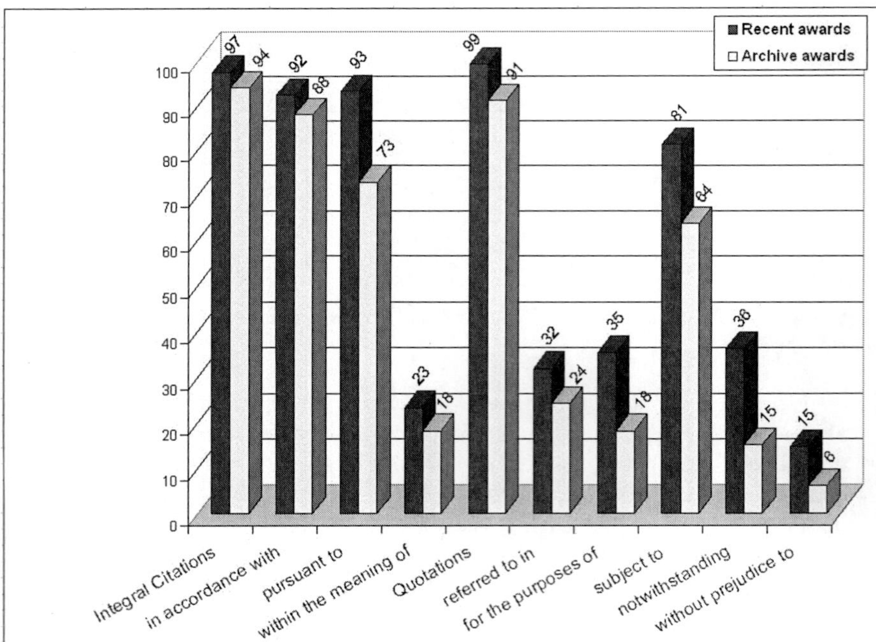

Graph 2. Comparison of dispersion values of intertextual markers in the subcorpora.

Thus, in general, in the Archive subcorpus recourse to intertextuality seems less homogeneous than in the Recent subcorpus. This might be due to a recent attempt at making arbitration texts more explicit, precise and unambiguous, possibly under the influence of litigation texts.

6. Analysis of sample awards

Two sample awards were subsequently analysed, CAS award #1448, issued in 2008, and CAS award #122, issued in 1996. These awards were selected because they are quite representative of their respective subcorpus, each of them featuring a number of words close to the average of its subcorpus. Furthermore they were chosen among others with similar total number of words also because of their issuing dates: award #1448 is among the most recent ones, and award #122 is among the least recent ones. Occurrences of intertextual markers in the two sample awards were computed and their intertextual functions identified and compared.

6.1. Functions of intertextual markers in the sample awards

The analysis of functions of the intertextual markers in the two awards shows a few differences from the corpus as a whole, as predictable. Mainly, a close-up look at these texts highlights the variety of realisations of intertextuality.

Textual authority is mostly signalled through the use of integral citations and of devices such as *in accordance with* and *pursuant to*, but also of equivalent devices such as *according to (article...)*, *under* and *in application of*.

Terminological explanation is mainly provided by quotations, but not through the use of *within the meaning of*, and only once through the use of *under the notion of*.

The function of facilitating textual mapping is performed by *referred to in,* as well as by *as provided in* and other similar devices, or sometimes by other types of expressions, such as *see above*, *see below*, *as set out in the following paragraphs* etc.

As in the whole corpus, *for the purposes of* is used to generically define legal scope, and *subject to* is used as conflict avoiding textual link, while no conflict-resolving textual links (*notwithstanding* and *without prejudice to*) were found in either of these awards. This might be due to the fact that the Panel chooses clarity over the conciseness of complex prepositional phrases, preferring to explain in full details how they intend to resolve possible conflicts, or simply that in the cases under examination there are no legally-relevant conflicts to be resolved.

6.2. Quantitative analysis and comparison of intertextual markers in the sample awards

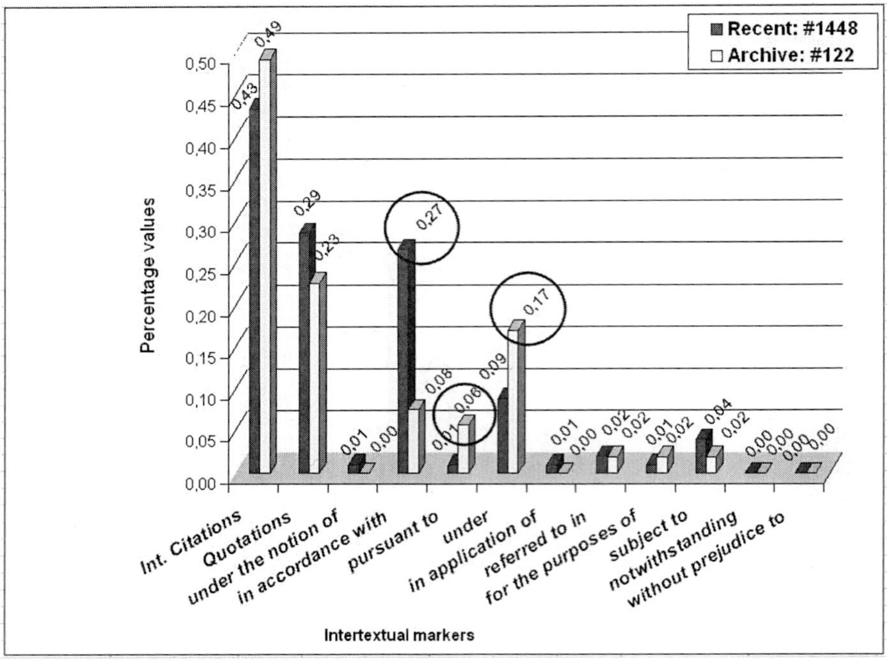

Graph 3. Comparison of percentage values of intertextual markers in the sample awards.

Graph 3 shows a quantitative analysis of the occurrences in the two awards of the above intertextual devices discussed above.

Few differences emerge from the comparison between the sub-corpora (Graph 3). Mainly, in the Recent Awards corpus there is a higher number of occurrences of *in accordance with* (and equivalent expressions), and a significantly lower number of occurrences of *pursuant to* and *under*. Besides, there seems to be a stronger presence of integral citations and a weaker presence of quotations in the Archive awards sub-corpus. Some explanations for such differences are offered in the next section, which presents the qualitative analysis along with some examples of markers of intertextuality and their functions from these two texts.

6.3. Qualitative analysis and comparison of intertextual markers and functions in the sample awards

In the following sub-sections, drawing on the classification introduced in section 5.1, the functions of intertextual markers will be explored more in detail, by means of qualitative analysis of the selected awards; examples from the texts will also be given and commented upon.

6.3.1. Signalling textual authority: integral citations, "in accordance with", etc.

The function of integral citations as intertextual devices is to explicitly signal the source of authority. There is no single specific recurring marker introducing integral citations, but some phrases, typical of legal texts, were more often found preceding the citations. In the Archive award, for instance, integral citations are usually introduced by expressions like *the rules / the guides / the agreement* etc. *provide as follows*, as expected in legal quoting practice. Here is an example:

> (1) The ICC [International Coordinating Committee of World Sports Organizations for the Disabled] *Rules provide as follows*: "Rule 1.1.3: Any competitor refusing to submit to a medical control or examination or who is found guilty of doping shall be excluded." [7] [award #122]

In the Recent Award corpus, integral citations are similarly introduced by expressions like: *the regulations / the code/ the statutes* etc. *provide as follows*, with the same function of signalling and explicitly referencing to textual authority, as in the following example:

> (2) *Article 17 paragraphs 3 and 4 of the FIFA* [Fédération Internationale de Football Association] *Regulations provide as follows:* "In addition to the obligation to pay compensation, sporting sanctions shall also be imposed on any player found to be in breach of contract during the Protected Period." [award #1448]

[7] In all the examples, italics and underlining have been added.

But in this text there are also cases (about one third of the occurrences) in which the citation is from one of the parties' submissions, as in (3) below, where a declaration by the appellant (*the Player*) is reported:

(3) […] given that the Player was not present at the Hearing, *the Panel may not disregard the Player's declaration in his appeal brief that he* "perfectly knew that he could have been called to serve the military service; however, he was absolutely confident that he would receive an exception according to Art. 37 of the Law no. 127/1980, due to his particular status of professional football player, who was playing abroad" [award #1448]

There are such cases in the Archive award too, but they only appear in the section of the parties' requests and contentions, which are cited in most CAS awards. In general, in the Archive subcorpus the appellant's submissions are basically never quoted in the legal analysis section, and integral citations are almost exclusively taken from rules, codes and precedents. Moreover, as we shall see, this specific Archive award focuses on the way ICC rules are written, more than on the parties' submissions.

Other intertextual devices used to signal textual authority are *in accordance with* and *under*, which in the Archive award are usually followed by *rules/law/Charte*r, etc., as the sources of authority backing the Panel's decisions or statements. This function is exemplified in excerpt (4) below:

(4) The Panel found it possible and appropriate to resolve the dispute *in accordance with the relevant rules* of the International Coordinating Committee, there having been no allegation that said rules would not be effective *under Swiss law*. [award #122]

Similarly, in the Recent Award corpus we find *in accordance with*, *according to* and *under* performing the same function, usually referring to *rules/law/article* etc. as in the following examples:

(5) *In accordance with mandatory Egyptian Law*, he was then obliged to stay in his country for 3 years. [award #1448]

(6) The Panel is of the opinion that the FIFA Statutes provide *under Article 61 para.3 (b)* a clear indication of cases where CAS would not deal with an appeal arising from a suspension imposed by a FIFA body. [award #1448]

Pursuant to is also used in similar expressions and with the same function in both these awards.

6.3.2. Providing terminological explanation: quotations

As in the corpus in general, quotations are actually mostly used not as intertextual devices, but as *intra*-textual devices to establish naming conventions and references within the text. In fact, in the sport arbitration corpus a wide use of acronyms emerged, especially in the initial part of the awards, where parties are introduced (such as CAS, WADA, IOC, FIFA and all other Federations and Sports Clubs' names). Hence the necessity to present acronyms in short quotations, as in this example from the Archive award:

> (7) The medals were sent to the International Wheelchair Basketball Federation (*"IWBF"*), which represented that it would hold the medals until the dispute had been resolved on appeal to the Court of Arbitration for Sport (*"CAS"*). [award #122]

This award also offers interesting examples of quotations used as intertextual devices, with the function of referring to and explaining words or expressions of other texts, in this case ICC Rules. In fact, the Panel comments (here and elsewhere in this text) on the phraseology of such controversial and ambiguous ICC Rules, and these recurring remarks and references might explain the higher frequency of citations in this award compared to the rest of the subcorpus:

> (8) In the expression of the ICC Rules, he was therefore *"guilty of doping"*. This is perhaps **unfortunate phraseology**, because the word *"guilty"* suggests reprehensible conduct and does not allow the outsider to distinguish between cheaters and inadvertent violators. [award #122]

Here follows another example of the interesting "textual analysis" (award #122) that the Panel was somehow forced to carry out:

> (9) The Panel notes in passing that the word *"excluded"* in Rule 1.1.3 was presumably intended to cover forfeiture of a result already obtained in an individual sport as well as prohibition from continuing in an on-going competition, whether an individual or a team sport. **It is unfortunate that such basic issues are dealt with by implication rather than by clear declarative language**. [award #122]

As can be seen in the previous example, along with providing explanations of expressions (in this case the word "excluded"), the arbitrators also comment on the unsatisfactory, imprecise language used by the drafters of the Rules. This goes on and on in the text, even to the point of contesting the very source of authority previously quoted, stating that: "The Panel does not endorse Rule 1.1.4" (award #122). This is an interesting characteristic of this older award, probably related to its dating back to a time (1996) when some sport and anti-doping rules had been recently drafted for the first time, and some sport federations and associations were themselves relatively "young" and in the making.[8]

As for the Recent award, in the following example of intratextual reference the full name "Dispute Resolution Chamber" is duly followed by its acronym in brackets and quotations:

> (10) On 11 March 2005, the FIFA Dispute Resolution Chamber (*"DRC"*) issued a decision on a claim that had been presented by Club X. against the Player and Club Y. [award #1448]

In such parts of the CAS corpus awards introducing acronyms, we also usually find the expression *hereinafter referred to as* before the actual acronym, but this was not the case in either of these awards.

There are cases of quotations used as intertextual reference in the Recent award text too, as in the following examples, in which a legal concept ("impossibility of performance") is introduced in quotations, and subsequently commented and discussed, also with the use of the complex prepositional phrase *under the notion of* (which corresponds to the more common expression in the corpus *within the meaning of*):

> (11) […] on 25 April 2006 it became impossible (*"impossibility of performance"*) for the Player to comply with his contractual performance towards Club Y […] [award #1448]

> (12) In the present proceedings the Player claimed that the same facts fall *under the notion of subsequent "impossibility of performance"* which constitutes a just cause to terminate (or even void) an employment contract. [award #1448]

As can be seen, the point at issue is whether the appellant did have a just cause to terminate his contract, and in this respect the notion of "impossibility of performance" that is being commented and explained in

---

[8] The ICC (International Coordinating Committee of World Sports Organizations for the Disabled) was actually replaced by the International Paralympic Committee in 1992, immediately after the 1992 Paralympic Games in Barcelona, when the events of the case dealt with in award #122 took place (see <http://www.paralympic.org/sites/default/files/document/120209104900153_2012_02_History+of+Paralympic+Movement.pdf>).

this part of the text is crucial. The arbitrators seem thus very keen on precision, even to the point of redundancy, in the attempt to be clear and exhaustive in their references and explanations of the necessary legal notions.

6.3.3. Facilitating textual mapping: "as provided in", "referred to in"

The function of facilitating textual mapping is generally introduced by markers such as *referred to in*, *as provided in*, etc. In the Recent award the complex prepositional phrase *as provided in* is used with this function, followed by the article or the law it refers to:

> (13) The Player submitted in his appeal brief and accepted during the Hearing that the "impossibility of performance" (either as a generally recognised principle of civil law or *as provided in Art. 119 of the Swiss Code of Obligations*) may qualify as a reason to void a contract or to terminate it without consequences for any of the contracting parties, in case the following two criteria are met: [...] [award #1448]

In this example the explanation of a legal notion (the "impossibility of performance", mentioned also in the previous two examples, of which (13) is a continuation) also offers an intertextual reference to the legal text where the notion itself is defined and coded. Thus, for further clarity and precision the arbitrators explicitly point the readers to the article of law where that notion is properly defined, using the intertextual marker *as provided in*.

In the Archive award the function of facilitating textual mapping is performed by the complex prepositional phrase *referred to in*, and is used in example (14) for the sake of brevity as well as clarity:

> (14) Rule 1.1.5 provides that the issue of such continued participation (without the individual offender) is a matter of discretion, to be decided after consultations with the bodies *referred to in the Rule*. [award #122]

Both in the Archive award and in the Recent award textual mapping is also facilitated through the use of non-formulaic expressions, functioning as intratextual references, such as *see paragraph above*, *see below*, *as stated above*, etc. However, these expressions were not considered nor computed as intertextual markers in this study, as the identification of all of them in all their possible variations would have needed a long and time-consuming manual analysis, and intratextual references were not the main focus of this study.

6.3.4. Defining legal scope: "for the purposes of"

For the purposes of is the intertextual marker typically used with the function of defining legal scope in the whole CAS corpus. In example (15) from the Archive award it allows the Panel to clarify that, although the ICC Rules are ambiguously drafted, their core meaning and function are still clear enough and valid, and the Rules are applicable and binding:

> (15) **These hesitations suggest an unmistakable need for clearer rules and more predictable practices**. But *for the purposes of this Panel*, the imperfections of the text and its application are important only if they prejudiced the rights of K. or his team mates. The Panel finds that they did not. The Panel has held that Rule 1.1.4 requires automatic forfeiture of the game, and that a team which forfeits a final match cannot retain its gold medals. It may have been a source of irritation and frustration that various official statements suggested that there was room for discussion and therefore discretion or clemency, but such statements could do nothing to change the fact that as of the determination that K.'s test was positive, there was no hope for him or his team mates – barring a failure to apply the Rules – to retain their gold medals. [award #122]

The Panel is thus allowed to decide on the case even if the ICC Rules are not clear enough, precisely because they don't "prejudice the rights of the Appellant" in the case under examination, which is all that is needed for the Panel's decision and its legal scope.

As for the use of *for the purposes of* in the Recent award, in example (16) the Panel uses it in reference to an article of law, to re-define and re-consider the compensation received by the Second Appellant as "transfer fee", rather than as simple "compensation":

> (16) Firstly, Club Y. paid on 18 July 2005 to Club X. the amount of USD 250,000 (approx. EUR 184,010.16, see above 7.2.4a) as compensation for the breach of contract determined by the DRC. *For the purposes of article 17 para.1*, such compensation may be calculated as a transfer fee. [award #1448]

7. Concluding remarks

As far as intertextuality can tell us, the diachronic analysis carried out here suggests that colonization by the litigation practice has not (yet) conspicuously touched sport arbitration. However, few but interesting differences among older and recent awards in terms of intertextual features might be taken to indicate that a recent trend in this sense is under way.

Differences, as revealed by quantitative analysis, can be summed up as follows:

- the dispersion of intertextual markers is definitely more uniform in the Recent subcorpus;
- unlike in older awards, the legal analysis section of the Recent awards includes integral citations of parties' submissions;
- some markers occur with different frequency in the two subcorpora. *Within the meaning of* (used to provide terminological explanation) is four times more frequent in the Archive subcorpus, while *notwithstanding* (used as conflict resolving textual link) is twice more frequent in the Recent subcorpus.

The use of integral citations seems particularly interesting, as they are concentrated in specific sections and even completely absent in some of the Archive awards, but almost invariably present, and distributed more evenly through various sections, in the Recent ones. Since integral citations as markers of intertextuality in awards perform the function of signalling textual authority, such even small differences show that authority and its sources (typically rules, codes, previous cases, etc.) are expressed and claimed in a slightly different way in the older awards, where references to sources of authority are not considered as necessary as they are in Recent awards. Along the same line, the more uniform distribution of intertextual markers in general in the Recent Awards subcorpus seems to testify a recent attempt at making awards more precise, clear and unambiguous. These results might generally indicate an incipient concern for arbitrators to assert authority and make their decisions as explicit and conclusive as possible, which might be seen as an effect of litigation influence.

Quantitative analysis has been complemented with a close-up analysis of sample awards selected from the two ends of the time span taken into consideration, which has revealed interesting aspects that had not been detected by means of automatic corpus interrogation. First of all, intertextuality resulted to be realized through a greater variety of forms than emerged from quantitative analysis. Secondly, qualitative analysis shed further light on the explicitly dialogic orientation of both the awards, but, again, with some differences. In the Archive award the Panel acted as commentators of rules, wishing for uncontroversial phrasing of articles and rules, at a time (1996) when some sports rules and some sports federations and associations were relatively new. In the Recent award, qualitative analysis showed that the Panel quotes and discusses the

Appellant's submissions to explain their legal analysis and clarify the terms and scope of Rules. In both cases, however, it seems clear that intertextuality is aimed at achieving a higher degree of clarity and precision, a trend which, as suggested by qualitative analysis, seems to have become slightly more marked in recent awards.

References

Allen, Graham. 2000. *Intertextuality*. London: Routledge.

Bakhtin, Mikhail. 1981. *The Dialogic Imagination: Four Essays,* edited by Michael Holquist and translated by Caryl Emerson and Michael Holquist. Austin: University of Texas Press.

—. 1984. *Problems of Dostoevsky's Poetics,* edited and translated by Caryl Emerson. Minneapolis: University of Minnesota Press.

Bauman, Richard. 2004. *A World of Others' Words: Cross-Cultural Perspectives on Intertextuality*. Malden, MA: Blackwell Publishing.

Bhatia, Vijay K. 1998. "Intertextuality in Legal Discourse". *The Language Teacher* 22, no. 11. Available at <http://www.jalt-publications.org/tlt/files/98/nov/batia.html>.

—. 2007. "Interdiscursivity in critical genre analysis". In *ANAIS Proceedings of the 4th International Symposium on Genre Studies*, edited by Adair Bonini, Débora de Carvalho Figueiredo and Fábio José Rauen. Tubarão – Santa Catarina: CD-Rom Publication ISSN 1808-7655, University of Southern Santa Catarina, Tubarão, Santa Catarina, Brazil - August 15th-18th.

—. 2008. "Genre analysis, ESP and professional practice". *English for Specific Purposes* 27, no. 2: 161-174.

Court of Arbitration for Sport. <http://www.tas-cas.org/>

Evangelisti Allori, Paola. 2004. "International Arbitration in Different Settings: Same or Different Practice?" In *Intercultural Aspects of Specialized Communication,* edited by Christopher N. Candlin and Maurizio Gotti, 223-240. Bern: Peter Lang.

—. 2010. "Content as Indicator of Genre Identity. Key Concepts in Sports-related Arbitral Awards". In *Discorse, Identity and Roles in Specialized Communication*, edited by Giuliana Garzone and James Archibald, 139-161. Bern: Peter Lang.

Fazio, Alessandra and Michela Menghini. 2010. "Professional Identity in Sports-Related Arbitration Discourse: A Study on the Modelling of a Dynamic Conceptual Structure". In *Discorse, Identity and Roles in Specialized Communication*, edited by Giuliana Garzone and James Archibald, 163-190. Bern: Peter Lang.

Flowerdew, John (ed.) 2002. *Academic Discourse*. London: Longman.

Gibbons, John. 2003. *Forensic Linguistics. An Introduction to Language in the Justice System.* Oxford: Blackwell.

Gotti, Maurizio 2003. *Specialized Discourse. Linguistic Features and Changing Conventions*. Bern: Peter Lang.

Fløttum, Kjersti, Trine Dahl, and Torodd Kinn. 2006. *Academic Voices Across Languages and Disciplines.* Amsterdam / Philadelphia: John Benjamins Publishing Company.

Kristeva, Julia. 1980. *Desire in Language: A Semiotic Approach to Literature and Art.* New York: Columbia University Press.

Hunter, Martin. 2000. "International Commercial Dispute Resolution: The Challenge of the Twenty-First Century". *LCIA Arbitration International* 16, no. 4: 379-392.

Menghini, Michela. 2011. "Intertextual Devices in Sports-related Arbitration Discourse". In *Genre(s) on the Move: Hybridization and Discourse Change in Specialized Communication*, edited by Srikant Sarangi, Vanda Polese and Giuditta Caliendo, 425-444. Napoli: Edizioni Scientifiche Italiane (ESI).

Nariman, Fali S. 2000. "The Spirit of Arbitration: The Tenth Annual Goff Lecture". *Arbitration International* 16, no.3: 261-278.

Scott, Mike. 2009. *WordSmith Tools 5.0*. Oxford: Oxford University Press.

Swales, John M. 1990. *Genre Analysis: English in Academic and Research Settings*. Cambridge: Cambridge University Press.

CONTRIBUTORS

DONELLA ANTELMI is a Tenured Researcher in Linguistics at Libera Università di Lingue e Comunicazione IULM, Milan (Italy). Her earlier research work focused on language acquisition and sociolinguistics, with special attention for Italian standard language use and its varieties. Her recent and current research activity is based on interdisciplinary approaches to discursive practices, applying pragmatics, argumentation and rhetoric to several varieties of discourses, namely political, legal and media discourse. She took part in a few national and international projects, and is currently involved in a research project on the Metalanguage of Linguistics (PRIN 2009). Her research work has been published in book chapters and refereed journals. Her published books are: *La prima grammatica dell'italiano* (1997), *Lingua d'oggi* (with G. Garzone and F. Santulli,1998), *Fisiologia e patologia dell'apprendimento del linguaggio* (1999), *Il Discorso dei Media* (2006), *Pragmatica della comunicazione turistica* (with G. Held and F. Santulli, 2007) and *Comunicazione e analisi del discorso* (in press 2012).

VIJAY BHATIA has research interests in genre analysis of academic and professional discourses in legal, business, newspaper, advertising contexts. He has widely published in all of these areas: research articles, books chapters, edited volumes, and individually written books. Two of his books A*nalysing Genre: Language Use in Professional Settings* (1993) and *Worlds of Written Discourse: A Genre-based View* (2004), are widely used by researchers in genre theory and practice. Some of his recent research projects include *Analyzing Genre-Bending in Corporate Disclosure Documents*, and *International Arbitration Practice: A Discourse Analytical Study*, in which he leads research teams from more than 20 countries.

CHIARA DEGANO (PhD) is a Tenured Researcher in English Linguistics and Translation at Università degli Studi di Milano, Italy. Her research is centred on discourse analysis, which she has integrated with the quantitative approach of corpus linguistics and with aspects of argumentation theory (she is a member of ILIAS - International Learned Institute for Argumentation Studies, and CLAVIER - Corpus and Language Variation in English Research Group). Within this framework she has pursued a twofold line of research, focusing on the representation of international conflicts in the media publishing research aricles and a monograph (*Discorsi di guerra: il prologo del conflitto iracheno nella stampa britannica e italiana* [War Discourses: The Prologue to the Iraqi conflict in the British and Italian Press], 2008), and on professional discourse, which she investigated in the perspective of ideological and evaluative elements, with specific reference to issues of identity. She has taken part in two national research projects (PRIN 2005 "Identity and Culture in English Domain-specific Discourse" and PRIN 2007 "Tension and Change in English domain-specific Genres") and in the international research project *International Arbitration Practice: A Discourse Analytical Study* led by V. K. Bhatia, investigating generic tensions in international awards.

PAOLA EVANGELISTI ALLORI is Full Professor of English at the Italian University of Sport and Human Movement – IUSM, Rome, Italy. Her main research interests are in the language/culture interaction in domain-specific discourse, both academic and professional. She has published extensively on the comparative analysis of specialized discourse in various disciplinary areas and fields of action (Economics, Psychology, Politics, History, Journalism), both cross-linguistically and cross-disciplinarily. Her current research includes the comparative analysis of legal discourse in international arbitration practice with special emphasis on Sports related Arbitration. Recent publications include *English in Academic and Professional Settings*, Special Issue of *TEXTUS*, co-edited with Eija Ventola (2002); "International Arbitration in Different Settings: Same or Different Practice?" (2004); "Metaphors They Report by. The Construction of National Identity through Sport Commentaries in Different Cultural Communities" (2005); "Arbitration in Sport. Rules and Practices from Two Different Codes" (2008); and *Language, Culture and the Law. The Formulation of Legal Concepts across Systems and Cultures*, co-edited with Vijay K. Bhatia and Christopher N. Candlin (2008).

MANLIO FRIGO is Full Professor of International and European Law and of International Contracts and Arbitration Law at Milan State University (*Università degli Studi di Milano*), Department of International, Juridical, Political and Historical Studies. He is a member of the Steering Committee of the PhD in International Economic Law of Bocconi University, Milan, and of the Committee on Cultural Heritage Law of the ILA (*International Law Association*). A Consultant for Unesco, Unidroit and the EU Commission, he is active as arbitrator in national and international commercial disputes. He has authored several publications concerning contractual obligations, international cooperation in the field of civil and commercial procedure, the applicable law and the linguistic factor in the circulation of arbitral awards, and the protection of cultural property.

GIULIANA GARZONE is Full Professor of English Linguistics and Translation at Università degli Studi di Milano, Italy. Her main field of investigation is specialized discourse in its different domains, which she has explored in a discourse analytical perspective, integrating it whenever necessary with computerized interrogation routines, also in light of her work on the theoretical issues involved in combining Critical Discourse Analysis with Corpus Linguistics. She has co-ordinated several research projects and published extensively on legal language, on scientific discourse, and on business communication. She has also (co-)edited several volumes (most recently, *Discourse, Ideology and Specialized Communication*, with S. Sarangi, 2007; *The Use of English in Institutional and Business Settings,* with C. Ilie, 2007; *Discourse and Identities in Institutional, Professional and Academic Communication,* with J. Archibald, 2010; *Discourse, Communication and the Enterprise: Genres and Trends*, 2011, with M. Gotti). Her other research interests are in translation and interpreting studies, on which she has also published extensively (among others: *Interpreting in the 21st Century,* with M. Viezzi, 2002; *Esperienze del tradurre*, 2005). She is general editor (with A. Cardinaletti e F. Frasnedi) of the book series *Lingua, traduzione, didattica*.

DIANA GINER is a part-time lecturer at the Department of English and German Philology in the Faculty of Arts of the University of Zaragoza. She graduated in English Studies at the University of Zaragoza in 2003. Later, she obtained the Postgraduate Certificate in Secondary Education at the University of Nottingham and an MA in Textual and Cultural Studies in English at the University of Zaragoza. She is now working on her doctoral thesis on Arbitration practices within a PhD programme at the University of Zaragoza. Her research focuses on the rhetorical strategies present in the argumentation of arbitral awards through qualitative discourse analysis tools. She is also familiar with the analysis of interpersonality in research academic articles ("Writing with Conviction: Modelling Persuasion in Academic Discourse", 2009, with I. Vázquez; "Beyond Mood and Modality: Epistemic Markers as Hedges in Research Articles. A Cross-disciplinary Study", 2008, with I. Vázquez). Her other research interests include genre analysis, applied linguistics, professional legal practices and ESP.

JANE LUNG holds a PhD in legal and business discourse from City University of Hong Kong. She has been working closely with language specialists, subject specialists, ESP practitioners and language teachers in a number of research projects. She has interests in discourse analysis, genre analysis, corpus linguistics, professional communication such as legal, business, newspaper, advertising and other promotional genres, as well as language teaching and learning. Projects she has worked on with Professor Vijay Bhatia include *International Arbitration Practice: A Discourse Analytical Study* in which more than 20 international research teams participated. She is an associate professor at Macao Polytechnic Institute.

MICHELA MENGHINI is a Tenured Researcher in English Linguistics and Translation at the University of Rome "Foro Italico", and is part of the PRIN 2007 national research project "Tension and Change in English domain-specific Genres", Rome Unit's topic: "Tension and Change in English Juridical Genres: a Discourse Analytical Study of Variation in International Arbitral Awards". She has a university degree in foreign languages and professional training in computer science. Her main interests are corpus linguistics, and the application and development of computer tools for language analysis in general. Among her publications, there are: "Professional Identity in Sports-Related Discourse: a study on the Modelling of a Dynamic Conceptual Structure", 2010; and "Italian-English Correspondences in the Juridical Discourse of Sports Arbitration: an Electronic Glossary", 2008, which was a product of her work within the project "Linguistic and cross-cultural features of legal texts in professional fields: the case of international arbitration in Sport", financed by the Italian Ministry of University in 2003-2005.

CHIARA PREITE is a Tenured Researcher in French Language and Translation at the University of Modena and Reggio Emilia. She holds an MA in Legal Translation from the University of Genoa and a PhD in French Linguistics from the University of Brescia. Her main research interests lie in the fields of textual and discursive analysis, legal French, specialized lexicography and terminology. She has published widely on these topics and is the author of the recently published volume *Langage du droit et linguistique. Etude de l'organisation textuelle, énonciative et argomentative des arrêts de la Cour (et du Tribunal) de Justice des*

Communautés européennes. She is currently carrying out work on law dictionaries from the jurilinguistic perspective.

MICHELE SALA, PhD (University of Bergamo), MA (Youngstown State University, Ohio), is a Tenured Researcher in English Language and Translation at the University of Bergamo (Faculty of Foreign Languages and Literatures), where he teaches English linguistic courses at graduate and undergraduate level. An assistant editor of *The European English Messenger* and a member of CERLIS (Centro di Ricerca sui Linguaggi Specialistici, coordinated by Prof. Maurizio Gotti) and CLAVIER (the Corpus and Language Variation in English Research Group), his research activity and major publications are mainly concerned with ESP varieties, with a specific focus on the application of genre and discourse analytical methods to a corpus-based study of academic communication and legal discourse (*Persuasion and politeness in academic discourse*, 2008). These research interests are also reflected in his work on the analysis of the semantic, textual and pragmatic aspects of legal translation. He has also published articles in the area of pragmatics and cognitive linguistics, literature and narratology.

FRANCESCA SANTULLI is an Associate Professor of Linguistics at IULM University, Milan. Her research has focused on various aspects of language and linguistics, ranging from the history of linguistics to philology, from phonetics to language contact. She published many articles and a book (*L'opera di Hermann Paul tra linguistica e filologia* [*Herman Paul's work between linguistics and philology*], 1995) on the theoretical aspects of language change, with specific reference to the fundamental work of German philologist and linguist H. Paul. Her research also focused on phonetics and phonology, with particular emphasis on the didactic implications (*La voce e la macchina. Fonetica, glottodidattica, multimedialità* [*Voices and machines. Phonetics, language teaching, multimedia*], 1999, with G. Garzone). She has also published on translation and interpreting, as well as on interference and borrowing. She has applied linguistic and rhetorical models of analysis to *corpora* of texts belonging to different genres, combining qualitative and quantitative methodologies. In a book on political discourse (*Le parole del potere, il potere delle parole. Retorica e discorso politico* [*Power of words, words of power. Rhetoric and political discourse*], 2005) she integrates different theoretical approaches and presents a detailed analysis of political texts belonging to different sub-genres. Her most recent book (*Pragmatica della comunicazione turistica* [*The Pragmatics of tourism communication*],

2007, with D. Antelmi and G. Held) applies the principles of pragmatic analysis to texts produced in the realm of tourist communication (travel guidebooks, websites, advertisements).

GIROLAMO TESSUTO is an Associate Professor of English Linguistics at the Law Faculty of Seconda Università degli Studi di Napoli where he teaches Legal English and Specialized Translation. He also teaches in the Law Faculty of the University of Naples 'Federico II'. His main research interests focus on legal discourse and genre analysis in academic and professional settings from a synchronic and contrastive perspective, legal terminology and translation, and plain language issues. Besides a research monograph, he has published several research and conference papers in collected volumes. Among his latest publications: "US Commercial Arbitration Rules and Mediation Procedures: Linguistic and Discoursal Features of a Genre in Action', 2010; "Legal Problem Question Answer Genre across Jurisdictions and Cultures", 2011; "Developing Genre-based English Legal Writing Literacy in Italian Law Faculty Contexts: *Law Essays*. Research Principles and Pedagogic Applications", 2011; "US *Agreement to Mediate Forms*: Exploring Discursive and Generic Features", 2011.

IGNACIO VÁZQUEZ is Full Professor of English Linguistics at the Department of English and German Philology of the University of Zaragoza. His research interests include Pragmatics and Discourse Analysis, Systemic Linguistics, Translation and Contrastive Studies (English-Spanish). He has recently been involved in research on generic integrity in academic and professional discourse and its uses in the construction, expression and popularisation of scientific knowledge in English (2009-11). He is currently responsible for a research group called INTERLAE, which explores interpersonality in academic and professional discourse from a socio-pragmatic perspective. He focuses on writer stance in academic and one specific variety of professional discourse, the discourse of arbitration. He is particularly interested in the study of professional legal discourse. He is also interested in the translation of English legal documents into Spanish, and is a sworn translator of English into Spanish or viceversa.

HAN ZHENGRUI is an English lecturer in the College of Foreign Studies, Jinan University (Guangzhou, China). He acquires his PhD from City University of Hong Kong and his thesis investigates the generic structure of Chinese judges' written opinions. He is particularly interested in the discourse analysis of conventions and variations of legal texts, persuasive strategies of business negotiations, evaluation and engagement of bureaucratic talks, and semiotic construction of social-political issues. From 2007 to 2011, he is a participant of *International Arbitration Practice: A Discourse Analytical Study* (Project No. CityU 1051/06H). He publishes in *the Journal of Pragmatics*, *Discourse & Society* and *the International Journal of Speech, Language and the Law* (IJSLL). Contemporarily, he is conducting two researches on Chinese professional discourse. One attempts to examine Chinese business experts' negotiating strategies by reconstructing the process of the corporate power reorganizing of a highly-profiled Chinese public company. The other explores identity construction by Chinese university presidents in official situations.